600 Blessings and Prayers
from around the world

600 Blessings and Prayers
from around the world

compiled by

GEOFFREY DUNCAN

TWENTY-THIRD PUBLICATIONS
A Division of Bayard   MYSTIC, CT 06355

Geoffrey Duncan is the compiler of three popular anthologies of prayers and worship resources: *Seeing Christ in Others* and *Wisdom is Calling* are both published by the Canterbury Press, and *Dare to Dream* is by Harper Collins. He is the Church and Society Consultant for the Thames North Synod of the Uniterd Reformed Church. He lives in East Hertfordshire.

The Scripture passages contained herein are from *The Revised English Bible.*

Third printing 2005

Twenty-Third Publications
A Division of Bayard
P.O. Box 180
Mystic, CT 06355
(860) 437-3012 or (800) 321-0411
www.twentythirdpublications.com

ISBN: 1-58595-134-X
Library of Congress Catalog Card Number: 00-135771
Printed in the U.S.A.

Dedication

Blessings and Prayers from Around the World is dedicated with love and admiration to the resilient and resourceful children, women, and men who live in the remote, rural communities of Karnataka, south India. Also, to the many fine people that I met working in various projects, for their vision and commitment to improve the health and education of many people.

Royalties from *Blessings and Prayers from Around the World* will be given to projects which aim to improve the quality of life for villagers and the marginalized in Bangalore City.

Contents

Author's Acknowledgments   x

Introduction   1

Living God, Loving God   3

Aspects of Worship   15

  Shalom of God   16

  Praise and Thanksgiving   35

  Biblical Perspectives   42

  Baptism, Blessing, Eucharist   57

  Consecration and Dedication   66

  The Sacred Three   69

  Holy Wisdom   72

  To Be Silent…   83

  Saints Still Alive!   88

  Places of Worship   93

Fruits of the Spirit   97

  Encourage and Challenge   98

  Let Justice Flow…   108

  Protect Peace   122

  Joy, Perfect Joy   130

Festivals 133

The Christian Year 134

Advent 134

Christmas 135

Epiphany 139

Ash Wednesday 140

Lent 142

Good Friday 143

Easter Day 145

Pentecost 147

Harvest 148

God of Times and Seasons 157

Changing Splendors 158

Take Us through the Day, Lord 166

Creator God 177

Awaken our Senses 178

Beauty in Creation 184

Lands and Peoples 207

Community Lifestyles 231

Grow Together 232

Riches in Relationships 242

Learning and Working 254

Modern Technology 263

Being Creative! 268

Eat Drink and…Share 275

Hearth and Home 284

All the Days of My Life 292

Toward Wholeness 309

Toward Health 310

Treasured Memories 321

Always on the Move 329

Inner Strength 330

Journeys and Pilgrimages 339

Index of Titles/First Lines 357

Index of Authors and Sources 368

Acknowledgments 371

Acknowledgments

I am more than grateful to my daughter, Ruth, who before her return to south India put much of the text into the computer. Later, while I was away in India for six weeks, Pat, my wife, continued this valuable piece of work. I am sure this took up many hours during the summer of 1999. Then, when I needed calming because of a glitch or some problem which caused immediate panic, my daughter Jane offered support. My family are definitely a part of this work. Also, it is wonderful to express my thanks to the many friends and acquaintances from all over the world who willingly send contributions for my anthologies. The network continues to grow and my life is enriched as a result of the excellent material which lands in a variety of colorful envelopes through the letter box or as attachments to an e-mail message. As one who enjoys contact with a variety of people, culturally and globally, I find this activity delightful and stimulating. Christine Smith, my publisher at Canterbury Press, continues to keep me well occupied and is always ready to listen and offer advice. I am tremendously grateful for her support.

Geoffrey Duncan
Advent 1999

Introduction

Throughout the world, women and men live, love, enjoy relationships, learn, work, communicate, relax, laugh, cry, worship, explore spiritual resources, protest, campaign, and discover the challenges of a fast changing world. Children and young people develop according to the environment and opportunities, cultures and sub-cultures experienced in their formative years. Communities and nations are inextricably linked and need the impact of spiritual development and religious faith as an integral part of their structures and lives.

Today we can look around and see encouraging signs:

- there is an increasing valuing of people in our multicultural, multi-faith communities;
- there is an increasing interest in spirituality;
- many churches and other groups are developing new liturgies which are relevant and meaningful for women and men in contemporary society.

I heard recently of a family whose two-year-old son died of a very rare illness. At the funeral, poems were read, bright colors were worn—no black by request—and favorite songs were sung. The brightness at the funeral was symbolic of how the child was surrounded by light to try and stimulate his senses as blindness set in—a part of his illness. Although their son's funeral was not a traditional one, I believe this caring and loving family showed fresh insights into spirituality.

If we are to live effective Christian lives in our world, I believe many more local congregations need to become more aware of such insights into spirituality and relate them to the social, justice, and economic issues which have a wide impact upon people wherever they are in the world. Church and faith communities should challenge positively—radically when necessary—the context, the structure, and the content of worship and liturgy.

Blessing and benediction have a key place in contemporary living. When we invoke God's blessing, it embraces people who are to be found in our supermarkets and shopping malls, pop concerts, hospitals and care centers, schools, places of work, and the remotest parts of the world. God's blessing is not confined to the church.

When using the blessings in this book for private prayer by an individual, the plural pronouns can be changed to me and I. Many of the blessings in this book can also be read responsively. For example in Richard Becher's *Hold Me Lord* (p. 335) *me* can easily be changed to *us* and *we:*

Leader	Hold me in your arms, Lord
All	*Bless me with your Love*
Leader	Whisper in the quietness, Lord
All	*Bless me with your Word*

This is not a book to be read from beginning to end, but one to dip into again and again, to find nourishment for yourself and for others. Be bold and adventurous in the way you use these blessings and let them inspire you with confidence to write your own blessings. You will find yourself drawn to the heart of local, national, and global needs. This will be a blessing to you.

I trust that *Blessings and Prayers from Around the World* will draw us all a little closer to God who calls each one of us to serve Christ in others so that the whole earth may be free to enjoy the many blessings which God lavishes upon us in the world he has made.

Geoffrey Duncan
January 2000

Living God, Loving God

1 John 4:7–12

No one has ever seen God,
but if we love one another,
God lives in union with us,
and his love is made perfect
in us.

God of Love

The blessing of the God of Love
and laughter,
whose foolishness is the heart
of all goodness;

the blessing of Jesus Christ,
whose truth
is in the language
of every day;

the blessing of the Holy Spirit
who is a paradox...
ever present yet unpredictable...
breathing new life into communities
everywhere...

be upon us all.

Joy Mead
England

God of Life

God of life,
 May the promise of the sunrise be echoed in our minds.
 May the warmth of the midday sun flow through our hearts.
 May the peace of the sunset touch our souls
 And when life seems dark teach us to remember even then you are
   with us, and that we will again see your light.
 In the name of Christ.

Nick Fawcett
England

Living God

Living God,
   We have come to you,
      to seek your help,
      offer our worship,
      and declare our faith.
   Now we go for you,
      to work for your kingdom,
      proclaim your love,
      and make known the gospel of Jesus Christ.
   Go with us and grant us grace to serve you,
      even as through him you have served us.

Nick Fawcett
England

May God Who Is Light

May God who is light shine in your darkness.
May God who is love be the love between you.
May God who is life be your life everlasting.
And the blessing of God, Creator, Flesh, and Spirit
Is with us and all people,
Now and forever.

E. A. S. Gray-King
England

A Life Blessing

May God, the author of life,
give you strength.
May Jesus, the bread of life,
give you hope.
And may the Holy Spirit, the staff of life,
lead you, ever deeper,
into the mystery
of the one with everything
who gave it all up for you.

Duncan L. Tuck
Wales

God for All

For orphans in their loneliness
God bless them as their Father.
For widows in their bereavement
God bless them as their Husband.
For children without mothers
God bless them as their Mother.
For human beings in their sinful state,
God bless them as their Savior.
For prisoners in their captivity
God bless them as their Redeemer.
For patients in their suffering
God bless them as their Healer.
For church attenders in their duty
God bless them as their Shepherd.
For worshippers in their love of God
God bless them as their Lord.

Frances Ballantyne
England

The God of Life

We know life is great:
Being loved
Giving love.
A fun night out,
A quiet night in.
Fresh fruit and salad,
Another cream pie,
Being a child,
Having a child.

We know life is dull:
Waiting in lines,
Filling in forms,
Reruns on the television,
Football again.
Bored children,
Grumpy parents,
Being told what to do,
Thinking of something to say.

We know life is hard:
Debt and depression,
Being at home on the street,
Living with loss,
Being thrown out of work,
Families divided,
Being treated like dirt,
But we declare
that in all of life
The God of Life is there.

Peter Cruchley-Jones
Wales

Gift of Life

God has to be so different from all that I have known.
But yet I wonder how he coped with life on earth, with all the hurtful
words and spiteful allegations, being hounded out of many towns and
villages.
God has to be so different from all that I have known.
But yet I wonder how he coped with life on earth, with all man's
greed and selfishness, the love of self instead of love of God.
God has to be so different from all that I have known.
But yet I wonder how he coped when stripped of all his clothes
and spat upon and hung in shame upon the cross.
God has to be so different from all that I have known.
But yet I wonder how he coped when on his own, and suffering
pain, for me and you, an agony of death to give us life.
God has to be so different from all that I have known.
But yet I wonder with amazement that he blessed us with his life,
the greatest gift, his Spirit dwelling in our hearts.

God has to be so different from all that I have known.
But yet I wonder with such love, who blesses God, and even thinks
to offer him our heartfelt praise and gratitude.
God is so different from all that I have known.

Frances Ballantyne
England

Summit of Blessings

God, you brought us out of the valley,
We believe we've started to live again,
We can remember the day it all began,
We felt we died, we descended fast,
We couldn't make sense of life,
We were thrown into confusion and fear,
We wanted to believe in life,
We needed help from people and God,
We were disappointed by everybody,
We somehow climbed the valley sides
We realized somebody must have helped,
We can believe in God again,
We can see the summit,
God, we're standing there with you!

Frances Ballantyne
England

Thank You?

Thank you, gentle God...
Thank you?
Did I really say "Thank you"?
Thank you for plaited thorns, scourging, spitting and jeering?
Thank you for the nakedness, the piercing, the bleeding?
Thank you for that sense of abandonment,
those racking breaths, that blackness?
Thank you for all this?

Thank you, gentle God...
Thank you?
Did I really say "Thank you"?
Thank you for the internment camp, the torturer's instruments,
the stinking prison cell?
Thank you for this twisted limb, that damaged brain,
these wounded hearts?
Thank you for abuse, terror, disease, bereavement, despair?
Thank you for all that?

Yes, thank you!
Thank you for being there

at the very heart of it all—
not the perpetrator,
but the recipient of the cruelty,
suffering with each one who suffers,
alongside and at one with us all.

Kate Compston
England

Your Very Best

God bless us with your very best.
The best wine of the kingdom
and seated as your guest,
a celebration, of good things.

The best of meat,
the spread of excellence,
and filled with satisfaction.

The best of life,
with fun and festivities,
abounding full and free.

God bless us with your very best.
Frances Ballantyne
England

A Generous Mercy

May the mercy of God be yours
to absolve and transform you revealing
the triune love society that is God.
May you, in turn, offer mercy
a mercy which is lasting, generous and fruitful—grace from grace.

In the munificent, magnificent spirit of the merciful Christ
we pray this blessing.

Glenn Jetta Barclay
Aotearoa New Zealand/Northern Ireland

Claim the Treasures

Leader   Sisters and brothers,

Let us claim the treasures Christ holds
    out to us,
    let us claim the freedom he
    gives us
    by his own self-giving on
    the cross.

All   May he enable us to live and serve
in faith, hope and love.

Leader   Let us, in times of sorrow, as in
    times of joy,
    celebrate the goodness of God.
    Let us go in peace.

All   Thanks be to God.

Kate Compston
England

The God of All Time

The God of all time bestow upon you space;
The God of all love free you from hate;
The God of all flesh hallow your body;
The God of God; Creator, Flesh and Spirit
Loves you,
Accepts you
And sends you forth,
Love living for all humanity.

E. A. S. Gray-King
England

Blessing of Heart and Breath

Every beat of your heart, every breath of your mouth
Be blest as an act of love and bind you forever with God.

Adapted by John Shevlin
England/USA

May God Rain on You With His Blessings

May God rain on you with his blessings,
May God shine on you with his mercies,
May God blow onto you his wind of life,
May God protect you with his presence.

Prince Dibeela
Botswana

Forgiving God

To God who is always forgiving,
    always loving,
    always offering a new beginning,
    be honor and glory,
    praise and thanksgiving,
    this day and forever.

Nick Fawcett
England

Everlasting to Everlasting

May God as father guide you
    as mother feed you
    as son befriend you
    as spirit inspire you
From hour to hour, day to day, everlasting to everlasting.

Henry Rack
England

Blessing of the One who Brings Laughter

And now may the blessing of the One who gives, the One who loves justice and the One who brings laughter be with us all now and forever.

Gertrude Lebans
Canada

Loving God, Lead Us

Loving God,
 Lead us out into the world,
  renewed in vigor,
  in hope,
  in faith,
  and in purpose.
 Send us back to live and work for you,
  sharing your love
  and living your life.
 Through Jesus Christ our Lord.

Nick Fawcett
England

Thank You, Most Loving God

We thank you, most loving God,
for the blessings you have given.

For calling us to be your people.
 Blessed are you, O God.

For forgiving us our shortcomings, our failures and our sins.
 Blessed are you, O God.

For revealing your love through Jesus Christ.
 Blessed are you, O God.

For the gift of life that we possess.
 Blessed are you, O God.

For families and friends to nurture and to comfort us.
 Blessed are you, O God.

For challenges and opportunities
to build new dreams out of past failures.
> **Blessed are you, O God.**

For the wonder and mystery of love.
> **Blessed are you, O God.**

For the salvation of the world
and the promise of eternal life.
> **Blessed are you, O God.**

For the call to bear witness to Jesus Christ.
> **Blessed are you, O God.**

For these and all the blessings of this life.
> **Blessing, honor and glory are yours,**
> **O God of love.**
> **Glory to you forever and ever.**
> **Alleluia!**

Vienna Cobb Anderson
USA

Living, Loving God

One Voice   Living God.

All Voices   Loving God,
we thank you
and we praise you
for your presence deep in our hearts,
for your presence here in our midst,
for this opportunity to come together
to affirm our identity
and to celebrate our common vision.
We thank you for the quality of achievement
that is represented here,
for the many and diverse efforts
that contribute toward the building of a better world.
Refresh our spirits.
Confirm and strengthen our vision.
Sustain us and strengthen us
in these changing times.

One Voice   May God bless us,
embrace us and send us forth
Renewed
Refreshed
Revitalized.

The peace of God

All Voices   The peace of God's people
be upon each thing our eyes take in,
be upon each thing our ears take in,
be upon bodies and souls
evermore and evermore.

Ken DeLisle
Canada

Aspects
of Worship

Psalm 95

Come, let us praise the Lord!

Shalom of God

The Shalom of God

The blessing of God,
The eternal goodwill of God,
The shalom of God,
The wildness and the warmth of God,
be among us and between us
Now and always.

St. Hilda Community
England

The Story

This litany for two voices is a blessing we might offer each other before we share in reading/hearing/acting the Word as part of our worship together.

Voice One   The universe began as a story.

Voice Two   God the Story-maker, together let us bless Love's story.

Voice One   The infinite life of a beautiful story.

Voice Two   We bless the beginning: chaos, light and dark.

Voice One   Creativity is love, a very high kind of love.

Voice Two   The blessing of creative love extended to us.

Voice One   Creativity is a form of prayer, and the expression of a profound gratitude for being alive.

Voice Two   We are grateful for life in all its fullness.

Voice One	Stories do not belong to eternity. They belong to time. And out of time they grow.
Voice Two	We celebrate Love's story, growing through time.
Voice One	Storytelling hints at human unease and human imperfection.
Voice Two	We acknowledge our humanity; we are uneasy, dis-eased, imperfect.
Voice One	Stories can heal profound sickness of the spirit.
Voice Two	We seek the healing promise of Love.
Voice One	Stories are either dangerous or liberating because they are a kind of destiny.
Voice Two	We affirm Love's liberating story which has given us new life.
Voice One	Stories are always a form of resistance. A good story keeps on growing, a good story never dies.
Voice Two	Praise to the Loving God for Love's endless story.
All	Glory to the Creator, who makes the Story, Glory to the Son, who tells the Story, Glory to the Spirit, who inspires the Story. Glory to God, Three in One and One in Three, Together may we share Love's blessing forever. Amen.

Janet Lees
England

Bless our Worship

Bless, O God, our worship this day, that it may fill our hearts with the gladness and holiness of the Sabbath. Let us receive from it increased strength and guidance for our life and work. So shall the spirit of this day spread blessing over all days.

Traditional Jewish Blessing

In Every Place

"In every place where I cause my name to be mentioned I will come to you and bless you." Bless, O God, those who are assembled here in your name. Grant that we may all draw from this service a renewed consciousness of your presence, a deeper loyalty to our faith, and a stronger resolve to order our lives in harmony with your will.

Traditional Jewish Blessing

Implant the Love of God

It has been said: "If God is not in your hearts, you will not find him in the whole universe." May this service help to implant the love and reverence of God in the hearts of all who worship here this day. May the beauty of our faith lead many to find God and to serve him in all their ways.

Traditional Jewish Blessing

Renew the Whole Creation

Go in faith to renew the whole creation.
And may the goodness of God's creation
be found in the little and the least,
Christ be present in the longings in the face of our neighbor,
and the Spirit show us the way toward true peace.

Dorothy McRae-McMahon
Australia

Lord, Inspire Us

Lord, inspire in us
A true longing
For holiness,
So that we can sense you
in the depths of our being;

A true desire
To renew our lives,
So that we can rejoice in you
in every moment of the day;
A true yearning
To love others,
So that we can see you
Especially in the faces
Of the poor.

Thomas McMahon
England

Hold Firm!

In the midst of conflict,
may your peace comfort us.
In the midst of pain,
may your comfort strengthen us.
In the midst of uncertainty and fear,
may your strength reassure us,
that in the midst of life with all its troubles,
we may hold firm to you, O Lord,
confident that you hold firm to us.

Dorothy M. Stewart
England

May God Challenge your Ability

Blessings from God
who creates and carries life
who loves and struggles
who renews and gives life.
May God surround you with rest and comfort

and challenge your greatness and ability
in the name of the Father,
the Son, and the Holy Spirit.
Amen.

Per Harling
Sweden

Faith in God

May faith in God uphold you,
the hope of God uplift you,
and the mighty love of God surround you,
as you go into the world as his people,
in the name of the Father, the Son, and the Holy Spirit.

Dorothy M. Stewart
England

Go in Faith

Leader   Go in faith, for there is God,
riding in the light on the water,
singing in the songs of the birds,
sitting in the midst of the feasts of life.

All   We go in faith
to live in joyous freedom,
to play in the creation
and to drink deeply of the gracious cup of life.

Dorothy McRae-McMahon
Australia

Trust in God

Trusting in you, Lord God,
who alone is worthy to be trusted,
we ask your blessing on us,
our homes, our work, and on all we love,
in Jesus' name.

Dorothy M. Stewart
England

Go in Peace

We may leave our worship
with faith in our hearts,
with a song of praise on our lips,
with love in our minds
and with caring in our hands.
Go in peace.

Per Harling
Sweden

A Bulwark of Strength

May the wonderful grace of our Lord and Savior Jesus Christ
be with you;
May the unfathomable love of God the heavenly Father envelop you;
and
May the undefeatable power of the Holy Spirit
be your bulwark of strength;
Now and forevermore.

Author Unknown
Nigeria

The Seeds of your Kingdom

Gracious God,
Send us back to the world with your eyes rather than ours.
Help us to see not only the bad but the good,
not simply the ugly but the beautiful,
not just the worst but the best.
Help us to see around us the seeds of your kingdom,
and to nurture them lovingly
until that day comes when your will is done
and you are all in all.

Nick Fawcett
England

The Fullness of Joy

May our world be flooded with the grace of your coming and the whole universe experience the fullness of your joy.

Ancilla Dent
England

Free Samples

Go out from here with a pocket of free gifts
    to give to those you meet.
Give freely your love and concern
    as a token of the greater love of God.
Give freely your time and effort
    as a token of the sacrifice of Jesus.
Give freely your help and friendship
    as a token of the upholding Spirit.
And may all you give and all you do
    cause others to seek the true gift
    of the God who blesses without end.

Duncan L. Tuck
Wales

Your Kingdom Come

Into our hearts,
    your kingdom come.
Into our lives,
    your kingdom come.
Into our churches,
    your kingdom come.
And may the blessings of that kingdom
overflow from us into all the world,
in Jesus' name.

Dorothy M. Stewart
England

Go in Faith and Hope

Let us go from our worship in faith and hope,
to serve God and the world with love and joy.
So may the blessing of God who is Father, Son,
and Holy Spirit, be upon us and radiate from
our lives, now and always.

David L. Helyar
England

Guests of Jesus Christ

Leader   We have been guests of Jesus Christ
we have received God's good gifts.
Now we go to our homes,
to our neighbors, to our work
equipped to put Jesus' words and being into action
to be salt of the earth,
light of the world,
to seek justice,
to make peace,
to preserve the creation,
to gain life.

All   Thanks and Amen.

Per Harling
Sweden

Go Forth

Go forth in the miracle of the grace of God.
And may you be touched by the fire of the
Spirit,
the gentleness of the Christ
and the wisdom of your Maker.

Dorothy McRae-McMahon
Australia

Go out to Change the World

We go out with God's message.
We go out with Christ's love.
We go out with the Spirit's power.
We go out to change the world
As we go out in Christian service.

Marjorie Dobson
England

In Whose Name We Have Met

Lord Jesus Christ,
in whose name we have met
    and whose presence has blessed our fellowship;
take the words we have spoken,
    and our quest for faith, hope, and love,
    into the purpose of your love for us
    and for all people
that we may hasten the day
    when everyone shall live in the power of the Holy Spirit
    and every knee shall bow and every tongue confess
    that you are Lord and Savior;
    to the glory of our God and Father.

Graham Long
England

Blessing for a Missionary Congregation

God make you a holy people
    ready to learn God's ways
    and eager to witness to God's generous love.
And the blessing of God Almighty,
    the Father, the Son and the Holy Spirit
    be with you now and forever. Amen.

Michael Turnbull
England

Our Offering

Accept, O God, this money we bring.
Bless the ways in which we make it,
bless the ways in which we use it,
and bless this part which we give back to you
that, with it, we may give you
our lives, body and soul,
to work for you, here on earth.

John Stewart Murray
Aotearoa New Zealand

Unity in Christ

Christ's love enfold you,
the Spirit inspire you,
and God the Father lead you
as children of one family,
united as Christ's body on earth,
till he brings you safely
into his heavenly kingdom.

Dorothy M. Stewart
England

Worship Does Not End

On leaving this place,
the worship does not end,
the presence of God is not taken away,
nor is the community when we are disbanded.

On leaving this place,
do not forget the holiness of worship,
matched only by the holiness of your life.

On leaving this place,
you go to live among people created by God,
you go to discover the companionship of Jesus,
you go to follow the Spirit.

On leaving this place,
carry the music of God with you,
carry the prayers of your friends with you,
carry the Spirit of adventure with you.

You are the instruments of God,
the hope of your community,
the beginner of tomorrow,
on leaving this place.

John Ll. Humphreys
Wales

Blessing of the Protector of Life

Leader May God, the creator of the world, bless us,
may God, the protector of life, keep us,
today and for all time.

All Thanks and Amen.

Per Harling
Sweden

Love Be with You

Joy be with you to take to those in sorrow.
Peace be with you to take to those in trouble.
Love be with you to take to those whose lives are empty.
God be with you to take your hand
and guide you in his work.

Marjorie Dobson
England

Go to Serve

As you have come to worship,
so now (we) go to serve,
showing the truth in your lives
of what you have declared with
your lips,
in the name of Christ.

Nick Fawcett
England

Sing We, Sing of a Blessing

Leader	Sing we, sing of a blessing
All	Sing we, sing of a blessing
Leader	Sing we, sing of a blessing
All	Sing we, sing of a blessing
Leader	A blessing of love
All	A blessing of love
Leader	A blessing of mercy
All	A blessing of mercy
Leader	Love will increase
All	Love will increase
Leader	A blessing of peace
All	A blessing of peace

The remainder of this blessing follows this pattern.

Pray now, pray for a blessing
Repeat
A blessing of joy
A blessing of justice
Love will increase
A blessing of peace

Share now, share in a blessing
Repeat
A blessing of hope
A blessing of courage
Love will increase
A blessing of peace

Live, live, live as a blessing
Repeat
A blessing within
A blessing among us
Love will increase
A blessing of peace

Send forth, send forth a blessing
Repeat
A blessing to all
Now and forever
Love will increase
A blessing of peace

Rise up, rise for a blessing
Repeat
A blessing be yours
Now and forever
Love will release
A blessing of peace.

Miriam Therese Winter
USA

Blessed Be

Blessed be.
In the name of all that is good and growing,
In the name of all that is loving and living,
In the name of all that fires our passion,
Blessed be.
Blessed be.

Jan Berry
England

Blessed with all Heavenly Benediction

May God, the Lord, bless us with all heavenly benediction,
    and make us pure and holy in his sight.
May the riches of his glory abound in us.
May he instruct us with the word of truth, inform us with
the gospel of salvation, and enrich us with his love.

Gelasian Sacramentary

Candle Blessing for Shabbat

God began the world by saying,
"Let there be light."

We begin Shabbat with candlelight,
saying *"Baruch ata, Adonai."* *

God finished creating the world
by making *Shabbat* a holy day.

We make *Shabbat*
a holy day for ourselves.

May the warm glow of these candles
remind us of God's light.

And may this *Shabbat* be
a special, holy time for us.

Baruch ata,
Adonai Eloheinu,
melech ha-olam,
asher kid'shanu
b'mitzvotav
v'tzivanu l'hadlik
neir shel Shabbat.

We praise You, God,
for the *mitzvah* to
light *Shabbat* candles.

A Jewish Blessing

*We praise You, God
Shabbat is Sabbath
mitzvah means blessing

Blessing with Seeds in our Hands

Leader   As you brought with you the seed in your hand
so believe that it always lies within you.
As you have received the life of Christ,
so take these small loaves
as the sign of the work of the Spirit in your midst
bringing forth the fruits of grace.

The loaves are passed around.

All   Go in peace
for Christ is risen!

Christ is risen indeed!

Dorothy McRae-McMahon
Australia

God's Blessing

May God bless you and keep you.
May God watch over you in kindness.
May God grant you a life of good health, joy, and peace.
Traditional Jewish Blessing

A Selection of Blessings from
Sinfonia Oecumenica

Sinfonia Oecumenica is an ecumenical collection of liturgies in four European languages entitled *Worship with the Churches in the World.*

May God's breath stream within me,
may God's breath renew me,
may God's breath invigorate me.
I walk
with confidence
into this day.

*

Leader	Glory to you, O God, our hope, glory to You.
	May Christ our true God, as a good,
	loving and merciful God,
	have mercy upon us
	and save us, through the intercessions of his
	most pure and holy Mother;
	the power of the precious and life-giving cross;
	the protection of the honorable, bodiless
	powers of heaven,
	the supplications of the honorable, glorious
	prophet and forerunner John the Baptist;
	the holy, glorious and praiseworthy apostles;
	the holy, glorious and triumphant martyrs;
	our holy and God-bearing forefathers;
	the holy and righteous ancestors Joachim and Anna;
	the holy (Name of the day's saint and patron saint of
	the church) whose memory we commemorate today,
	and all the saints.
All	Amen.

Leader	May the blessing of the Lord descend upon you
	by his grace and love,
	now and forever, and unto ages of ages.
All	Amen.

*

We Set Off

Presented as mime

Speaker 1	It's time to go!
Speaker 2	It's time to go!
Speaker 3	It's time to go!
Speaker 4	It's time to go!
Leader	Let go of what you have—
	say goodbye and turn your face to what lies ahead.
	You have a long way before you.
	God says: I will be with you.
	Let us encourage one another on our way together.
	Let us rise and say together:

All

Let us go in the strength
which God gives us.
We will go gently into the land
that you, O God, will show us.
We will go together,
looking out for signs of your presence.
Christ has gone before us.
He is waiting for us, there where we are.
Amen.

*

Leader

May the Lord of creation bless your animals:
your cows and bulls, your sheep and goats,
your chickens and pigs, your camels and donkeys.
May the Lord of the harvest bless your crops:
your maize and beans, your potatoes and rice,
your coffee and tea.
May the Lord of all life bless your families,
your ancestors and descendants,
your grandfathers and grandmothers,
your husbands and wives,
your sons and daughters.
And may the blessing of God Almighty,
the Father who made us,
the Son who redeemed us
and the Holy Spirit who renews us,
be among you,
keep you safe,
and remain with you always.
Amen.
Go in peace
to live and work for Christ.

All   Thanks be to God!

*

Leader	Go in peace and grace.
	And may God lift up new possibilities before us,
	the face of Christ be seen in our neighbors
	and the Spirit lead us into the celebration
	of a new community.
All	Amen.
Leader	Let us say together:
All	Let us go in the strength which has been given us.
	keeping watch for love,
	and for the dignity of each individual.
	Christ has gone before us,
	He is waiting for us, where our tasks are to be done.
	Amen.

*

May God bless you.
May God renew in you every day
your courage and your love of life
your strength and your imagination,
that, out of an inexhaustible source of life,
you too may develop your talents
and realize your dreams,
that you too may become your whole self,
and give your gifts to others,
that your life may be fulfilled.
May God lead you into a fulfilled life,
that you can be and become who you are.
And so may God bless you.

Word of Benediction

May God go before you to show you the right way.
May God be beside you to wrap you in his arms and protect you.
May God be behind you to keep you safe from the treachery
    of evil persons.
May God be beneath you to catch you when you fall
    and pull you out of the trap.

May God be within you to comfort you
    when you are sad.
May God surround you to defend you,
    when others attack you,
May God be above you to bless you.
Blessed be the God of Goodness.

after Sedulius Caelus
Sinfonia Oecumenica
Germany/Switzerland

Praise and Thanksgiving

Praise and Glory

To the one whose goodness is without equal,
   whose love is beyond comparison,
   whose mercy is beyond understanding,
   and whose power is beyond words,
   be praise and glory,
   worship and thanksgiving,
   now and always. Amen.

Nick Fawcett
England

Praise Forever and Ever

May the name of our God,
      Creator,
         Redeemer
            and Savior be praised
               forever and ever.

May the name of our holy Father
who gives us the great privilege of living
      at this special time in history
when so many changes are taking place,
challenge us to make decisions that bring glory to our Lord Christ.

May God's Holy Spirit open to us
the beauty and knowledge of
Our Lord and Savior Jesus Christ.

May the Church for which Christ died proclaim
His holy and precious name
and may we be a channel of blessing to those
who are yet to receive your love and grace.

May your great and holy name be forever praised.
Author Unknown
Ukraine

Inhabited Praise

Praising, you inhabit our praise.
Praising God, from whom all blessings flow.
Praising Jesus, from whom our salvation comes.
Praising Holy Spirit, God with us today.

Lifting hearts and voices in worship.
Raising hands and hearts in wonder
Dancing, and clapping in wordlessness.

Praising God as individuals in thankfulness.
Praising Jesus as communities in fellowship.
Praising Holy Spirit, as peoples in harmony.

Praising, you inhabit our praise.
Frances Ballantyne
England

Prayer over the Gifts

Lord, pour out on us the Holy Spirit who filled your apostles, that we
may acknowledge the gifts we have received through them and offer
this sacrifice of praise to your glory. We ask this through Jesus Christ our
Lord. Amen.

Giles Harcourt
England

A Blessing for Christian Unity

This prayer of thanksgiving uses the simple act of lighting candles. The first one should be taller than the others, and placed in a central location. Each sentence is offered by a different voice, and the prayer works best if people are gathered in a circle.

I light a candle for Jesus, the Christ.
Thanks be to God.
I light a candle for the apostles, sent out to be Christ's Church.
Thanks be to God.
I light a candle for the Scriptures, Hebrew and Christian, in which we may discern the word that enlivens us.
Thanks be to God.
I light a candle for the wise thinkers—the Fathers and Mothers—of the early Church.
Thanks be to God.
I light a candle for theologians through the ages: for their learning and study and new insights.
Thanks be to God.
I light a candle for the faithful people of God, in whose love and lives the ongoing Church of Christ is realized.
Thanks be to God.
I light a candle for worship—colorful and quiet, exuberant and contemplative: for word and silence, movement and stillness, singing and sighing.
Thanks be to God.
I light a candle for Christian art and literature and music, and for symbols which point us to God.
Thanks be to God.
I light a candle for strength of conviction.
Thanks be to God.
I light a candle for questioning, for journeying in the wilderness, and living on the edge.
Thanks be to God.
I light a candle for our rich diversity.
Thanks be to God.
I light a candle for our blessed connectedness in the love of Christ.
Thanks be to God.

Kate Compston
England

God Has Given Us Every Moment

To God who has given us every
moment
    to celebrate,
    to savor
    and satisfy,
    be heartfelt praise,
    and joyful thanksgiving,
    now and always.

Nick Fawcett
England

The Wonder of God

Let the love of the Father course through our veins.
Let the goodness of Christ pulse through our bod-
ies.
Let the power of the Spirit flow through our souls.
Let the wonder of God resonate through our minds.
Glory be to God,
    Father, Son, and Holy Spirit,
    now and for all eternity.

Nick Fawcett
England

Blessed Is the Spot

Blessed is the spot and the house and the place,
And the city and the heart and the mountain,
And the refuge and the cave and the valley,
    And the land and the sea and the island,
    Where mention of God has been made,
    And his praise glorified.

The Bahá'í Community of the United Kingdom

Ascribe Greatness to our God

May greatness be ascribed to our God
May his name be glorified by all creatures
May all that has breath bow before him
and may he reign in our hearts,
now and eternally.

Prince Dibeela
Botswana

Bless My Soul and All that's in Me

Can be sung to the hymn tune Geneva.

Bless my soul and all that's in me,
Blessings on God's holy name.
Ever mindful of God's mercy
We are striving to remain.
Bless the Lord who knows our failings,
Yet ignores our constant shame.
Rather, God will send us healing;
Grace instead of fixing blame.

Even at our weakest moment,
Mired in all that life can give,
God crowns us with love and mercy,
Seeks us out that we may live.
God is always seeking justice,
Making known God's saving way,
Acting through a chosen people,
Bringing us God's realm today.

God is seeking to create us
in a heav'nly form once more.
Bless my soul and all that's in me,
Open hearts God will restore.
Blessed is our worthy maker,
Blessed too the Holy Child,
Blessed is the Spirit's movement,
Heavenly breath and touch so mild.

Michael Jacob Kooiman
Canada

Praising God in the Four Quarters of the Earth

Face South

O Great Spirit of the South,
Spirit of all that is warm
and gentle and soothing,
we ask you for the spirit of growth,
of creativity, of fertility.
You caress us with a cool breeze and give us
succulent fruits when the days are hot.
Help us nurture the water of life as she nurtures us
and not to contribute to its decay.
Give us seeds that the flowers,
trees and fruits of the earth may grow.
Grant us the seed of what is life-giving at all times.
We love the land.
We respect all of earth's creatures.
We praise you for diversity and harmony
and the richness of your creation.
Sustain us through the warmth of
good friendships and sisterhood
especially on this day of celebration
and sharing of presence and persons.
Keep our spirit moist with life.
Spirit of the South,
send the comfort and assurance
of your abundant blessings.

Face East

O Great Spirit of the East,
we turn to you where the sun comes up,
From where the power of refreshing light
and the promise of a new day comes.
Everything that is born comes forth in this direction—
the birth of children,
the birth of ideas,
the birth of movements and
the birth of relationships.
Let there be Light.
Spirit of the East,
let the subtle colors of fresh rising
and new beginnings in our lives
be in praise of your glory.

Face West	O Great Spirit of the West,
	where the sun goes down each day,
	we turn to you in praise of sunsets
	and in thanksgiving for changes.
	Your bright colors are awesome as they are inspiring.
	You are the powerful force that
	pulls us into constant cycles
	of transformation and renewal.
	We ask for the grace of completeness.
	Keep us open to life's processes,
	attentive to its natural laws,
	grant us the wisdom to know when to be with the flow
	and when to let go.
	Spirit of the West,
	do not desert us,
	when it is time for us to return to mother earth
	receive us in the arms of our loved ones.

Face North	O Great Spirit of the North,
	we come to you
	and ask for the strength and the humility
	to bear what is cold, uncertain and harsh in life.
	We come to you, ready to receive the winds
	that truly could be overwhelming at times.
	Do not let the winds of adversity blow us away in
	surrender and alienated from each other.
	Grant us resilience to help us bend without breaking apart.
	Do not let that which seems to ask us to wait
	be completely lost in mystery.
	Spirit of Life and Spirit of the North,
	keep us open to the darker hues of life
	as we ask for the
	gift of courage and endurance
	to act justly and keep the balance of life.

We thank you for the blessings of women and men and the wisdom of your *anawim*. May these be a source of mutual empowerment, peace and wholeness.

Agnes N. Miclat-Cacayan
Philippines

anawim means "the poor people of God"

Biblical Perspectives

Abound in Hope

May the God of hope fill you with all joy and
peace in believing, so that by the power of the
Holy Spirit you may abound in hope.

Romans 15:13

The God of Blessings

Leader   The God of blessings is a child in a cradle.
All   Give us strength to give the child a future.
Leader   The God of blessings has wounded hands.
All   Give us courage to be vulnerable.
Leader   The God of blessings is the way, the truth and the life.
All   Give us strength to walk the way of truth.

Per Harling
Sweden

The People of the Book

May the God of the living Word
bless those who read the written Word.
May the Book that is shared
by Jews, Christians and Moslems
be a source of blessing for all peoples.

May it be a guide for conduct
encouraging compassion for the widow and the orphan
and generosity toward the hungry and the poor;
may it be an inspiration in the quest for knowledge,

encouraging honesty in the search for true wisdom
and insight in the seeking of the will of the Creator;
may it give strength to those who make a prophetic stand
in speaking for justice and for peace.
May those who are the people of the Book
delight to share with all on the spiritual journey,
respecting those of different traditions
and joining in a common search for truth.
May the people who received a blessing through Abraham
delight to be a blessing to all people of goodwill.
May the God of the living Word bless with wisdom
all those who teach the written Word.

John Johansen-Berg
England

Peniel

"I will not let you go unless you bless me," Jacob replied. (Genesis 32:26–30)

There are many wrestlers, who, through the night,
argue and question and make demands on God.
Distraught people who have lost what is precious,
worried people who wonder where sorrow will strike,
guilty people who fear they will be found out,
uncertain people who have found no solid rock,
people in pain and people in hunger.
These wrestle through the night
till morning comes.

But Jacob was blessed and called the place
Peniel, "because," he said, "I have seen God
face to face yet my life is spared."

Bless the wrestlers, God of Jacob,
God of Gethsemane, midnight God.
Bless with light,
Bless with sanity,
Bless with courage,
Bless with each new day.

Bernard Thorogood
Australia

A Version of the Aaronic Blessing

May the Lord bless you,
May the Lord keep you,
Make his face to shine upon you.
May the Lord bless you,
May the Lord keep you,
Make his face to shine upon you.
May he lift his countenance upon you,
Fill your heart with his joy and peace.
May the Lord bless you, May the Lord keep you,
Make his face to shine upon you.

Declan Smith
Ireland

The Blessing of the God of Miriam

The blessing of the God of Miriam, Aaron and Moses,
The blessing of Jesus born of the woman Mary,
The blessing of the Holy Spirit who flies on before us,
Be with you all, now and forever.

Adapted by Jean Mayland
England

The Blessing of the God of Deborah

The blessing of the God of Deborah, who promises justice,
The blessing of the Son, who appeared to Mary Magdalene,
The blessing of the Holy Spirit, who breathes new life
into the community of men and women in the church
be with you all.

Suzanne Fageol
USA

The Blessing of the God of Sarah

The blessing of the God of Sarah and of Abraham,
the blessing of the Son, born of the woman Mary,
the blessing of the Holy Spirit who broods over us
as a mother with her children,
be with you all.

Lois Wilson
Canada

Generous, Loving God
Based on Ephesians 4:12–13

May the generous, loving God,
who loves each one of us,
however unlovely we believe ourselves to be,
help us to mature to our full potential,
see God's gift in others
and help them grow in Christ's image, too.

Lesley Husselbee
England

To Whom, Jude?

This blessing is designed to be read by a number of voices, the questions coming from among the body of worshippers in response to the leading statements.

Now to him who is able to keep you from falling
    But, if I still fall?
Then to him who is there when you stand
    But, if I cannot rise?
To him who will lift you up
    But, if I fear the journey?
To him whose arm is around you
    But, if I cannot walk?
To him who carries you on
    But, if I fail at each attempt?
To him who loves you, took your place, walks your way, and
    presents you
without blemish before the presence of his glory with rejoicing,
to the only God, our Savior through Jesus Christ our Lord,
be glory, majesty, dominion and authority,
before all time and now and forever.

Duncan L. Tuck
Wales

The God Who Sang in Mary

May the God who sang in Mary
sing a new song within us,
the God who surprised Paul on the way
meet us on the road,
and the God who led the church in every age
lead us forth in courage and joy.

Dorothy McRae-McMahon
Australia

Hail Mary!

Hail Mary, full of grace!
All generations bless
our highly favored sister
and her holiness.
Rejoice with her
who first received
the Word made human, and believed

Marnie Barrell
Aotearoa New Zealand

Exalt the Humiliated

May God the Father, who exalts the humiliated,
Jesus Christ, the son of Mary, whose praise overturns the powerful,
and the Holy Spirit, who breaks every barrier,
making each man and each woman a child of God,
bless you and keep you.

World Council of Churches
Brazil

Blessed Be God

"I form light and create darkness,
I bring prosperity and create disaster;
I, the Lord, do all these things."
Isaiah 45:7

Blessed be God in the dark and the light,
in trouble and joy, sorrow and delight.
Blessed be God for still center in the storm,
Blessed be God for relief in pain.
Blessed be God in the refugee camp,
Blessed be God in the aid worker's strife.
Blessed be God in the man in the street
lying in a shop doorway out of the rain.
Blessed be God in the woman at the corner,
plying her trade as life is so hard.
Blessed be God who creates and who saves,
who corrects and leads on to the ultimate good
of a kingdom where all will find room
and the dark and the light will be one.

Jean Mayland
England

Blessed Are the Poor in Spirit

Blessed are the poor in spirit.
Blessed are those who are at the end of their tether.
Blessed are those who have no one else to turn to.
Blessed am I when I realize how much I need Jesus,
For then Jesus is mine.
To a woman with an alabaster jar who comes, breaking the jar,
breaking her heart, he says, "I forgive."
Blessed are the poor in spirit.
To an intellectual too nervous to come to him by day, who
tentatively asks, "How can it be?," he says, "Because God so loved
the world."
Blessed are the poor in spirit.
To a centurion with a hopeless longing for the well-being of a sick
child, who comes pleading, "I am not worthy, but just say the
word," he says, "There is healing."
Blessed are the poor in spirit.

And to me, this day, coming to him with all the uncertainty of the twenty-first century full of dilemmas, aware of failures, wondering what the future holds, fragile—to me he says,
"You are the one for whom blessing is on its way.
Never mind the others!
You!"
For this is the gospel of Christ.

Peter Graystone
England

A Paraphrase of the Beatitudes
Matthew 5:3–10

How liberated are those who have learned to let go—
They shall experience the mystery of God.

How strong are those who are not afraid to admit their weaknesses—
Their tears shall heal their grief.

How beautiful are those who reverence life—
The Earth shall rejoice in their presence.

How satisfied are those who seek to serve God—
For God shall be their delight.

How happy are those who are willing to forgive others—
They shall find release from guilt and fear.

How enlightened are those who know oneness with all things—
They shall see God everywhere.

What an inspiration are those who work for justice and peace—
For they shall live as children of God.

What an opportunity there is for those who suffer in the cause of right—
For their rejection can become the doorway to new life.

W. L. Wallace
Aotearoa New Zealand

A Beatitude Reflection

Leader Blessed are those who hunger
and thirst for righteousness.
All They will be filled.
Leader Blessed are the merciful.
All They will receive mercy.
Leader Blessed are the peacemakers.
All They will be called the children of God.
Leader Walk with righteous hearts,
merciful hands, and peaceful minds.
All Amen.

Per Harling
Sweden

The Blessing of Poverty

"Lord Jesus Christ,
you became poor,
that through your poverty
we might become rich."

Thus enriched,
we shall not be afraid to become poor again:
poor as we sit light to possessions;
poor as we refuse privilege and share power;
poor as we identify with the downtrodden;
poor as we give away our time to others;
poor as we bear ridicule for the stand we take;
poor as we shed masks and accept our vulnerability;
poor as we carry our aloneness with courage;
poor as we acknowledge our not-having, our not-knowing;
poor as we walk the way of the cross;
poor as we surrender our lives to God.

We shall not be afraid to die, in Christ,
to our obsession with self, our prejudice, our greed,
for in such dying
we richly live.

We bless you for this assurance of life
given through the death of Jesus—
treasure beyond price.

Kate Compston
England

Blessing of Salt

Leader *(passes around a bowl of salt)*

Jesus said: "You are the salt of earth."

Now, each one takes a pinch of salt from the bowl and holds it in their palm as the salt is blessed.

As the bowl of salt is returned to the leader, all say:

Leader   We bless this gift of the lowly salt, O God.

People   That makes our soup and food tasty;
that preserves our catch of fish, our harvest of
vegetables and meat, thereby extending its availability
on our tables.

Leader   We bless this gift of the lowly salt, O God.

People   That cleanses and heals our wounds,
that helps us remember the tears of the suffering
and moves us to work for justice and peace.

Leader   We bless this gift of the lowly salt, O God.

People   Salt takes the risk of becoming invisible in food or
water, reminding us to learn the gospel of humility
while challenging us to become a presence
that makes a tasty and pleasant difference
in our communities and wherever we go.

Leader   We take this lowly salt to taste its saltiness.

Everyone puts the salt on their tongue.

We are now one with the salt. We are now the salt of the earth.

All   Gracious God, You who took all the risk
just to make your love for us known,
thank you for the gift of the lowly salt.
Bless it and bless us that we may humbly seek always
to become the salt of the earth.
In Jesus' name.

Muriel Orevillo-Montenegro
Philippines

Bodily Blessed

You are the Body of Christ.
Go and be hands:
    reaching out to the needy;
    holding the friendless;
and willingly receiving God's love.
Go and be feet:
    walking the extra mile;
    striving for others;
and humbly letting Jesus wash you.
Go and be tongues:
    chatting the good news;
    welcoming all;
and allowing God's Spirit to speak to you.
You are the Body of Christ. Praise God.

Duncan L. Tuck
Wales

Bible Blessings

I will bless you
So that you will be a blessing.

Genesis 12:2

May the Lord make your love increase and overflow
to one another and to everyone…
May he make your hearts firm,
so that you may stand before our God and Father
holy and faultless
when our Lord Jesus comes with all those who are his own.

1 Thessalonians 3:12–13

May God himself, the God of peace,
make you holy through and through,
and keep you sound
in spirit, soul and body,
free of any fault when our Lord Jesus Christ comes.
He who calls you keeps faith;
he will do it.

1 Thessalonians 5:23–24

May God make you worthy of your calling,
and confirm every good resolve and work of your faith
by holy power;
that the name of the Lord Jesus may be glorified in you,
and you in him,
according to the grace of our God and the Lord Jesus Christ.

2 Thessalonians 1:11–12
Adapted by Roberta Rominger
USA/England

May our Lord Jesus Christ himself
and God our Father,
who has shown us such love,
and in his grace has given us
such unfailing encouragement
and so sure a hope,
still encourage and strengthen you
in every good deed and word.

2 Thessalonians 2:16–17

Now to the One who can keep you from
falling
and set you in the presence of his glory,
jubilant and above reproach,
to the only God our Savior,
be glory and majesty,
power and authority,
through Jesus Christ our Lord,
before all time, now, and forevermore.

Jude 24–25

God's Soil

Go and die to yourself.
Let your selfishness rot,
decompose,
become part of the soil of God's creation,
that new life may sprout from you.
Be recreated in the image of Jesus,
sharing in his resurrection now,
a foretaste of your resurrection to come,
in glory.

Duncan L. Tuck
Wales

Blessed Are the Steadfast

Blessed are the steadfastly enduring, they that are
Patient under ills and hardships, who lament not
over
Anything that befalleth them, and who tread the
path
    Of resignation.
The Bahá'í Community of the United Kingdom

A Metaphor Blessing

Bless you, Wise and Holy One,
for your Word made metaphor—
for meaning that reads deep
between the lines—

wings of the morning
bright morning star
shepherd and sheep
vine and branches
bread of life
oil of gladness
oaks of righteousness
trees of the field that
clap their hands
stones that cry out
and a mother-hen-God
who gathers her brood
under her wings
bless you, Wise and Holy One,
for your Word made metaphor—
inexpressible truth
made flesh
in expressible form

Norm S. D. Esdon
Canada

Go Forth as the Children of God

Leader   Go forth as the children of God.
All   **In the power of the Spirit,**
    we will be the people of love and sharing.
Leader   And may the God who sang in Mary
    sing a new Magnificat within you,
    the God who danced in Miriam
    move your feet on the road to freedom
    and the God who led the church in Phoebe
    be your wisdom and guide.

Dorothy McRae-McMahon
Australia

Girl Talk

1 Corinthians 12:12–27

Bless my mind for all it is,
and for being there when times are rough.
Bless my arms that help me climb.
Bless my heart that helps me love.
Bless my consciousness for telling me what's right.
Bless my lips that help me talk and ask questions.
Bless my nose that smells the freshness of spring.
Bless my hands that touch with care.
Bless my eyes that see beauty.
Bless my toes that keep me balanced.
Bless my hair that sways in the wind
and keeps my head warm.
Bless my ears that hear the sound of
all things that go round and round.
Thanks for the faces that show feelings
when words cannot.
Thanks for the vertebrae that let me
crack my back which feels good.
Be good, arms. Be good, legs. Be good, eyes.
Be good, body.
Do I really have to say this?
One can't say, "Hand, I have no need of you,"
or "Eye, I have no want for you."
There are many parts, but one body.

Cora, Kalea, Lauren, Meg, and Rachel (ages 11-12)

USA

The Rich Variety of Women in the Bible

Let us lift up in prayer the rich variety of women in the Bible,
the diversity of female characters,
the strength and power of their stories; and give thanks for
    Eve's curiosity, Miriam's dancing,
    Ruth's loyalty, Esther's courage
    Mary's vision, Lydia's hospitality.
May their example free women to be who they are,
    and all they are called to be.
Let us lift up in prayer the unnamed women in the Bible,
identified only by an action or a relationship,
not granted the dignity of their own status, and give thanks for
    the women on the Ark, Lot's wife,
    the Levite's concubine, Jairus' daughter,
    the woman who anointed the feet of Jesus,
    the women and children not counted
        among the five thousand.
May their memory be kept alive,
may all women treated as invisible and dispensable
be awarded their rights of acknowledgment and personhood.

United Church of Canada

May Others Meet with Christ

Go now and proclaim the gospel,
    not just through words but deeds—
    through what you say,
    what you do,
    and who you are.
May others, as they meet with you, meet with Christ,
    and know his living presence for themselves. Amen.

Nick Fawcett
England

Baptism, Blessing, Eucharist

The Welcome

This blessing can be said at an infant baptism by the children and young people who are present there.

Welcome to our church!
We hope you will soon feel part of our church family.
We have gifts, friendship and love to share with you.
Please share with us and be our brother/sister in God's family.
We know you will make new friends here—
we know because we have all made new friends here
and we try to love and care for each other as Jesus asked us to.
So, come, play, have fun, learn and let us all grow together
And may you always know God's love.

Shiregreen United Reformed Church
England

A Blessing for a Newborn Child

Dear God, there is so much potential in this small creation. Bless this new life, that all the promise we see here is fulfilled.

Grant love, discipline and encouragement in even measures, that growth may be strong and steady.
When the learning curve dips, or experience seems too harsh a teacher, or love fails, wrap your caring arms around her/him until the weeping stops and the future begins to offer hope again.

Strengthen the love, the will and the nerve of those who will care for this young life and nourish it, for they are so aware of the weight of their responsibilities.

Help us all to see in this small scrap of humanity, so new to this world, yet another image of your many-faceted face.

Marjorie Dobson
England

Welcome to the World

A Blessing for a Newborn Child

Angels hold their breath; for you, child of morning,
The Spirit of the Lord moves anew;
There in the room, as you meet the light of day,
Our Father God rejoices over you.

Welcome to the world! Your journey has begun.
What will it bring? I don't know;
But the One who was there in the moment you were born
Will be waiting for you everywhere you go.

Later you will learn the language of living,
The words to think and speak, the deeds to do;
But for now, just to be is to know God's loving touch—
Creation sees its joy fulfilled in you.

Welcome to the world…(continue as above)

Let us tune our hearts to hear heaven singing,
And share our joy with those dear ones we knew—
They are safely home, with God whose love is all,
But I believe they see and welcome you.

Welcome to the world…(continue as above)

Jenny Dann
England

Bless this Child

The child's name can be used instead of "child."

Bless this child, innocent and pure
Start on your journey, safe and secure
Surrounded by family, cradled soft in love;
Child, we welcome you to this world.
Bless this child, precious and so dear.
We, as God's servants, will raise you with care
And bring out your goodness, guiding you in truth.
Child, we welcome you to this world.
Child, we welcome you to this world.

Radha Sahar
Aotearoa New Zealand

Blessing of the Child

Leader (Name) we bless you and welcome you into this community. May the Holy One be your Guide, may the Beloved be your friend and may the Spirit fill you with grace. May your place with us be safe and wide enough for your growth.

Response Blessed be God, now and forever. Amen.

To the child and family

Leader We light this candle for you to burn in your home as a sign of our unity, our solidarity and the Light which illuminates all life.

Response May God be always present in our joy and in our sorrow. May God be ever welcome and present in our midst.

Prayer

Leader Source of life and hope, today we place before you our dreams. Help us to live, seeing in each other your Beloved, acting with honesty, speaking with integrity and responding in your love. May the Spirit of wisdom and understanding guide us all so that our homes may be signs of reconciliation, havens of peace and warm with delight and inspiration.

Blessed be God now and forever. Blessed be the Beloved who calls us and reminds us that we are created from the Divine Essence. Blessed be the Spirit who weaves families together in community.

Response Blessed be God, now and forever.

Gertrude Lebans
Canada

The Naming of a Child

Using the Yoruba Tradition

The baby is carried to a table where the symbols highlighted below are placed.

Elder Here are symbols of the good things of life,
the things which people seek.

As the elder names each symbolic item, the symbol may be given to the child, or the parents, to be tasted where appropriate.

We offer you the good things of life!
Water runs deep, gives refreshment and calm.
May you find the depths that offer you the quenching of your thirst,
the satisfaction of your desire.
Salt is for seasoning and taste
—to save life from dullness and drabness,
to freshen things and to preserve the good.
Honey is tasty too.
A strength and a sweetness at the center of life.
May you find in you the qualities which make you special.
Pepper has many seeds
to offer you plenty, as your mouth will tell you by the taste
and a warning against our desires to get more and more.
May God create in you riches, in mind and spirit, so that you may be creative.

We offer you the good things of life!

Here is **cloth.**
May you be sheltered and protected by care and love.

Here is **food.**
May you never be hungry for the good things or for love.

We offer you the good things of life!

Here is **Spirit (glass of wine).**
A symbol of permanence in taste and in power,
the link with the living and the living-dead.

But the symbols of our desires are also those of our division.
So we offer you **Sugar,** for sharing
The sweetness of life to be shared, with justice, for peace.
We offer you **Oil**
for soothing and healing, for peace.
May you find the peace which God gives in confusion,
the peace which comes after discord and strife.

The Lord bless you and keep you.

We have God's covenant of peace.
God will make it true for us and for this child.

Donald Pickard in association with Adeolu Adegbola
England/Western Nigeria

A Place of Blessing and Salvation

Eternal God,
whose Spirit moved over the waters in creation,
who saved Noah and his family from the flood,
and who led the Exodus people through the sea,
make these waters a place of blessing
and salvation for *(Name)*,
and give to him/her/them
that same life-giving Holy Spirit.
We make our prayer through Jesus Christ,
your Son, our Savior,
who lives and reigns with you
and the Holy Spirit,
one God forever and ever.

Paul Sheppy
England

Baptismal Blessing

Bless, O God,
bless this child
with the gift of your life.
Bless these parents
with the gift of your love.
Bless us all, your family,
with the Christ Spirit
of life and love and peace.

John Stewart Murray
Aotearoa New Zealand

Blessing of a Font

Lord, you have adorned the day with the beauty of the morning where-in all life begins; at this fountain of rock where true and eternal life begins, we humbly beseech you to bless, hallow, and consecrate (here make a sign of the cross over the font) this gift of beauty, fashioned with love and care to your honor and glory.

Let all who come to this font to be baptized be mindful of your pres-ence, and purposed to worship you in the beauty of holiness.

And let all who are gathered here, be ever mindful of and faithful to the vows they have made in the power of the grace you have given, in the name of your blessed Son Jesus Christ our Savior, who is alive and reigns with you and the Holy Spirit, ever one God, world without end. Amen.

Giles Harcourt
England

Parting Prayer

Order of service for anointing

Be at peace!
God be your comfort, your strength;
God be your hope and support;
God be your light and your way;

and the blessing of God,
Creator, Redeemer and Giver of life,
remain with you now and forever.

Graham Long
England

Approaching the Communion Table

At this table we are not the only people to receive the invitation of Jesus
to share the bread and drink from the cup.
The spaces around us are not just empty voids
which we sometimes try to ignore or remember as once filled!
The invitation goes to all,
to the hungry and the thirsty in all places,
to the lonely, homeless and friendless,
to the people whose glances disturb us on TV or on the street,
and for whom we pray, so very briefly.

Picture one or two of these—
them.
They sit with us at this table,
the bread is theirs, too;
the cup is for them, too.

That they can be with us,
that they must be with us belongs to the blessing God offers
in this bread and wine moment. They are his gift,
precious to him, may they become as precious to us.
So as we receive, may we imagine that the least
of his sisters and brothers also receives.
Lest we remain in imagination, remember this sharing is for them,
this sharing equips us for them,
blesses us with the love of God teeming through our veins—
for them.

John Ll. Humphreys
Wales

Blessing of the Bread

Let us pray to the Lord…

Lord, Jesus Christ our God! As you blessed the five loaves and satisfied the five thousand hungry in the wilderness, so now bless this bread and all the fruits of the earth; sanctify the faithful who partake of them, and let there always be plenty not only for us here, but for all your people everywhere. For you are the one who blesses and sanctifies all things, Christ, our God, and we give glory to you, your eternal Father, and all-holy, good and life-giving Spirit: now and forever, and unto ages of ages.

World Council of Churches

Eucharistic Benediction

Celebrant   All life is holy, all life is one.

All   Awaken us, O God, that all life may be Holy Communion and the whole creation Eucharist.

W. L. Wallace
Aotearoa New Zealand

At the Lord's Table

Leader   Lift up your hearts.
All   **We lift them to the Lord.**
Leader   Let us give thanks to the Lord our God.
All   **It is right to give our thanks and praise.**

Leader   God of many names,
We thank you for all that you are
and for all that you do in the world.
As Creator you made all things
and are continually creating.
As Father and Mother you nurture and sustain us.
As the One Holy Trinity,
You invite us to dance with you
To the lilt of life and time.

And through Christ,
You have named us as your adopted children.

Therefore, with all your people, in every time and place
we sing the triumphant hymn of your glory:

All **Holy, Holy, Holy Lord**
God of power and might.
Heaven and earth are full of your glory.
Hosanna in the highest!

Leader Blessed is he who comes in the name of the Lord.

All **Hosanna in the highest.**

Leader And we come to this table
To remember how you became human
under the name of Jesus.
Who on the night when his name was betrayed
shared food and wine with those he loved.
He took bread,
Sign of health and life,
Broke it and shared it with them naming it as his body.
And he took a cup of wine,
Sign of celebration and joy,
Shared it with them naming it
as his blood that would be spilled.

We come here to do the same in memory of Christ.

Come, Spirit of God,
Move over these signs of life and celebration,
This bread and wine,
That we may take them as your body and blood.

As we stand around this table,
May we be your people,
Committed to your kingdom
Whose name is justice, peace and love.

All **Amen.**

Peter Colwell
England

Consecration
and
Dedication

A Blessing for Anglican Ordinands
Written in the Celtic tradition

May the God of guinea fowl gather with you each morning.
May the God of processing ants keep you in step.
May the God of spiders spin patterns of meaning.
May the God of sparrows sing you out of sorrow.

May the God of the storm guard you in the eye of it.
May the God of the wave unfurl insight and wisdom.
May the God of seals flip you into playfulness.
May the God of whales carry you on her back.

Grow and be suckled in the curl and lick of mother bear.
Fly and be free in the careful talons of the eagle king.
Roar out truth in the opening jaw of the prophet lion.
Bless and be blessed in the name of the Creator God.

Viv Stacey
South Africa

Blessing of a Newly Professed Nun

Send out your Spirit, Lord, upon this child of yours
who has left everything for you.
Set her, Father, in the full radiance of the face of your Son,
that she may catch his beauty, and by what she becomes
show all the world that Jesus is living in his Church.

Free from every selfish care
may she take into herself the cares of her brothers and sisters,
realizing that in allaying the sorrows of others
she is comforting the Lord himself suffering in them.

May the great human scene be lit up for her and given meaning
by the vision of your providence at work always and everywhere.

May the gift she makes of herself
hasten the coming of your kingdom,
and may she find her true place with all who love you
in the heavenly fatherland.

We ask this through Christ our Lord. Amen.

Elizabeth Obbard
England

Blessing of a Brother before Leaving the Monastery to do Outside Work

Versicle The Lord watch over your going out and your coming in.

Response From this time forth forevermore.

Superior May the God of peace, who raised up from the dead our Lord Jesus, the great shepherd of the sheep, by the blood of the eternal covenant, make you perfect in everything good that you may do his will, working in you that which is pleasing in his sight:
through Jesus Christ, to whom be glory forever and ever. Amen.

Community of the Resurrection
Mirfield, England

For Judith,
On the Occasion of Her Ordination

May the rainbow God,
the colorful Christ,
and the paradoxical spirit
that is the lightness
of all being,
be with you
today and always.

Joy Mead
England

Dedication of Those Who Work with Children

This can be used to commission catechists, as a prayer for parents,
or with any group who works with children.

Minister or Child   In the name of the Lord Jesus Christ, the head of
the Church, we commission you for service as ministers for children in
this church.
We pray that you
will be enriched with the Holy Spirit;
will find grace to be faithful in your work;
will be led to a deeper understanding of the gospel
and sustained in your sense of calling to proclaim it by word and
example.

The congregation is then asked to support and encourage those commissioned
and to hold them in prayer.

Prayer
Nurturing God, we seek your blessing on these your servants. Grant
them vision and courage, patience and persistence, enthusiasm and
devotion. Give them the heart and mind of Christ, that they may understand and care in love for those committed to their charge.
Deepen their knowledge
hold them in times of difficulty
and give them a sense of joy in their calling.

Rosemary Johnston
England

The Sacred Three

Triune God

Triune God
Father all loving
Son all compassionate
Holy Spirit source of all life
Embrace us
Cleanse us
Renew us in your life
To be to your glory
Triune God

Community of St. Peter
Woking, England

One in Three, Three in One

The blessing of God who creates and upholds,
The blessing of God who redeems and endures,
The blessing of God who inspires and leads on,
The blessing of God, one in three, three in one,
be with you this day and into the night
and guide all you love to the kingdom of light.

Jean Mayland
England

The Blessing of the Three

The blessing of God and the Lord be yours,
The blessing of the perfect Spirit be yours,
The blessing of the Three be pouring for you
Mildly and generously,
Mildly and generously.

Carmina Gadelica

A Trinitarian Blessing

God the Father, who created you
help you value all that is.

God the Son, who died and rose for you,
help you say "Yes" to all that can be.

God the Holy Spirit, thrilling through every fiber of your being,
help you make each "Yes" come true.

And the blessing of God Almighty, Father, Son, and Holy Spirit,
be with you and remain with you always.

John Petty
England

The Trinity Blessing

Yours be the blessing of God and the Lord;
The perfect Spirit his blessing afford;
The Trinity's blessing on you be outpoured
With gentle and generous shedding abroad,
So gently, gen'rously just for you stored.

Source Unknown

Strength, Light and Love

God the Father give you his strength,
God the Son give you his light,
God the Holy Spirit fill your heart with his love.
So may the one true God, Father, Son, and Holy Spirit,
Bless, guard, guide and keep you
Now and forever. Amen.

Mark Santer
England

The Place

This is an adaptation of a Celtic ritual called caim *which is an encircling ritual with pre-Christian origins. Turn around in a circle to your right, drawing a circle with your right index finger, saying:*

May God the image maker bless us,
May God the image bearer bless us,
May God the image grower bless us,
May the Holy Three bless us, now and forever. Amen.

Janet Lees
England

The Great Mystery

May the Great One who is both mother and father bless you
May the Suffering Servant who is both brother and sister bless you
May the Great Spirit who is neither male nor female bless you.
The blessing of the Trinity, the Great Mystery,
be yours now and always.

John Johansen-Berg
England

Lullaby

Rest in the love of the Father
Rest in the love of the Son,
Rest in the love of the Spirit,
The love of the sacred Three
Your rest-place be.

Ann Lewin
England

Holy Wisdom

Holy Wisdom

May Holy Wisdom,
kind to humanity,
steadfast, sure and free,
the breath of the power of God,
may she who makes all things new, in every age,
enter our souls,
and make us friends of God,
through Jesus Christ.

St. Hilda Community
England

The Purpose

You are embraced by the love of God
You are accompanied by the Son of God
You are called out by the Spirit of God—
listen—She is calling you in the streets!
Take with you the peace of Christ,
the love of God and the fellowship of the Holy Spirit,
with you now and forever.

Janet Lees
England

Blessed Be God, My Guide

Blessed be God, my guide
who trains my hands for justice
and my fingers for healing,
my safe haven and my home,
my imagination and my passion,

the word who opens the doors of the soul,
    who connects me to other beating hearts.
O Wise and Holy One, how carefully
you made us so that we might
be clay with color, full of divine
radiance, yet open for all the
earth to fill.
Our days are but a moment
through which your breath passes,
sanctifying body and soul.
Burst from our hearts, Sister and Friend,
unite us to one another like forests
sharing sunshine and rain.

Gertrude Lebans
Canada

Keep your Worship True

May the Lord of wisdom
guide
your every
action;
May the Lord of glory
keep your worship
true;
May the Lord of justice
fire
you with his
passion;
May the Lord of mercy
grace
his world
through
you.

Mike Hollow
England

A Glass of Blessings

May God the giver of all good things bless you with:
The understanding of friends
The lessons of experience—painful and pleasant
The testimonies of believers
The questionings of seekers
The examples of saints
The instructions of teachers
The wisdom of thinkers
The visions of spiritual guides
The sacrifices of givers
The service of helpers
Now and always.
Amen.

Henry Rack
England

Fountain of Living Water

May the blessing of God, fountain of living water,
flow within us as a river of life.
May we drink deep of her wisdom.
May we never thirst again.
May we go through life refreshing many,
as a sign of healing for all;
through the One who is Life eternal.

Miriam Therese Winter
USA

Information, Knowledge and Wisdom

All-knowing God,
The folly of God is wiser than the wisdom of humankind.
Such knowledge is too wonderful for me.

Creating God
we give you thanks for the inventiveness of the human mind
which explores the far boundaries of knowledge
and makes connections and proposes theories
to add to the quantity and quality of life

We thank you for the thirst for information
which makes learning pleasure
and discovery delight;
which draws us beyond the familiar and the known
to the very edge of understanding.

We thank you for the skill of mind and hand
which originated computer technology
that smooths and speeds our way through many tasks
and gives us access to immense stores of information
and immediate communication.

But information is not the same as knowledge
nor is knowledge wisdom.

Forgive us the folly and greed for power
which hook us into a web of overwork
and mesh us in an exclusive community
which divides the powerful from the powerless.

Show us how to find ways of sharing knowledge
and opening ideas to one another
so that the superhighway is also a way
of just trade and peaceful communication.

And teach us the difference between
a web of information
a body of knowledge
and a God of wisdom.

Heather Pencavel
England

Beatitudes of a Still-Seeking Christian

Blessed are those who ask difficult questions:
they are honoring their God-given brains.

Blessed are those who don't have glib answers:
they offer a refreshing change.

Blessed are those who are not afraid to say
"I do not know for sure" or "I could be wrong":
their integrity will be rewarded.
Blessed are those who do not judge others
by their sexual orientation, gender or beliefs:
God will cherish their compassion.

Blessed are those who respect different ways of praising God:
gifts will be given to them.

Blessed are those whose coming to faith was gentle
and unspectacular:
they are good to be with.

Blessed are those who listen quietly to others' hurts:
they will be known as sensitive friends.

Blessed are you when you are awed by the Mystery of God,
can find few words to describe your highest experiences, and so love
your neighbor that you can be supportive of others while they take different paths from yours. Some may tell you that you are not a proper
Christian, but you will be on the way to wholeness as a human being.

Kate Compston
England

May All Beings

May all beings be at ease
Whatever living beings there may be
Whether they are weak or strong, omitting none
The great or the mighty, medium, short or small
May all beings be at ease

May all beings be at ease
Whatever living beings there may be
The seen and the unseen, those living near and far away
Those born and to be born
May all beings be at ease

Radha Sahar
Aotearoa New Zealand

Someone Said...

Someone said:
"We've always done it this way. Do not try something new."
Someone said:
"We must have another yard sale: it keeps the church going!"
Someone said:
"Pick some hymns that we know!"
And someone said:
"This church is too small, it is better to close it down."
But I heard a different voice say:
"Sovereign Lord, can these dry bones live?"

Spirit of Wisdom,
yelling in the street,
upsetting our easiness,
calling us to change:
show us the way of risk,
give us life,
lead us to the joy we will find in the recklessness of your foolishness.

Peter Colwell
England

A Sabbath Blessing

O Wise and Holy One
bless you for the Sabbath
we used to have—
A day of rest
    from checkout lines
    and sorry-sir-this-line-is-closed,
    from how-are-you-today
    did-you-find-everything-you-want?
    and have-a-nice-day,
    from piling up more and more
    to burglar-proof and insure
    from buying and selling time
    and rushing to beat time

A day of relief
    from our infinite loop of
    Monday to Monday—
    week after week of
    endless beginnings

O Wise and Holy One, bless us with
    the courage to redeem
    from our seven days of racing
    time against time
    your one day of
    time-out-of-time

Bless us with
    the wisdom to see
    the humility to admit
we need a Sabbath day—
    Sunday, Saturday, Friday
    or middle-of-the-week-day
a day of exodus
    from stocks and bonds
    of pay-out and pay-off
pay up and pay back
a day of recreation
    to take stock of our souls
    to rediscover ourselves
    as shareholders
Wise and Holy One
    in your company.

Norm S. D. Esdon
Canada

May the Longtime Sun

May the longtime sun shine upon you
All love surround you
And the pure light within you
Guide your way on.

Traditional

Green Leaves in a White Jug

Blessed is the judgment
        of this white jug
on its dun background
        with its green leaves
Blessed is the green leaf and the dry
Blessed is the clay
        in the hands of the potter
Blessed is the filled jug
        solid, cool, the thirst-slaker
lightening held to the parched
        lips of the juice-taker

Blessed are they who share this jug
        and this juice
who partake of this life-giving gouache
        water, honey, and gum.

Blessed is the
man who walks humbly
in the sight of this white jug
Blessed is he who abases
        in the presence of these green leaves
        in the silence of this jug
welling, spilling
        running over with love
from the deep river
        flooding through all our lives.

Blessed is he who can see
in the life brought, pulsating, to a still
        the presence
of the invisible
        uttering
the unspoken

Blessed is the traveler who sits still
        and sees
sunlight on folded hands
        in railway carriages

white petals, patches
red, yellow, flick
in the passing flower gardens:
patches of light reflected
from women standing by clotheslines
      forms in adventure playgrounds
flecks reflected from walls
      of white and brown washed houses

into the white jug with them whence they came.
Brian Louis Pearce
England

A Blessing on Opposites

A blessing on the light
and a blessing on the dark.

A blessing on beginnings
and a blessing on endings.

A blessing on the open
and a blessing on the closed.

A blessing on friends
and a blessing on strangers.

A blessing on the known
and a blessing on the hidden.

A blessing on consistency
and a blessing on upheavals.

A blessing on the living
and a blessing on the dead.
Kate Compston
England

Paradox

The Christian faith is full of it,
And so is all of life.
Lord, bless our state of paradox;
Let it not end in strife.
Lord, bless our world of opposites
And weave them into one.
Lord, bless us as we live with this—
A task scarcely begun!

Sister Michelle, OHP
England

A Blessing

May we sow seeds of justice,
May we nurture holy visions,
May we harvest gentle wisdom,
May patience be our grain.

May we mix in grace and courage,
May we kindle fires of truth,
May we share the bread of healing,
May God's banquet fill each hand.

Keri Wehlander
Canada

Woman of Wisdom

Written on the occasion of the 70th birthday of my mother-in-law.
(This can be sung to the hymn tune: Gift of Love (8888)).

Woman of wisdom, Spirit-filled,
May we stand with you at the well.
May the new life you come to know
Rest upon all who seek to grow.

Woman of wisdom, without fear,
Reach out to touch the Savior's hem.
Share with us healing you receive.
Show us anew we can believe.

Woman of wisdom, seeking yet
A place at table to be fed.
Claim your desire for spiritual food.
We seek with you to be renewed.

Woman of wisdom, coins in hand,
Striving to follow faith's demand.
Generous widow, help us to give.
Through your example, many live.

Woman of wisdom, at Christ's feet
Learning and sharing words of life.
Beside you there we find a space
To know the blessings of his grace.

Michael Jacob Kooiman
Canada

To Be Silent...

Blessing Prayer for a Place to Be Used as a Hermitage

My Lord and my God,
     you did call, from their busy daily lives,
     your servants Moses, Elijah, John the Baptist,
     Mary of Nazareth and your Son, Jesus,
     to come apart and to spend time in solitude.
Some you have called to the desert,
     some to mountain peaks,
     others to the hidden hermitage within their homes.
I have heard that ancient desert call
     and seek to be alone with you.

Since I lack a nearby mountain or desert,
     I will use this space I have.
My Lord, you who are the creator of all space,
     you who make lonely desert places holy,
     come and consecrate this place
     as a temporary hermitage for me.
Cleanse it of noise
     and anything that might call me out of its stillness.
May this space, sacred by your blessing,
     become for me a waiting room
     where I shall wait upon you,
     my Lord, my beloved, my friend.

May prayerful peace flow outward from here,
     touching with grace all those whom I love
     and all the earth as well.
May all dark powers be impotent,
     unable to cross the sacred circle
     that surrounds this holy hermitage.

Help me, my Lord, to leave outside this hermitage
      my plans for tomorrow, my memories of yesterday,
      as I live fully and completely
in the wonder of your present moment.

Lord, may my prayer be one with that of all persons
      who throughout this earth are in solitude and stillness,
      forming a luminous and silent hymn of glory to you.

May your blessing, Almighty God,
      Father, Son, and Holy Spirit,
      be upon this hermitage and this solitary time.

Edward Hays
USA

Prayer before Leaving a Hermitage or Ending a Time of Solitude

My Lord, it is time for me to return.
I thank you for this quiet time apart,
      unburdened by my normal duties of life.
This time alone
      has been renewed and re-creating for me
      as body and spirit have been healed.
Its rest has given a boost to my body.
Its silence has been as a salve to my spirit.
This time apart from others
      has renewed within me a desire to be in communion
      with all those whom I love.
Fire within me the desire
      to join them and all others
      on the crowded journey of life.

I thank you, O Secret One,
      for the graces of this time in solitude.
Each time I withdraw to be alone,
      I learn more not to fear being alone,
I thus prepare myself for that final moment
      when I shall pass through the desert of death,
      with its absolute aloneness,
      and come to absolute communion of life eternal
      with you.

My Lord, I treasure this time now ending.
Help me, as I return to the flow of daily life.
    the good and the bad
    mistakes and successes—
    whatever you have laid out for me.

May this holy time of prayerful solitude
    fill me with the necessary energy
    to once again take up the challenge
    of finding holiness in the midst of my work,
    in the center of my home.
Come, my beloved,
    and accompany me as I return
    to the crowded and noisy crossroads of life.

Edward Hays
USA

Wallis House Blessing

Frederic Wallis House is an Ecumenical Retreat and Conference Center in the heart of Hutt City, near Wellington, Aotearoa New Zealand. This blessing can be used in similar situations around the world.

On the house and the land
the blessing of God,
on the trees and the pathways
the moving of God,
in our talking and praying
the listening of God,
in our troubles and laughter
the company of God,
on the community and the guests
the peace of the Spirit of God.

John Stewart Murray
Aotearoa New Zealand

A Blessing Inspired by Coleg Trefeca

A Christian training and conference center in Wales

God's blessing be on you as you enter this place.
In the stillness and the beauty,
in the solid, simple welcome of stones,
built on faith and vision,
hallowed by prayers and pilgrim lives.

Christ's blessing be among you as you stay in this place.
In shared laughter and common tasks,
in the meeting of minds and hearts,
in the healing touch of community.

The Spirit's blessing be with you as you go from this place.
In energy restored and vision focused,
in the stirring of your heart, tumbling into prayer and action,
in the knowledge that you are not alone.

May the blessing of God's presence be with you and go with you.
This day and every day.
Amen.

Fiona Liddell
Wales

Saints Still Alive!

The Love of Christ Embrace You

After the vision of Mechthild of Magdeburg

May the love of Christ embrace you,
The divinity of the Creator infuse you,
And the joy of the Spirit lead you
always
Further into all bliss.

Christina Rees
England

Hildegard Blessing

Based on her Hymn to the Spirit, "O ignis Spiritus"

May the strengthening Spirit bear fruit in your creating;
May the anointing Spirit touch your brokenness;
May the breath of the Spirit infuse your heart with the beautiful
    perfumes of goodness;
May the flowing Spirit spring up as Wisdom's fountain in your heart;
May the enfolding Spirit become your well fitting garment;
May the sword of the Spirit defend your vulnerability;
May the guiding Spirit lead you through the heights and the depths;
May the elemental Spirit connect you to the natural world;
May the joyful Spirit temper the solemnity of our knowing,
So that you may become a song within the Divine creation.

June Boyce-Tillman
England

Blessing from Saints of the North

Blessings of Hilda, God's battlemaid, and her beacon-monastery
high on cliff top;
> of Aidan, wise teacher, strong leader, gentle friend;
> of Columba, exile for Christ, radiant light beaming out from Iona
>> into dark reaches of unbelief;
> of Caedmon, herdsman-poet, first to hymn the Creation in
> common speech;
> of Bede, scholar, translator, devoted chronicler of Church's story;

Blessings of Colman, Chad, Oswald, and of all God's saints, who wove
Christ into the warp and weft of life's fabrics in this northern region;

Blessed be God for their presence and prayers today!

Sister Catherine, OHP
England

A Franciscan Blessing

Leader   Blessed be God, Father, Son, and Holy Spirit.
All   And blessed be his kingdom now and forever.

Leader   We have been crucified with Christ.
All   It is no longer we who live, but Christ who lives in us.

Leader   We count everything as loss.
All   Because of the surpassing worth of knowing
             Christ Jesus our Lord.

Blessed are you Lord, God of all life and author of all creation.

Blessed are you in the life of your servant, Francis, the little poor man
of Assisi, who in his compassion poured out your love to the outcast
and forgotten, the sick and the dying, the humble and the hungry.

Blessed are you in Francis' humility, wherein he was taken by others
and spent in your name.

Blessed are you in Francis' joy in your Spirit, and his union with you in
his work for the whole of creation.

Blessed are you in our brother the sun, our sister the moon and in mother earth and in all that sustains life, and brings us the hope of salvation.

Blessed are you for the gifts of the earth; for life-giving water, for the warmth of fire, and for the wind and rain that sustain all that lives and grows.

Blessed are you in the love we receive from our brothers and sisters and in whom Christ is ever present to greet us.

Blessed are you in the kindness and gentleness of death in which you will finally bring us into your arms and embrace us in your love as our creator, our redeemer, and our eternal keeper.

Blessed are you in all things, at all times, and in all places, as Francis taught us through his ceaseless giving and love.

Blessed be God, Father, Son, and Holy Spirit.

Blessed be God, Blessed be God, Blessed be God forever.

Stephen Platten
England

Let Nothing Disturb You

Let nothing disturb you;
let nothing dismay you;
all things pass:
God never changes.
Patience attains
all it strives for.
Those who have God
find they lack nothing:
God alone suffices.

Teresa of Avila

A Petition for the Life of the Martyrs and the People

Originally written and read with Guatemalan Christian Action at a meeting of the Commission of Accompaniment for the Fulfillment of the Peace Accords, October, 1997

We invite ourselves to hold a moment of silence to remember all of those brothers and sisters, all of those families, who died by blows of the stick, flames of the fire, wounds from the machete; for those who gritted their teeth in the fire; for all of those who were banished from their homes—the heart of the family—and those who were pulled away from the wombs of their mothers.

Today it is they who are the witnesses, who are the stars in the firmament.

Silence

That they should be the bearers of presenting our petitions, our problems, before *Ajaw*—God, the Mother and the Father—for us, for we shelter so much sorrow, pain, forgetfulness and death.

Aye, *Ajaw*, Mother and Father! We no longer want any more difficult roads to travel, afflicting roads, thorny roads, roads that wound and kill, roads that drain our hope. No more detours or straying. Now no more with the persecution of indigenous peoples and the dispersed in the jungle, mountains, cities and the countryside. Enough! We do not want more authority, more "power" placed over us.

Oh, *Ajaw*! may the forces of the wind drive away the darkness so that, unobstructed, we can have a voice and a force, so that we may participate and talk of justice, of liberty and of democracy from the four cardinal points, so only joy invades the heart of the child, the woman, the man, the elder.

Oh, *Ajaw*! so that when the new dawn arrives all of your sons and daughters will be ready to lay down these pains and to proclaim you in those places in which you are invoked.

That it may be so.

Juan Ixchop Us
Guatemala
Translated by Garry G. Sparks, USA

Ajaw: Lord

Preserve and Instruct Us

May the strength of God pilot us
May the power of God preserve us
May the wisdom of God instruct us
May the hand of God protect us
May the way of God direct us
May the shield of God defend us
May the hosts of God protect us
Now, and always.

Attributed to St. Patrick of Ireland
5th Century

Places of Worship

Blessing a Place of Worship

Almighty God and Heavenly Father bless and hallow (make a sign of the cross here) this place of worship, that all who come to it may find in you the delight of new life and a strengthened faith, with their joy and happiness in him who gave himself for others, even Jesus Christ our Lord. Amen.

Giles Harcourt
England

Blessing a Banner

Heavenly Father, as with the disciples of your blessed Son you gathered the fragments of humanity and food, that none might be lost, so we thank you that in the careful and patient making of this banner, in all its beauty and color, you hold us close to your most loving servant *(Name)* in whose memory we bless and dedicate this wonderful creation made by *(name artist/s)*. We joyfully offer this in the name of him who gives himself continually for others, Jesus Christ our Lord. Amen.

Giles Harcourt
England

Blessing an Altar Frontal

Heavenly Father, giver of all gifts, bless we pray this altar frontal as a delightful expression of new life and abundant creation in your blessed Son. Let those who made it, and all who see it, marvel at the patience and care and joy that went into its making; so that these same qualities may shine in our lives, for the furtherance of your love and the extension of your kingdom, through Jesus Christ our Lord. Amen.

Giles Harcourt
England

Refurbishment of a Chapel

Heavenly Father, you bring the brightness of morning and the gift of each new day; you renew the beauty of nature and the hopes of our lives. We give profound thanks for the refurbishment of this chapel, for all who gave so generously of their time, skill and money, and for those who have cared for us in the transition. Sanctify what has been retained and bless all that is new, as we continue in your love and dedicate ourselves anew to your service. Fill our hearts with such wonder and thanksgiving that we may fill this house of prayer with true worship and praise, through him who makes all things new, the same Jesus Christ our Lord. Amen.

Giles Harcourt
England

Service for the Re-opening of a Church Hall

All glory and praise are yours,
Lord God,
creator of the universe and Father of all:
we thank you for calling us in Jesus
to be your beloved people
and temples of your Holy Spirit.

Remember the promises of the Lord Jesus
and listen to the prayer we offer in his name.

Bless us in all we do
and bless once more this hall (these halls)
in which your people will meet,
and work, and play.
Help us to recognize your presence among us,
fill us with your joy,
and guide us at all times.

We give you praise and thanks, heavenly Father,
through Jesus Christ our Son
in the love of your Holy Spirit,
now and forever.

Roy Williamson
England

Blessing for Church Cleaning

Bless, O Lord, our task of making this church clean and fit for worship. May its brightness be a witness to your glory and an aid to the reverence of those who enter here. Take our hands, and use them in your service.

Raymond Chapman
England

Blessing for Churchyard Work

Almighty God, eternally present in the beauty of nature, and with whom the souls of the faithful departed are at peace, bless our work in caring for all that lies around our church, that it may be a fitting approach to the worship within.

Raymond Chapman
England

Blessing a Garden Seat in an Area of Remembrance

Lord of all Creation, of the earth in all its strength and fragile beauty, we give to this ground now hallowed again in your name, the gift of this seating which encircles this tree, that, as with your Holy Spirit, all who rest here may find solace and comfort and renewal.

We remember especially your servant *(Name of donor and/or person in whose name the seat is given)*, beloved of *(Name)* and the family, and held close in our hearts. The strength of his/her kindness, his/her courage and fortitude remain with us. The grace of his/her personality and spirit enliven us. The steadfastness of his/her love and purpose inspires.

By the power of your Spirit and the sanctity of your name, we ask you to bless and sanctify this gift of the open air, in the name of him who gave rest and refreshment to others, Jesus Christ our Lord. Amen.

Giles Harcourt
England

Fruits of the Spirit

Galatians 5:22–23

The Spirit produces love,
joy, peace, patience, kindness,
goodness, faithfulness, humility
and self-control.

Encourage and Challenge

Risk Everything

May the blessing of God who risked everything for our sake, the blessing of Jesus Christ—the indignant youth—who cleanses everything and releases in us new visions of hope, and the blessing of the Holy Spirit who guides and directs us into new forms of obedience, be with us all.

Usha Joshua
India

God Has Given Us a Dream

God has given us a dream:
a tree whose leaves are for the healing of the nations.
And into our hands God places the seeds
to give birth to such a tree.
Go forth with that dream inside you.
Go forth with hope burning bright.
Go to be planters of seeds,
nurturers of hopeful things.
And may God bless you with the vision
of that hope come to fruition before your eyes.

Roberta Rominger
USA/England

Go as Far as You Dare

Go as far as you dare, for you cannot go beyond the reach of God.
Give as extravagantly as you like, for you cannot spend
    all the riches of God.
Care as lavishly as you are able, for you cannot exhaust the love of God.
Keep moving on for God will always be with you.

Marjorie Dobson
England

Move Us to Change

God of holy process
move us to change
our ways
as well as our language,
that our weapons
may become ploughshares
in practice
as well as in poetry,
that we may see our uncertainties
and insecurities
not as worries
but as blessings.

Joy Mead
England

Stir Up a Divine Restlessness

May God the Father who called the world into being name you with his love;
May God the Son who harrowed hell and dragged Adam from the grave
    lead you into life;
May God the Holy Spirit who troubled the waters of creation stir up a
    divine restlessness in your hearts;
And the Blessing of God Almighty, the Father, the Son, and the Holy
    Spirit be upon you and remain with you this Holy Day and
    forevermore.

James E. Atwell
England

A Blessing for Strength

O God, where hearts are fearful and limited:
Grant freedom and daring.
Where anxiety is infectious and widening:
Grant peace and reassurance.
Where impossibilities close every door and window:
Grant imagination and resistance.
Where distrust reshapes every understanding:
Grant healing and transformation.

Where spirits are daunted and dimmed:
Grant soaring wings and strengthened dreams.
Keri Wehlander
Canada

It Is So Easy to Say

God bless you—
    It is so easy to say,
    a clerical word, a cheap comfort.

But to mean it and believe it,
that's different.

May God stir you with the Spirit
    to adventure and risk and dream;
May God wash from you
    all old prejudice and fear;
May God heal within you
    broken promises and relationships;
May God challenge your compromise
    with the spirit of the age;
May God lead you into obedience
    and service for the kingdom.

May God bless you—
    not cheap, not easy at all,
    but a cross-carrying word,
    a word from the upper room.
Bernard Thorogood
Australia

Courage Blessing

Fall in love with living
Wrestling with the chaos and the pain
Within yourself and within the world.
Join the celebration of life,
Dancing with the angels and the clowns.
And may the God of peace and joy,
Who is continually making all things new,
Embrace you
As a partner
In the divine creating.

June Boyce-Tillman
England

Bless Me!

Bless me, Lord
when my mind is closed to the ways you meet others
that I may loosen the parameters which I place around you.
Bless me with the willingness to listen to you through the insight and
thoughts of others who also listen and receive and are a blessing from you.

Bless me, Lord
when my heart is closed to the ways your love is felt by others
that my heart may expand beyond the protective shield of my unloving.
Bless me with the desire to be at ease in the breadth and depth and
marvel at the way you touch the different who are blessing for me, too.

Bless me, Lord
when I from my own special and particular pilgrimage deny
the pilgrimage of others
that I may be sensitive to your presence in lives very different from mine.
Bless me with openness to the abundance of your spirit in the
wonder of human variety, your creation and your delight.

Bless me, Lord
when I seek to limit the nature of people's lives through which
I'm prepared to see you
that I may be bold in my confidence that you are the one
who shapes and moulds and creates through each and all waiting on you.

Bless me with such a welcome for the different and unusual
that my world may grow toward the world you know.

Bless me, Lord
when I hide in the culture and among the people with whom I'm familiar
so that I cannot appreciate or even imagine and least of all enjoy
the glitter of the peoples and cultures who surround me, close by
and far away.
Bless me so that I may soar above my small world, familiar and safe
to enjoy you so present and glorious among the many and the varied.

Bless me, Lord
so finite and fixed and placed.
Bless me, Lord
so closeted and bound.
Bless me, Lord
so small
that even I might rise toward you
through the richness of your friends, the generosity of your blessing.

John Ll. Humphreys
Wales

Make a Difference in the World

May God bless you with discomfort at easy answers,
half-truths, superficial relationships,
so that you will live deep within your heart.

May God bless you with anger at injustice,
oppression, and exploitation of people,
so that you will work for justice, equity, and peace.

May God bless you with tears to shed for those who suffer from pain,
rejection, starvation, and war,
so that you will reach out your hand to comfort them and change their
pain to joy.

And may God bless you with the foolishness to think that you can make
a difference in the world,
so that you will do the things which others tell you cannot be done.

Source Unknown
Canada

Release Us

Release us, O God,
from the temptations and the lies of evil,
from the culture of superficiality,
from the sensation-seeking media,
from artificial needs,
from speculation in our longing for love,
from over-consumption,
from violence in all its shapes,
from xenophobia,
from degradation of people,
from the hell of loneliness,
from indifference to the need of the world,
from the slavery of drugs,
from restlessness and anxiety,
from superficial spirituality,
from a life without you.
Release us in your grace,
restore us in your love,
guide us in your truth,
you who are the way,
the truth,
and the life.

Per Harling
Sweden

Give Us the Courage to Change

I look at my world, our world,
a sign of wonder,
a symbol of God's creation:
populations are displaced,
mud slips, decisions are made,
satellite dishes are installed,
boundaries are re-located,
countries are re-named, and I
realize that nothing
stays the same—change is painful,
change is frightening, yet
change can also bring new life.
I look at our world.

I look at our churches: my church,
sign of wonder,
symbol of your creation, O God.
Let your holy Spirit, weaving, moving,
threading, living and breathing,
among us,
give us the courage to change,
so that we may move forward together
in life, in death and in new life
and draw us to the Cross, to the
sign of wonder, symbol of your creation,
as fragile as a leaf—your son
Jesus Christ.
I look at a leaf.

Ruth Harvey
England

New Ways

Bless us, Lord, as we try to work out new ways
of encouraging others to consider
whatever is true, whatever is pure,
whatever is lovely, whatever is admirable,
whatever is excellent or praiseworthy.
Lord, there are so many people
who want to make a meal of lesser things.

Help us to praise the things that are precious.
Help us to put into words, pictures, actions
and so much more, great deeds that will pull others
toward higher aspiration and inspiration.

Help us all, Lord.

Peter Comaish
England

We are Encouraged

Leader Now go forth all of you who have received God's power and grace. May the God who has become our Father, the source of life; our Mother, the nurturer and giver of joy, empower us all. Live a life worthy of your calling. Plant the seed of hope amidst hopelessness and despair. Work for peace amidst all that hinders the working of the Holy Spirit. Together, heal the broken world and restore order amidst chaos, remembering that God is always at our side to encourage us, behind us to push us ahead, in front of us to lead the way, and above us to shelter us and give us strength.

All Amen and Amen!

Angeling B. Esquierdo
Philippines

To Work for Change

God who weeps at injustice and oppression,
    genocide and crucifixion:
we grieve the state of our world—
so much brokenness and violence,
so much pain and unfairness.
God who aches for a different way,
    a peaceable respect, a community of equals and a realm of love:
we ask for hope in order to work for change;
we ask for courage to resist in the face of opposition;
we ask for faith to believe in the possibility of peace.

United Church of Canada

Jesus, Courageous and Vulnerable

Jesus, courageous and vulnerable, you broke into the vicious circle.
  May we break into cycles of violence?
Jesus, bold and brave, you confronted the traditional customs.
  May we confront patterns of hatred and prejudice?
Jesus, assertive and strong, you challenged the perpetrators.
  May we challenge victimizers and abusers in our day?
Jesus, clear and direct, you drew a line in the sand.
  May we refuse to accept injustice?
Jesus, amazing and powerful, you got them to drop their stones.
  May we find ways to be in the world
  that increase safety, establish fairness and promote peace.
United Church of Canada

Blessing of Flame

May the fierce breath of God
  blow through our lives
  and set us ablaze.

May the brilliance of her presence
  kindle courage in us
  for every wilderness.

May the fervor of her calling
  continually disturb us
  and draw us forth.

May her fiery faith in us
  be the spark that takes hold
  teaching us to do the same.
Keri Wehlander
Canada

Go with Courage

Take up the task with hope and faith!
We believe that we are the children of God.
The world is always waiting for us to emerge:
so, go with courage into the costly path of Christ,
go with imagination into the creative life of God
and go with freedom into the life of the Spirit.

Dorothy McRae-McMahon
Australia

Go Forth...Ask...Share!

Go forth now to live life to the full.
Where you've got questions, ask them!
Where you think you've found answers, share them!
And may our gracious God meet you,
with peace and hope and joy.

Roberta Rominger
USA/England

Let Justice Flow...

A Blessing for Speaking Out

May we leave the land of silence,
May we bring our truth to voice,
May hope be ours in every step,
May healing flow in every word,
May others stand with us in grace,
May God grant us peace.

Keri Wehlander
Canada

Stir Up!

Stir up, O God, our wills and kindle our understanding; that we may discern the way to a just society, where all may work and all may find a fair reward, serving Thee and one another in peace and goodwill, in the spirit of Jesus Christ our Lord.

Bob Knight
England

Blessing for Those in Mission

Go now and take your place on holy ground.
All God's creation is holy ground.
May peace be your dream,
justice be your vision on the way,
and God's freedom open before you
like a pathway of hope.

Dorothy McRae-McMahon
Australia

The Gathering

As we have been gathered, so we must be sown back into the world to witness to the power of God's transforming love, to support and challenge each other, to bring healing and justice to the world around us.

Gertrude Lebans
Canada

Open Eyes and Hearts

Leader   May God bless us with strength to seek justice.
All   Amen.
Leader   May God bless us with wisdom to care for our earth.
All   Amen.
Leader   May God bless us with love to bring forth new life.
All   Amen.
Leader   In the name of God, the maker of the whole world,
       of Jesus, our new covenant,
       and of the Holy Spirit who opens eyes and hearts.
All   Amen.

Catholic Organization for Development and Peace
Canada

A Justice Blessing

Judges 11:34–40
The God of Jephthah and his daughter
preserve us from exploitative relationships.

Genesis 16
The God of Hagar and Sarah
disrupt our patterns of humiliation.

1 Samuel 4:10–22
The God of Phinehas' wife and their child
bless and honor our longings for peace.

Exodus 1:15–21
The God of Shiprah and Puah
bless and strengthen us in all our action for justice.

Janet Wootton
England

God of Justice

God of all times and places,
who brings light into the world's darkness,
we come to you with our prayers:

So that the children may no longer be denied education;
so that the sick may no longer die from curable diseases;
so that the workers may no longer be cheated of justice;
your kingdom come:
your will be done on earth as it is in heaven.

So that financial systems may no more burden the poorest;
so that our trade may no more deny a fair wage;
so that debt may no more trap nations in poverty;
your kingdom come:
your will be done on earth as it is in heaven.

So that the innocent will walk free from prison;
so that minorities will live without fear;
so that the whole earth will worship in freedom;
your kingdom come:
your will be done on earth as it is in heaven.

Peter Graystone
England

Open the Door

For one voice

Open the door, that Christ may come in.
Open the door, that we may go out to his world.
This is the house of God;

here is the home of the homeless.
Peace on all who enter,
blessing on those who depart.
Open the door!

Walk in and walk out;
find here, and beyond, the God of the years.

Open the door!
Bring hope to the no-future people.
Open the door!
It is Christ who is calling for bread.

Paul Sheppy
England

Open the Door

For two voices

Voice One	Open the door, that Christ may come in.
Voice Two	Open the door, that we may go out to his world.
One	This is the house of God;
Two	here is the home of the homeless.
One	Peace on all who enter,
Two	blessing on those who depart.
One	Open the door!
	Walk in and walk out;
	find here, and beyond, the God of the years.
Two	Open the door!
	Bring hope to the no-future people.
	Open the door!
	It is Christ who is calling for bread.

Paul Sheppy
England

God Who Dances in Creation

May the God who dances in creation,
who embraces us with human love,
who shakes our lives like thunder,
bless us and drive us out with power
to fill the world with her justice.

St. Hilda Community
England

Give and Take

As you go:
take Jesus in your hearts
        to offer his love to the loveless;
take God in your minds
        to speak his peace to the restless;
take the Holy Spirit in your lives
        to live in his power,
        for the sake of our Lord,
        and for all those he would reach
        through you.

Duncan L. Tuck
Wales

May the Grace of God Sweep through this World

May the love of God sweep through this nation,
releasing us from the need to claim our debts,
and leading us into freedom.
May the grace of God sweep through this world,
transforming the lives of those gripped by debt,
and leading them into justice.
May the blessing of God sweep through this place,
challenging us to act differently because we honor God,
and leading us into joy;
now and forever. Amen.

Peter Graystone
England

A Blessing

Unsettling God,
Dizzy with your vision,
May we craft our living
With realized mercies
And unfashionable hope.

Transformed by your message,
May we disrupt idolatrous norms
With the vigor of justice
And the plain language of faith.

Resolute in your embrace,
May we form new foundations
With the endurance of love
And a passion for grace.

Keri Wehlander
Canada

A Smile and a Tear

This blessing comes with a smile and a tear
To those afar and near
That they may lose fear
To smile and to shed a tear.

In a cruel, calculating, and shrewd world
Easily forgetful, a rigid world.
May the blessings pour like the monsoon
To soften the hearts to smiles and tears.

As the century passes
Leaving skulls and ashes
May automated bombs be drowned
By the smiles and tears of the masses.

May emotion drown reason
May harsh rule be treated as treason
And may each person
Roar with laughter, cry with emotion.

Tears of joy, tears of sadness
Rise above reason's madness
No more TV pictures with bombing planes
Human faces let's see again.

Rise, rise all hearts
Bless, bless this sad earth
Let this tragic century depart
Magic smiles and tears, come, come fast.

Basil Fernando
Hong Kong

Sweet Are the Blessings

Sweet are the blessings
Coming from the lips
Of the poor

Knowing life's betrayals
Happy lives they wish
For each other

Knowing life's paradoxes
They bless their children
Happiness limitless

Though life gave them
Nothing sweet
Their hearts are so sweet

A blessing of the cynic
Is a sweetened curse
He knows nothing of life's sweetnesses

Sweetness of running waters
Comes from those
Suffering has tempered

For a belief in tomorrow
Is a human need
From it comes the sweetnesses

Bitternesses of the prophets
Are sweet
Grounded in beliefs

The blessing of the matured
Not lured by greed
Is what humankind needs

Come—come—come
Voices—the noises—of the wise
Bless the sorrowing world.

Basil Fernando
Hong Kong

Do Justice—Love Kindness

Our worship has not ended—
    it has only just begun—
    for God is with us every moment of every day!
Go then, and offer the worship he desires—
    to do justice,
    to love kindness,
    and to walk humbly with him, every step along our way.

Nick Fawcett
England

For Those Who Live on the Margins

Living God, you sent your Son into the world,
not to be born in a palace but in a stable,
not to sit on a throne but to serve the poor,
not to rule with pride but to suffer in humility,
not to live in comfort but to die on a cross.

Bless those who live on the margins;
the families who crowd together in shanty towns
with a cardboard roof and a curtain of sacking
to keep out the harshness of wind and rain;
the children who live on the streets of crowded cities,
who sleep in shop doorways or damp basements,
who beg or steal to survive the next day's hunger;

the women who flee in terror from violence in the home,
who find a refuge where sisters share a common fear,
who seek to protect their children from abuse.
the people who are crippled by debt who share with many
fellow citizens a common burden imposed by the wealthy who draw
money from the poor.
those who face hunger in a world of plenty, who do not know
where the next meal will come from, who see their children dying
for lack of food.
God of the poor, Savior of the outcast,
bless those who live on the margins,
encircle them with your love.

John Johansen-Berg
England

God Bless

God bless the people who never had a voice, the ones who in silence
endured such pain and violation. God bless the people who never had
a chance, the ones who in innocence suffered in their vulnerability. God
bless the people who never had a hope, the ones who died within
themselves, a death before old age. God bless the people who caused
this pain, the ones who in their selfishness took life from someone else.
God bless the people who are left to cope, the ones who face a lifelong
toil of memories and pain. God bless the people who are needing love,
the ones who yearn for love, yet live in disappointment. God bless the
people who are created in your image, all your children, love them,
hold them and make them whole.

Frances Ballantyne
England

Just for Me

Count your blessings, it's a joke!
As people's words are said, in ignorance with little care.
Count your blessings, it's no joke,
As depression hits life hard, in desolation with despair.
Count your blessings, it's a laugh!
As days are full of tears of pain, in isolation without hope.
Count your blessings, it's no laughing matter,
As friends ignore and walk away, in selfishness with hate.
Count your blessings, it's so easy,
As life is full and festive, in carefree times with friends.
Count your blessings it's so hard,
As living loses meaning, in desperation with need.
Count my blessings? It's hard to see,
As cruelty is the way of life, in day-to-day familiarity,
Count my blessings? Yes I begin to see,
As love is found in Jesus, in new life of blessings, just for me.

Frances Ballantyne
England

Blessing of Liberation

Locked in a jail, prisoners within its walls,
the voices cry out in need and pain.
Locked behind manmade bars, against their wills,
the guilt of innocence, their crime.
Locked secure, denied their freedom, chained
and bound by guilt and fear.
Locked in for life, unless appeal is made
"Set us free, to worship God."
Unlocked, set free, their voices praise
"God sets the prisoners free to live!"

Frances Ballantyne
England

A Refugee Prays for a Blessing

Bless to me my feet
that they may create a path
where no path yet exists.

Bless to me my shoulders
that they may carry riches
when all my riches have been removed.

Bless to me my tears
that they might wash the dead
though the dead lie untended in the dust.

Bless to me my hands
that they might make a home
in every stopping-place away from home.

Bless to me my heart
that I may go on loving
when no loving is shown to me.

Bless to me my spirit
that it may rise in hope
even when reasonable hope is gone.

Bless to me my life
that it may defy the power of death
should death bend over me tonight.

Kate Compston
England

A True Blessing

This blessing comes
from the Cyber-Space Graveyard
of the disappeared persons
we who received no justice
wish for you
a world filled with justice
we who were taken blindfolded
wish the road rise to meet you

we deprived of the warmth
wish the wind be always at your back
and sunshine warm upon your face
from the earth wet with our blood
we bless
the rainfall soft upon your field
we the rejected and forgotten pray
may God hold you in the palm of his hand.

Basil Fernando
Hong Kong

A Blessing for the World's Children— The World that Might Be

This blessing is based on the Declaration of the Rights of the Child adopted by the United Nations General Assembly in 1959.

You are our gift.
We thank God for you.

We give back to you our wisdom
That you may all have education and knowledge
to empower you.
That is our wish.
May we live up to our responsibility.

We give back to you vibrant health
That you may grow strong in body and
work toward good.
That is our wish.
May we live up to our responsibility.

We give back to you protection and shelter
That you may feel safe in a place where
your needs are met.
That is our wish.
May we live up to our responsibility.

We give back to you our love
That you may feel cherished by the Creator
in whose image you are made.
That is our wish.
May we live up to our responsibility.

We give back to you our peace
That you may never know war or hatred or
loneliness or abuse.
That is our wish.
May we live up to our responsibility.

We give back to you our freedom
That you may live without fear or oppression
and may worship as you choose.
That is our wish.
May we live up to our responsibility.

We give back to you our joy
That you may experience a life
that is rich and full.
That is our wish.
May we live up to our responsibility.

We give back to you our hope
That you may know a world where all these gifts
are not just dreams and wishes,
but irrevocable truth and reality.
That is our wish.
May we live up to our responsibility.

For you are our gift and
We thank God for you.

Louise Margaret Granahan
Canada

Create a World of Equality

Leader   May God our creator continue to create a world of equality and just living where the whole of creation enjoys life at its fullest; where there is neither the ruler and the ruled; nor the powerful and the powerless; nor the dominant and the dominated, but where all experience God's grace and live happily knowing that it is God the giver of life, who cares for all of us.

All   Go therefore, and work together for the good of all.

Angeling B. Esquierdo
Philippines

On Racial Justice Sunday

May God's justice strengthen you,
the reconciliation of the Holy Spirit be in all your encounters
and the love of Christ live in you
as you go out into the world.

Norman Hart
England

Protect Peace

The Peace

Brother/sister, be at peace.

Peace and love are always alive in us, but we are
not always alive to peace and love.

Peace I leave with you,
My own peace I give to you.

May Christ's peace invade, flood and shake the
foundations of our hearts and lives, in this
Community, in our daily lives, in our witness
to the world; let peace break out.

We meet together to share this meal,
may it express our love for one another
our commitment to each other
and point us beyond ourselves
to the needs of the world.

God makes peace within us.
Let us claim it.
God makes peace between us.
Let us share it.

And our approach was in peace,
And we were established in the Spirit of unity.

St. Hilda Community
England

In Times and Places of War

Great God of justice and peace,
    we cannot ask you to bless guns and bombs
    and landmines and poison gas;
    we cannot claim your blessing on dictators,
    on the power-hungry, on the nation which chooses war.

But we plead for your blessing
    on those who are defenseless,
    those who wait for loved ones to come home,
    those who give loyalty and comradeship when death is near,
    and those whose vision is untouched by bitterness.

Desperate days, fearful nights, horrors beyond telling,
    and so many caught up in it who have no passion for war.

Bless all peacemakers in this broken world,
give them courage, patience and hope;
    they are children of God indeed.

Bernard Thorogood
Australia

Peace of God

    I will wait for your peace to come
    The battle zone is all around, the shocking sights,
    the sounds of war, the lack of calm and joy.

    I will wait for your peace to come
    The soldiers bravely march to win,
    under orders to destroy, to kill and maim.

    I will wait for your peace to come.
    The guns and bombs wreak havoc, refugees
    made homeless, casualties of war.

    I will wait for your peace to come.

Frances Ballantyne
England

God's Strength

Inspired by Lough Gill, Ireland, August, 1998,
the day after the Omagh bombing

May the blessing in the strength of
    these mountains,
    the calm of this lake
    the freshness of tree and flower

remain with you
and
may God's strength
peace
    and creativity
go with you always.

Audry Barnard
England

You Have Called Us to Peace

O God, you have called us to peace,
for You are Peace itself.
May we have the vision to see that each of us, in some measure,
can help to realize these aims;

Where there are ignorance and superstition,
Let there be enlightenment and knowledge.

Where there are prejudice and hatred,
Let there be acceptance and love.

Where there are fear and suspicion,
Let there be confidence and trust.

Where there are tyranny and oppression,
Let there be freedom and justice.

Where there are poverty and disease,
Let there be prosperity and health.

Where there are strife and discord,
Let there be harmony and peace.

A Jewish Blessing

The Road of Uncertainty

Leader May the God of peace and justice go with us as we travel the road of uncertainty and as we choose to deny ourselves so that we will be able to heed God's call. May his Son Jesus Christ, our Savior and friend, remind us of how we ought to live and may the Spirit sustain us whenever we become weak and doubtful.

All The road less travelled by is always scary. Strengthen and sustain us, O Lord. Amen.

Angeling B. Esquierdo
Philippines

Hilda's Blessing

Have peace with each other,
As children of one mother
Let each defer to other
And may your hearts be one.

Have peace with all around you
Sweet love of earth surround you
And may no harm confound you
Or break the peace within.

Have peace with God, your maker
In Jesus be partaker
And Spirit consecrator
God, three in one, grant peace.

The peace of God possess you
The love of God caress you
The grace of heaven bless you
Peace everlastingly.

Barrie Williams
England

Receive the Gift of Peace

As the dove gently settles on the tree,
receive the gift of peace.
As the flame rises with light and warmth,
receive the gift of life.
As the wind moves and dances around the earth,
receive the gracious gift of the Spirit,
through Jesus Christ, and to his praise and glory.

Dorothy M. Stewart
England

Peace Harmonious

May peace harmonious bless this land;
May it be ever free from maladies and war;
May there be harvest rich, and increased yield of grain;

May every one delight in righteousness;
May no perverted thought find entry to your minds;
May all your thoughts e'er pious be and lead
to your success religiously.

Milerepa—Tibet

Deep Peace

May the God who created the seas give you deep calm
May the God who created the stars give you radiant light
May the God who created people grant you many friendships
May the God who is your Father abide with you always.

The peace of the deep sea calm be yours
The peace of the deep forest quiet be yours
The peace of the mystic's inner silence be yours
The peace of the blessed Three be yours
To eternity.

John Johansen-Berg
England

Peace

Peace is never earned with easy words.
Tenacious tending of the wounded weak
and encouragement for honest anger help.
Sacrifice by those who hurt inspires
and standing with the grieving is a must.

Lord, when times are hard and we despair
of ever finding peace, help us to cry
with sighs too deep for words so you can hear.
Help us not to be broken by our fear.

In Jesus you have shown the perfect way
to change affliction, counter helplessness,
to strengthen those who don't know how to cope.
Help us, Lord, to follow on this road.

Lord, we need your guidance here today.
We need to wrestle for the peace you love.
Lord, we need your strength to battle on
And find the materials that will help us build.

Lord, bless us on our journey to this goal.

Peter Comaish
England

Discover the Riches of Christ

May God's Spirit send you out into the world.
Discover the riches of Christ in the poor, the sick,
and the stranger.

Share the treasures of Christ with those at work,
with your family, and among your friends.

Restore the glory of Christ to his earth and join
hands with all those who work for peace and justice.

Fill this world with the beauty of God's love,
that even in suffering and death,
we may come together to the living hope we find in Jesus.

And may the blessing of God Almighty,
the Father, the Son, and the Holy Spirit,
be among you and remain with you always.

Patrick B. Harris
England

Live Simply, Gently

Go in peace.
Live simply, gently,
at home in yourselves.
Act justly, speak justly.
Do not forget the depth of your compassion.
Do not forget your power in the days of your powerlessness.
Do not desire with great desire to be wealthier than your peers
and do not be reserved in extending your hand in charity.
Practice forbearance in all you do.

Speak the truth or speak not.
Take care of yourselves as bodies
for you are good gifts
and crave peace for all peoples in the world
beginning with yourselves and go from this place
with the dream of the peace aflame in your heart.

Mark Belletini
USA

Peace Be with Us

Let us go from here in peace.
We will accept the gift of peace.
May the peace be carried within all that is past,
may the peace be held within all that is present
and may the peace stay safely in all that is to come.

Dorothy McRae-McMahon
Australia

Go Home in Peace

God bless you;
God make your heart bright.
Go home in peace
in the name of Christ.

Traditional Ethiopian Blessing

The Joy of the Spirit

May the joy of the Spirit,
The compassion of Christ,
And the power of God
Lead you to the highest heights,
Where love reigns
And where fear has no place.
In the name of Jesus our Lord,
Who conquered death and gives us life forever. Amen.

Christina Rees
England

Joy, Perfect Joy

Laughter in your Eyes

Go now,
>With laughter in your eyes,
>>a smile on your lips,
>>a song in your heart,
>>and merriment in your soul,
>>and share the joy that Christ has given you.

Nick Fawcett
England

The Grace of God Thrill your Hearts

The grace of God thrill your hearts,
>the mercy of God transform your minds
>the peace of God flood your souls,
>and the love of God flow through your lives,
>to the honor of his name. Amen.

Nick Fawcett
England

All Your Days

May you spend...
All your days singing praise
All your nights in the light
Every hour being showered with blessings from above
All your time feeling sublime
All your life free from strife
Every minute basking in the joy of Divine love!

Radha Sahar
Aotearoa New Zealand

Go out Rejoicing

Go out into the world rejoicing,
    for God is waiting to meet you and surprise you with the
        beauty of his presence.
In the song of a blackbird, the hooting of an owl, the cry of a fox,
    in the opening of a bud, the fragrance of a flower, the falling
        of a leaf,
    in the murmur of the breeze, the rushing of the wind, the
        howling of the gale;
    in the babbling of the brook, the rippling of the stream, the
        crashing of the waves,
    in the peace of the meadows, the freedom of the hills, the
        grandeur of the mountains,
    in the cry of a baby, the laughter of children, the hum of
        conversation,
    in the pat on the shoulder, the handshake of welcome, the
        embrace of a loved one,
    in the noise of the factory, the routine of the office, the bustle
        of the shop,
    God is here,
    God is there,
    God is everywhere.
Go then,
    and walk with him,
    in the light of his love,
    and the fullness of life.

Nick Fawcett
England

May the Holy God Surprise You

Go in peace,
and may the holy God surprise you on the way,
Christ Jesus be your company
and the Spirit lift up your feet.

Dorothy McRae-McMahon
Australia

May the World Continue to Surprise Us

May the world continue to surprise us,
love continue to astonish us,
life continue to captivate us,
faith continue to sustain us,
and may God go with us always,
now and forevermore.

Nick Fawcett
England

Jeu d'Esprit

Flame-dancing Spirit, come
Sweep us off our feet and
Dance us through our days.
Surprise us with your rhythms,
Dare us to try new steps, explore
New patterns and new partnerships.
Release us from old routines,
To swing in abandoned joy
And fearful adventure.
And in the intervals,
Rest us,
In your still center.

Ann Lewin
England

Festivals

Matthew 28:1–9

He is not here;
he has been raised
just as he said.

The Christian Year

Advent

Advent Blessing

Let us go in faith
to ponder in our hearts
the mystery of this moment.
And may life be born within you,
Christ Jesus be seen among you
and joy surround you like the angel's song.

Dorothy McRae-McMahon
Australia

An Advent Blessing

Follow, where the Spirit of Hope leads you
Listen, as the child of Peace cries for you
Rejoice, as the Love of God embraces you
 and go now, with Hope, Peace and Love in your hearts
and the blessing of Creator, Child and Spirit forever with you.

Richard Becher
England

Christmas

A Christmas Blessing

May the love of the newborn Christ surround you,
and release in you compassion and care for others;
May the joy of the Holy Family enrich you
in your travelling through life, and in your discoveries;
May the hope of the baby of Bethlehem direct you
in your birthing, and in your departing;
May the insight of the Carpenter from Nazareth challenge you
in your struggles, and in your complacency;
And may the Peace of the risen Christ empower you
in your hearts, in your homes, and in all your longings:
And the blessing of God Almighty,
The Father, the Son and the Holy Spirit,
be among you and remain with you, your families
and all in the family of God's creation,
Now, throughout this Christmastime, and forevermore. Amen.

Edgar Ruddock
England

Blessing for Christmas

May we know in our hearts, and share with others, the simple joy of the shepherds, the praise of the angels, the love of the Holy Family.
    May the holy child of Bethlehem, true God and true Man, be close to us this day and every day.

Raymond Chapman
England

A Blessing of the Christmas Child

Travel safely,
and may you find your stable
with a manger and a child.
Listen carefully,
and hear the child cry to you
and take him to your heart.

Watch closely,
and see the guiding light
that shows you the road to travel.
And as you listen for the cry
and watch for the light on your journey
feel the presence of hope, peace and love
with the blessing of the Father, Son, and Holy Spirit
within you, beside you and before you. Amen.

Richard Becher
England

At the Heart of the Manger...

Let your body be the stable
Let your heart be the manger
Let your life be like the child's
with the blessing of the Father upon you
as the Spirit goes before you
and Jesus lives within you. Amen.

Richard Becher
England

The Babe of Bethlehem

May this Christmas be for each of us, a time of moving
Beyond reason to wonder,
Beyond grasping to letting go,
and beyond competition to cooperation,
In the power of the Babe of Bethlehem.

W. L. Wallace
Aotearoa New Zealand

Come to Us, Emmanuel

God, still come to us.
Emmanuel, you come to us, and touch our lives and change our plans.
Everlasting Father, you come to us and hold us in your loving arms.
Wonderful Counselor, you come to us, and walk along our path.
Prince of Peace, you come to us, and reconcile our differences.
Almighty God you come to us, and see and save our world.
God, still come to us.

Frances Ballantyne
England

Your Word Made Flesh

Mark 3:21

Bless you, Wise and Holy One,
for your Word made flesh—
For making holy and human
    more intimate
Bless you
for embodying your Word
    not as the founder of
    The-One-True-Religion
    but as a foundling in
    a garden variety family
    —its unwed mother-to-be
    its disputed paternity—
    a family that will wince
    at the public outcry
    over his table-turning words
    will try to take him out
    of the public eye
    to spare the family
    further embarrassment.

Bless you, Wise and Holy One,
for not keeping your distance
for making holy
    our garden variety.

Norm S. D. Esdon
Canada

Christmas Benediction

May the wonder of the shepherds,
the generosity of the wise men
and the compassion of Mary,
be in us and flow from us,
this Christmas and always.

W. L. Wallace
Aotearoa New Zealand

Orphanage

It was Christmas 1951. I was ten years old and had been in an orphanage about four months. There were ninety-eight of us kids and we had been lined up in twos. The older ones had to walk around the building to the chapel for midnight Mass. Even though, as you can imagine, I was not that enamored with my situation, I could not quell the feeling of excitement as we marched through the crisp white snow. On arrival we took our pews and waited expectantly as the occasional nun glided down the aisle, one into the sacristy. Having never experienced Christmas in the East End, you can imagine how I felt. The organ played a soft introduction for the service. Then the priest and altar boys entered. The choir stood up and filled the air with the strains of *Silent Night.*

I had finally arrived at Bethlehem.

Harry O.
England

Motivate Us

May the responsiveness of the shepherds,
the sense of adventure of the wise men,
the steadfastness of Joseph,
the commitment of Mary, both to her child
and the vision of a better world for all,
motivate us, now and always.

W. L. Wallace
Aotearoa New Zealand

Epiphany

Epiphany

O God, may the star we follow be the steady radiance of your mystery
which we discern only in part but can forever trust.

W. L. Wallace
Aotearoa New Zealand

Epiphany Blessing

Go in peace,
and may the God who protected the Holy Child
cover you and keep you,
the God who came to be with us be found beside you
and the love within you be called into safe places
by the gentle Spirit.

Dorothy McRae-McMahon
Australia

An Epiphany Blessing

"Star" child,
wanted and welcomed by the humble,
hated and hounded by power-seekers:
refuge and refugee,
we love you!

"Apple of God's eye,"
cherished and chosen by kingdom-travelers,
rejected and ridiculed by the earth-bound:
sacred and scarred,
we honor you!

"Light of the world,"
tended and treasured by the pure in heart,
shadowed and shunned by the deceitful:
peerless and pierced,
we exalt you!

Kate Compston
England

Ash Wednesday

Blessing of Ashes

As the green of palms became the dark of Calvary, so in these ashes which
we + bless in your Most Holy Name, let the power of this sign, in peni-
tence and purity, tell the world of the fire of your Spirit, and, in turn, the
uplifting power of your Presence to draw us from our darkness into your
marvelous light, now and forever through Jesus Christ our Lord. Amen.

Giles Harcourt
England

Suddenly, It's Wednesday

*On this day, Catholic Christians take upon themselves the sign of the
cross in ash as a symbol of repentance.*

Good Friday?
Green hill?
Holy timber?
Sweet iron?

And now the blessing of a fleeting, ashen cross?
How on earth
Do we wrestle righteousness
From blunt, outrageous torture?
Hope from helpless cruelty?

Only blessed faith, my dear,
Skin deep and five miles high,
Can do that...

Forgive the bitterness, the bile.
Religion wears me
Thin and raw

Especially when our sickened soul,
War piled on war,
Economy of sin
And life's petty, searing injustice

(Face drawn, longing)
Saps the last remaining drop
Of sanctity
From our hideous, artifact "crosses."

So today we will tear them down again:
Pile them high,
Burn them in the sanctuary—
Pyre on smoking pyre

It smells so sweet
So strangely blessed
To scorch our own hypocrisy."
To daub it on the brow
And wash away the history
of sacred "murder...

So paint my face blood black
With stardust, death, and memories."

Ashes in ashes,
Flesh on flesh,
Unsure, uncertain hope
Is resurrected, dreaming...

Yes, this sign is given,
Not wanted—given,
That God can take
Even the most markable,
Re-markable humanity
And draw it into the canvas...
Of a new heaven, new earth
In this blessed and haunted canopy.

Suddenly, it's
Wednesday.

Simon Barrow
England

Lent

For Waiting in the Wilderness

This is the wilderness time,
when every path is obscure
and thorns have grown around the words of hope.
Be the wings of our strength, O God,
in this time of wilderness waiting.

This is the time of stone, not bread,
when even the sunrise feels uncertain
and everything tastes of bitterness.
Be the wings of our strength, O God,
in this time of wilderness waiting.

This is the time of ashes and dust,
when darkness clothes our dreams
and no star shines a guiding light.
Be the wings of our strength, O God,
in this time of wilderness waiting.

This is the time of treading life,
waiting for the swells to subside
and for the chaos to clear.
Be the wings of our strength, O God,
in this time of wilderness waiting.

Keri Wehlander
Canada

Good Friday

A Good Friday Blessing

Bless you, Wise and Holy One,
for your enduring Word—the Word
that endures the cross of
    words heard
    but not understood
    palms bestowed
    for the wrong reason
    laurels withheld
    by home and family
    friends with us only
    until the cock crows
    peers who condemn
    our I-am-who-I-am—
    denounce our integrity
    as blasphemy
Bless you, Wise and Holy One,
for your enduring Word from the cross—
    whoever is true to I-am-who-I-am
    who risks I-am for others
    rises from affliction
    rolls away despair
    endures beyond
    even death itself

Norm S. D. Esdon
Canada

Blessing the Thorn in the Flesh

Bless you Wise and Holy One
    for your Word made
    thorn in the flesh
for answering No when I prayed
    to have my thorn removed!

Bless you
    for the thorn of alienation that
    drives me deep into inner desert
    to face my need to please—
    the desert where you re-create me
    deeper than popularity
    wider than the majority
    truer than hypocrisy

Bless you
    for the thorn of hardship that
    helps me get the point—
    that my thorn can serve
    as another's therapy
    that the best healer
    is a wounded healer
    that the hardship I cannot change
    and that threatens to embitter me
    can change me—for the better

Bless you Wise and Holy One
for this epiphany—
    that praying away Good Friday
    prays away Easter too

Bless you
for answering No when I pray
    to have a thorn removed
Bless you Wise and Holy One
    for your Word made
    "thorn in the flesh"

                Norm S. D. Esdon
                Canada

Easter Day

Easter Blessing

Broken the stone
of everyman's despair
the ultimate
ice cry of defeat

Broken the stone
of the sound of groping hands
fumbling with the cords
of tears

Broken the stone
of the dark stagnant deeps
twisting the shadows
of the dead

Shattered the stone
life's energies renewed
rising from nothingness
fullness from emptiness
the Word of the Easter tomb.

Ancilla Dent
England

The Power of Your New Life

Risen Lord,
    be with me in the power of your new life.
Open me that I may grow in the Spirit
    in love and understanding,
    in knowledge and self-giving.
Let me receive your strength
    that I may accept your trials
    which I must endure with you.
Help me to treasure the revelations you bring
    of the presence and power
    of God.

Give the the refreshment
of a new beginning
in his joy and glory.

Paul Iles
England

Risen Lord and Master

Risen Lord and Master,
you know me better than I know myself;
speak and help me to listen;
call me into your life,
that with you I may possess your Father's kingdom.
Give me insight to recognize you
in the moment of your speaking,
and to value the time of your calling;
that through all my days
I may rejoice with you
in the power of God,
and receive a share in the glory
of his victory and love.

Paul Iles
England

Love of Jesus, Fill Me

Love of Jesus, fill me,
Joy of Jesus, surprise me,
Peace of Jesus, flood me,
Light of Jesus, transform me,
Touch of Jesus, warm me,
Strength of Jesus, encourage me,
O Savior, in your agony, forgive me,
in your wounds hide me,
and in your risen life take me with you,
for love of you and of your world.
Amen.

Angela Ashwin
England

Pentecost

A Pentecost Thanksgiving

Thank you, kaleidoscope God,
for the strong colors of Pentecost!

Thank you
    for blue and green:
        rippling and raging, scouring and roaring
        in gales of the Spirit, winds of change.

Thank you
    for red and yellow:
        sparking and blazing, leaping and alighting
        in tongues of fire, torches of courage.

Thank you
    for white and silver:
        quieting and consoling, inspiring and soaring
        in dove of peace, messenger of hope.

Thank you for all these colors
    of love and longing,
    wildness and wisdom,
    challenge and compassion.

So color our lives by your mighty Spirit,
    that we change
    find courage,
    radiate hope,
    for this is thanksgiving
    more precious than words.

Kate Compston
England

Pentecost

And now may we all know the spirit of God within us and throughout the world that this day may be for us an experience of heaven, of stillness within the busyness, of hope within the pain, of peace beyond our anxieties, and a quality of life that is not limited to the competitive or the mechanical.

May this day be a spirited day for us all.

W. L. Wallace
Aotearoa New Zealand

Harvest

Lord of the Harvest

A blessing which may vary according to the local crops and livestock and which may be said outside the church, with the minister stretching out his hands toward the fields, etc.

May the Lord of the harvest bless your crops:
Your maize and beans,
Your potatoes and rice,
Your coffee and tea.

May the Lord of creation bless your animals:
Your cows and bulls,
Your sheep and goats,
Your chickens and pigs.

May the Lord of all life bless your families:
Your grandfathers and grandmothers,
Your husbands and wives,
Your sons and daughters.

The blessing of God Almighty,
   The Father, the Son, and the Holy Spirit,
   Be among you and remain with you always.
Church of the Province of Kenya

The Golden Rice Harvest

May we all live as grains of rice
Within God's sacred fertile farm;
Roots nourished by the holy earth,
Love's waters guarding us from harm.

May we all grow as shoots of rice,
The many lives that fill the field,
Each standing tall in gentle power,
A ripening harvest rich in yield.

May we all share this verdant gold,
The fruit of peasant farming ways,
With all the poor of every land
And join their seasoned song of praise.

Tune: Winchester New

W. L. Wallace
Aotearoa New Zealand

Seedtime and Harvest

God of yesterday, today, and tomorrow,
God of seedtime and harvest,
Father, Son, and Holy Spirit,
bless us and strengthen us
to live and blossom and bear good fruit
to his praise and glory.
Dorothy M. Stewart
England

The Fruit of the Land

Bless, O Lord, the plants, the vegetation, and the herbs of the field, that they may grow and increase to fullness and bear much fruit. And may the fruit of the land remind us of the spiritual fruit we should bear.

Coptic Orthodox Liturgy
Egypt

Blessing of Harvest Gifts

Most gracious and loving Father, giver of all good gifts, make holy all that we offer with gratitude from the harvest of the earth.

As our land has brought forth plentifully, make our hearts fruitful with your love, and make us always mindful of the needs of others, especially the poor and forgotten, through Jesus Christ our Lord. Amen.

Giles Harcourt
England

On the Land

May the Land be blessed by God.
may the earthy fields be full of goodness,
giving sustenance to all that grows.
May the sun shine on the farms,
encouraging life, giving warmth.

Response: *May God our Creator bless the Land.*

May the waters be given by God.
May the rain come in due season,
irrigating the earth for new growth;
may the rivers and lakes be brimming,
home to bright shoals of fish.

Response: *May God our Life-giver bless us with rain.*

May the animals receive God's blessing.
May the cows be healthy and strong,
giving wholesome milk each day.
May the sheep be numerous and fit,
each with a thick coat of wool.

Response: *May God our Shepherd bless our livestock with health.*

May the farmers be blessed by God.
May they be given wisdom and skill
to farm the land, making it productive.
May they be given compassion and sensitivity
to look after the animals placed in their care.

Response: *May God our Parent bless those who farm the land.*

May the land be blessed by God.
May sun and rain and earth combine
to give us the fruitfulness of the fields;
may human beings and animals be partners
to give us joy in the harvest.

Response: *May God our Vine-dresser bless our Land.*

John Johansen-Berg
England

Blessing of a Garden Field

Almighty God, you have created and blessed the earth that it may supply our needs:

Bless now, we beseech you, this field, granting seasonable weather for growth and health to those who labor to your honor and glory; through Christ our Lord.

The Community of the Servants of the Will of God,
Crawley, England

Blessing of an Orchard

Blessed are you, Lord God, for you give all the seed-bearing plants that are upon the earth, and all the trees with seed-bearing fruit, to be our food:

Let the seed of the Word of God which you have sown in our hearts, spring up and bear fruit unto everlasting life; through Christ our Lord.

The Community of the Servants of the Will of God
Crawley, England

A Blessing for the Wine Harvest

May the God who made the grape in all its varieties and flavors bless those who grow, cultivate and process the wine grape which decorates our tables, and makes glad our hearts.

Alan Nichols
Australia

Blessing of Beehives

Blessed are you, Lord God, who in these your creatures, the bees, grant us a living example of industry and unity of purpose. Pour down your blessing upon them; curb their desire to swarm; grant them freedom from disease and abundance of nectar in the blossom, that by the sweet savor of their honey we may bless you in the joy of festal days.

Glory to you, O Lord, glory to you.

The Community of the Servants of the Will of God,
Crawley, England

Blessing of Chickens

Blessed are you, Lord God, for you have created these birds for our use. Protect them from disease, and prosper the work of our hands, that we may bless you again in the fruit of your bounty; through Christ our Lord.

The Community of the Servants of the Will of God,
Crawley, England

Blessing of a Herd of Cows

All praise and thanksgiving be to you, Heavenly Father, that you have entrusted this herd of cows to our care.

Protect them from disease and every kind of harm, and grant that we may bless your holy Name, through Jesus Christ our Lord.

The Community of the Servants of the Will of God,
Crawley, England

For Those at Work in Food Production and Preparation

May God bless you in the sowing of the seed
and the reaping of the harvest.
May the sun shine on your fields
and the rain fall to water your crops.
May God bless you in the milling of the grain
and the baking of the bread.
May the smiles of heaven beam on the baking,
the making, the decorating and the selling.

May God bless you in the celebration of the Harvest,
in the songs of the reapers,
in the smiles of the shopkeepers,
in the satisfaction of the customers,
in the commerce of selling and buying.

May God bless you in the work of the kitchen,
in the cooking and the baking,
in the table setting and the gathering,
in the fellowship of the meal
and in the satisfaction of hunger.

All things work together for good with those who love God;
may all things come to culmination
for those who cooperate with the divine favor
in bringing bread to the hungry and food to the needy.

John Johansen-Berg
England

Agriculture Blessings

Speak these words before the prayers of blessing which follow:

In the name of The Father and of the Son and of the Holy Spirit. Amen.

O Heavenly King, the Comforter Spirit of Truth who art everywhere present and fillest all things; Treasury of blessings and giver of Life, come and abide in us and cleanse us from all impurity, and, O Good One, save our souls.

Let us pray to the Lord. Lord have mercy.

Prayer over a Sowing

O Lord, our God and Master, we offer this seed that lies before you, and which has come from your most pure and truly rich palms. And as this is handed to you, we pray: We would not have dared to enclose this seed in the bosom of the earth, if we did not heed the ordinance of your majesty, commanding the land to beget and germinate, and to give seed for sowing and bread for eating. Now we pray to you, O our God: Hear us who are praying to you and open to us your great, good and heavenly treasury; and pour out your blessing, to the utmost satisfaction, according to your true promise. Drive away all things eating the fruit of our land and all chastisement rightly directed against us, on account of our sins. Send down on us, your people, your rich bounties, by the grace and love for mankind of your only-begotten Son, together with your most-holy, good and life-creating Spirit, now and ever and unto ages of ages. Amen.

Prayer over a Threshing Floor or Barn

O Lord our God, Fountain of good things, who has commanded the land to yield fruit: for the sake of your deep compassion and graciousness, bless this barn and the harvest of your servants, and multiply it. Fill their treasury with all good fruit, grain, wine and oil, and preserve them and all present from every temptation, and enlighten to knowledge of you, those who have been well-pleasing to you, that they may become partakers of your eternal good things. For your name is blessed: of the Father, and of the Son, and of the Holy Spirit, now and ever and unto ages of ages. Amen.

Prayer to Bless a Herd

This prayer may be easily adapted for the blessing of other animals of a farm, with appropriate changes in the text.

O Master, Lord our God, who has power over all creation: We beseech you and we entreat you, that as you blessed and increased the flocks of the Patriarch Jacob, so too bless the *(herd of cattle)* of this your servant, *(Name)*; increase it a thousandfold, and strengthen it, delivering it from the violence of the Devil, from strangers and from all other snares of the enemies, and wasting infirmities. Fence it about with your holy angels, protecting it from all envy, temptation, enchantment and wild beasts, and from the action of the Devil which may come against it, driving these things away from it. For yours is the kingdom and the power and the glory: of the Father, and of the Son, and of the Holy Spirit, now and ever and unto ages of ages. Amen.

Blessing of Bees

O God the Creator of all, who blesses seed and increases it and makes useful that employed for our use: Through the intercession of the forerunner and baptizer John, who mercifully bears our prayers to you, be well pleased, out of your own deep compassion, to bless and sanctify these bees, that they may bear abundantly their fruit, with which your temple and your holy altars are adorned in magnificence, and that it be useful to us, in Jesus Christ our Lord, to Whom is due honor and glory unto ages of ages. Amen.

O God, having instructed us, out of your ineffable mercy, to use for our needs the fruit and work of these bees, and knowing how to do good through human labor and these wordless lives, humbly we pray to your majesty: Be pleased to bless these bees and increase them for use by the human race; preserve them and make them fat. Let everyone hoping in your majesty and the expanse of your compassions, who are laboring in the care of these living things, be granted to receive abundant fruit of their labors and to be filled with heavenly blessings, from Jesus Christ our Lord, to Whom be honor and glory unto ages of ages. Amen.

Prayer to Bless New Honey

O Lord Jesus Christ, Whose mercies cannot be contained and Whose bounties are ineffable; Who is wondrous in glory and Who works miracles, Who by the operation of the Holy Spirit once blessed Israel and nourished them with honey from a rock: As the same Lord, look down now from above on this your work, and with your heavenly blessing bless and consecrate this honeycomb and the honey that comes from it. Grant to it the action of blessings beyond all perfection, so that all tasting of it, receiving it and eating it, may find good health, and by this nourishment be satisfied and filled with all good things. For you are He Who bestows all good things, and to you we ascribe glory, together with your Father Who is without beginning, and your Most-holy, Good and Life-creating Spirit, now and ever unto ages of ages. Amen.

Blessing of Fish for Stocking Ponds, Lakes, or Rivers

O Almighty and Eternal God, Father of our Lord Jesus Christ, Father of mercy, Who commanded fish to increase and grow in rivers and the seas, we entreat you: Grant that these little fish with which we have stocked this pond *(lake, river)* increase and grow through your grace. For you are our God and to you we ascribe glory: to the Father, and to the Son, and to the Holy Spirit, now and ever and unto ages of ages. Amen.

Prayer for the Blessing of Fishnets

O Lord Jesus Christ our God, Who from a mere five loaves and two fish fed five thousand, and from the leftover morsels arranged that a multitude be gathered: As the same all-powerful Master, bless the nets laid before you: by the prayers of the truly blessed One, our glorious sovereign Lady, the Theotokos and ever-virgin Mary; of the holy glorious and all-praised apostles and the chief of the apostles, Peter. Preserve us, who by means of these nets may be partakers of fish, in peace and health of souls and bodies. For you are the Bestower of all good things, and to you we ascribe glory, together with your Father Who is without beginning, and your most holy, good and life-creating Spirit, now and ever and unto ages of ages. Amen.

Orthodox Church of the Holy Protection
Translation by the Orthodox Church in America

156

God of Times and Seasons

Genesis 8:22

There will always be
cold and heat, summer
and winter, day and night.

Changing Splendors

God of All Times and Seasons

God of all times and seasons:
I come to you, the God of Spring—the new leaf God, the new life
    God—blessed by your creation;
I come to you, the God of Summer—the color God, the growing
    God—blessed by your sustenance;
I come to you, the God of Autumn—the harvest God, the richness
    God—blessed by your fruitfulness;
I come to you, the God of Winter—the waiting God, the still and
    secret God—blessed by your mystery.
And so I surrender my seasons into your eternity;
I open my life to the edges of your timelessness;
And when I come to that place of stillness and silence,
There let me adore you.

Peter Graystone
England

Past, Present and Future

Gracious God, teach us to thank you for the past, to trust you for the future, to serve you in the present, celebrating every day you give us with glad and joyful praise.

Nick Fawcett
England

A New Year's Blessing

God our Maker, beyond all time,
    to whom the passing centuries are but an evening gone,
    yet caring for every detail of creation,
    breathe the breath of life
    upon all your work of building a world which God
    delights to share.

God the Son, born in time for us and dying in time for our salvation,
    reach out his arms to bless you with the time you need
    to redeem the time that is spent and to seek his glory in the present.

God the Spirit, breathing into every moment the freshness of new life,
    transform your fleeting seconds into worlds which are filled
    with love and joy and peace in the knowledge of God's goodness.

God the Holy Trinity, in whose company all time stands still,
    surround you with the arms of steadfast love,
    support you with a strength which never fails,
    and lift your hearts to a life which knows no death.

And the blessing of Father, Son, and Holy Spirit be your constant
    company forevermore.

Nicholas Coulton
England

Spring

Spring is full of energy—
like its name.
It coils and tenses and waits
and then jumps out at us,
bursting with vigor
and new life
and shouts its presence
with a this-is-what-you've-been-waiting-for attitude.

Spring blesses us in an aggressive new way.
Bare trees suddenly thrusting out new leaves.
Flowers shaking their defiant colors,
even at the occasional return of wintry weather.

Animals and birds proudly parade young ones.
Lawns and hedges cry out for mowers and trimmers.
And the sun gains strength and length of days
and by its energy
urges us to get out and do something.

Energetic God,
we thank you for the urgent message of renewal
that blesses us with each spring.

Marjorie Dobson
England

Signs of Spring

The blessing of the signs of spring be yours today:
The new life visible in the fields be a sign of new life in you,
The birds building nests be a sign of belief in the future for you,
The tiny flowers on grassy banks be a sign of the small but
significant things in your life.

May the blessing of God,
Sower of seed,
Nurturer of hope and
Gardener of harmony,
Stay with you today and always.

Rosemary Wass
England

Spring Thanksgiving

We have endured
The Order of Winter
The Hunger
The Winds
The Pain of Sickness
And lived on...
Once again we shall
See the Snow melt
Taste the Flowering Sap

Touch the Budding Seeds
Smell the Whitening Flowers
Know the Renewal of Life.

Found beside a Boreal forest display at the Museum of Man and Nature, Winnipeg, Manitoba. Boreal forests are just south of the treeline in northern Canadian Provinces and the southern part of the Northwest Territories.

Canada

Summer

May the openness that Summer brings be a gift to us—
To open the windows of our lives to other people,
To open our homes to share the hospitality of table and church.

Open our minds and revel in the beauties of nature—
The smell of newly mown grass
The morning dew on the rosebud
The scent of honeysuckle on the evening air
The open spaces offering relaxation and a change of pace.

Open our hearts to your love and may your Spirit rest with each one of us.

Rosemary Wass
England

Summer Is Extravagant

Summer is extravagant
and over-stated
and showy.

Summer colors are bright
and gaudy
and over-the-top.

Summer life is abundant
and prolific
and overwhelming.

Summer sun is dazzling
and brilliant
and hot—

sometimes.

Summer rain is warmer,
but just as wet
as at any other time.

Yet summer riots its colors loudest
where sun and showers combine
to ring out the glory.

Just as God's blessings abound
in the joy and sorrow
by which all growth comes.

Marjorie Dobson
England

Autumn Is a Blazing Time

Autumn is a blazing time,
a red and gold amazing time.
Trees maturing now display
fruit and leaf in fine array.
Trees prepared for winter's rest
show their glories at their best.

Autumn is a dying time,
a withering and a drying time.
Falling leaves are brittle rust
tumbling down into the dust.
Fallen leaves go back to the earth,
re-absorbed to bring new birth.

Autumn is a blessing time,
a God-will-keep-us-guessing time.
Emptying branches seem so stark,

stripped to bare and simple bark.
Empty branches on them bear
sleeping buds to wake next year.

Marjorie Dobson
England

Autumn

As morning air demands an extra layer
And dewy cobwebs decorate the thorn
The trees cast golden leaves to earth
And fruit is harvested and stored.

So comes the time for tidying up for rest—
And earth and we are truly blessed—
With all the colors, smells and glorious reminders
Of God's provision in abundance yet again.

Rosemary Wass
England

I Look at a Leaf

An Autumn Meditation

Each participant holds an autumn leaf in their hand.

I look at a leaf,
a sign of wonder,
a symbol of God's creation:
changing shape, color
with the seasons;
moving from bud to leaf
from green to red to
brown, black, decay,
fragmenting back into the earth
in death, bringing nourishment,
bringing new life.
I look at a leaf.

I look into myself,
a sign of wonder

a symbol of God's creation:
changing, growing, living, dying—
a year, a season passes—more change;
time moves and my body moves,
my thoughts change, my
perceptions alter, my taste buds
shift—and as I age, I pass on
wisdom, understanding, questions,
offering nourishment,
bringing new life.
I look into myself.

I look around me,
at the streets and homes,
towns, villages and cities,
signs of wonder,
symbols of God's creation:
yet nothing stays the same.
New neighbors, new streets,
new gaps, more dereliction,
more buildings, different shops—
and I think of the pain of change,
the fear of change—
and the new life that change can bring.
I look around me.

Ruth Harvey
England

A Winter Blessing

Winter has a dreary sound to it.
Fog, frost, snow, rain, and icy winds
all feature heavily.
They turn us indoors
to layers of warm clothing
and firesides and hot drinks,
which are all blessings in themselves.

But on bright winter days
there are unexpected joys.
Sunshine on snow.

Sparkling frosty air.
Tree outlines silhouetted by clear blue sky.
And piercing through the hardened soil
the sharp green points of new life.

We know it will always happen,
but it is good to see
God blessing us, once again,
with his promise of resurrection.

Marjorie Dobson
England

Winter

A hoary frost and breath upon the air;
A slower pace as nature needs to rest,
for every phase of season has its purpose:
Composting leaves to comfort the earth,
Migrated birds for sunnier climes,
Dark days, long nights, and a longing for light
And hope—the slightest sign of Spring—
A hint of green above the dark, dark earth,
The warmth of sun regaining strength and vigor,
And life begins to surge again—
In tree, to bursting bud and greening leaf.

So nature clothes the earth again
And Spring is here!

Rosemary Wass
England

Take Us through the Day, Lord

A Blessing to Begin the Day

In the shelter of new light
Before day's weight begins,
O God, hear my prayer.

As earth charts her course toward night
So may I chart mine:
with quiet clarity,
with visible compassion,
with clear integrity.

May the scope of this created journey
Run broad with recognition:
for each subtle miracle,
for each transparent mercy,
for each tender joy.

May the sweep of this day be steadied
By your gestures of presence:
Infectious grace,
Persistent love,
Outrageous vision;
Until an iridescence grows within
Marking my course with peaceful certainty.

Keri Wehlander
Canada

Blessing for the Morning

Go in peace into all that this day brings.
We go in faith and hope.
And may the face of God be turned toward you,
the hand of Christ be stretched out to hold you
and the Spirit be found as wisdom within you.

Dorothy McRae-McMahon
Australia

Morning Blessing

Bless me, O God
every moment of this day
each step that I take
every turn of my wheel,
each movement I make
every emotion I feel.

Bless me, O Christ,
every moment of this day
each temptation I face
every choice that I make,
each reaction I show
every fall from your grace.

Bless me, O Spirit
every moment of this day
each thought of my mind
every hour I'm awake,
each dream that I dream
every hour that I'm asleep.

May I dance for your glory
Holy One in Three
May I dance for your glory
As you dance in me.

Heather Johnston
England

Morning Affirmations

This day I shall let
        the hills embrace me,
        the trees comfort me,
        the waves wash over me.
This day I shall let the sap rise within me
and unfolding
      dance
      the music
      of the cosmos.

W. L. Wallace
Aotearoa New Zealand

May the freshness of the dawn enliven my spirit,
May the rising of the sun enlighten my mind,
May the noontide of the day warm my heart
May the benediction of sunset clothe my being
      with restfulness.

W. L. Wallace
Aotearoa New Zealand

Blessing for a Day

May the brightness of the morning light
      fill my heart with hope and vision.
May the bustle of the noonday heat
      fill my mind with wise reflection.
May the lull of evening's early calm
      fill my soul with contemplation.
May the darkness and the sleep of night
      fill my body with restoration.

Betty Lynn Schwab
Canada

A Celtic Blessing

May God the Father bless us in all that we do this day.
May Jesus, beloved Son of the Father, bless us, as we go our way.
May God's Holy Spirit bless us in every thought, in every deed,
in every word we say.
May Blessed Mary, Mother of Jesus, bless us, and protect us,
and draw us to pray.
May we be blessed by the Light of Christ.
May a spark be kindled in each heart, to flicker like a candle flame.
May Christ fill us with his light so that we may illuminate a dark
place, for his sake. Amen.

The Community of the Holy Name
Oakwood, England

Christ's Blessing to Start and End the Day

Loving God:
Pour into me the love of Christ;
Place in front of me the hope of Christ;
Surround me with the courage of Christ;
Nurture me in the spirit of Christ;
Protect me with the defenselessness of Christ;
Clothe me with the mind of Christ;
Entice me with the desire of Christ;
Enchant me with the vision of Christ;
Consume me with the passion of Christ;
Enable me with the gentleness of Christ;
Envelop me with the silence of Christ;
Affect me with the pain of Christ;
Attract me to the promise of Christ;
Inspire me with the understanding of Christ;
Engage me to the world of Christ;
Gift me with the will of Christ.
Open us all to Christ,

Open us to our neighbors,
Open us to our selves,
Open us to creation,
Open us to your presence in all, for all,

with all, to all, and enfolding all.
This day and forevermore.

Simon Barrow
England

In the Bath

And so to prayer,
Another breath gasped
as I pause to speak
words which were yours
before I thought them.

And so to breathe
Your love
And let it
Fall around today's tasks
And hopes.

And so to work,
My feet unique
My path shared,
Our prayers carried
Delivered.

Postal service, Spiritual dimension,
All first class, no stamp needed.

Val Shedden
England

Any Time of Day!

Gracious God,
Take this moment,
this minute,
this hour,
this day.
Take our lives,
and use them for your kingdom,
in the name of Christ.

Nick Fawcett
England

Blessing on Daily Living

May God bless you in your rising
and be with you throughout the day.
May you know his benediction as you travel,
keeping you safe amidst the hazards of the road.

May God bless you in your daily work
as you assist in production on the factory floor,
or use your skills in design at the office.
May God bless you in your relationship with people
as you offer service in personal caring ways.
May God grant you gifts in knowledge
as you teach the young and encourage them in discovery.
May God give you skill and compassion
as you engage in healing for those who are sick.
May God bless you, whatever your sphere of work,
granting you the gifts needed to fulfill his divine purpose for you.

May God bless you in the sharing of meals,
giving you sustenance sufficient for each day's need,
keeping you mindful of those who are hungry,
blessing you in your family links and friendships.

May God bless you in your taking rest at night;
may the restfulness of sleep renew your strength
and enable you to face each new day
with the needed energy and commitment.

May God, the Father, the Son, and the Spirit,
be with you in your daily living,
going with you where you go
and staying with you where you stay,
so that in his presence you may have
the peace that passes understanding.

John Johansen-Berg
England

An Evening Blessing

As the evening has come may this place be one that experiences
    God's presence.
May each of us here enter into the blessedness of God
May the troubles of the day flee from you
May the breath of the Spirit rest on you
May the calm of deep sleep fill your mind.

Philip Freier
Australia

Evening Blessing

Bless, O Lord, the rest of all who dwell in this house; bless, too, their
coming in and their going out. Keep them in health and send your
angels to be their defense. Grant them the light of your presence and
give them sufficiency in every good thing, enrich them in faith and
encompass them with love. When the stars look down, may stillness
and peace reign in the hearts of all who sleep here and make stronger
and stronger the sovereign gift of love which binds all hearts to you.
Amen.

Submitted by Richard Carr-Gomm
England

Goodnight, Lord

Goodnight, Lord,
protect us through the night
and as we sleep
bless our dreams
and may our rest
refresh and strengthen us
for what we will meet
at the dawn of the new day

Richard Becher
England

A Blessing for the Night

Lord our God,
restore us again by the repose of sleep;
after the fatigue of our daily work:
so that, continually renewed by your help,
we may serve you in body and soul;
through Christ our Lord.

World Council of Churches

A Night Blessing

Bless those
who are lonely tonight.
Bless those
who are cold tonight.
Bless those
who hunger tonight.
Bless those
who are homeless tonight.
Bless those
who fear the dark
for what it might bring.

May your light shine
upon their pain.
May your love burn
to warm them.

May they find shelter
in the shade
and the embrace
of the outflung arms
of your Cross.

Forgive me the nails
I hammer in,
when I don't stand up
and speak out
and act
in your Name,

against such injustices
and sin.
Please forgive me—
and bless me, too.
Susan Hardwick
England

Night Blessing

May the soft blanket of darkness be yours
as you face late night hours.
As you close blind and curtain
may you be secure from intrusion.
As clock chimes many times
may you relish private time.
May you supper on delight
before bidding a warm goodnight.
May your toilette be full-cleansing
day's dilemmas now releasing.
May your bedclothes not confound you
nor your mattress hound you.
May your pillow be sweet-scented
and your prayers fairly answered.
May your dreams be God-guided
and your spirit love-abiding.
May you sleep in deepest peace
as stars and moon reflect God's grace.
Glenn Jetta Barclay
Aotearoa New Zealand/Northern Ireland

The Guarding of the God of Life

The guarding of the God of life be on you,
The guarding of loving Christ be on you,
The guarding of Holy Spirit be on you
Every night of your lives.
To aid you and enfold you
Each day and night of your lives.
Carmina Gadelica

Resting Blessing

In name of the Lord Jesus,
And of the Spirit of healing balm,
In name of the Father of Israel,
    I lay me down to rest.

If there be evil threat or quirk,
Or covert act intent on me,
God free me and encompass me,
    And drive from me mine enemy.

In name of the Father precious,
And of the Spirit of healing balm,
In name of the Lord Jesus,
    I lay me down to rest.

Carmina Gadelica

Blessing for the Night

Go into the night in peace,
and may the God of eternity stretch out the heavens above you,
the God of each earthly moment be closer than breath
and the Spirit cover you with warm bright wings.

Dorothy McRae-McMahon
Australia

End of the Day

On Going to Bed

May sleep bring the mantle of peace
may dreams bring enlightenment
may forgiveness be my benediction.

Gracious God, I commit into your hands the joys and frustrations, successes and failures of this day; free me from its destructive force and grant that the power of its beauty and love may grow within me to make me a more effective "Friend of Jesus."

W. L. Wallace
Aotearoa New Zealand

The End of the Day

Bless the closing of the door
and the opening of the next.
Bless the ending of the day
and the beginning of the new.
Bless, Lord, what has gone
and what we know must come
as we journey on your road.
Amen.

Richard Becher
England

Blessing for Morning or Evening

As I enjoy and give thanks for all the blessings of my life, may I
remember that I am mortal, and live so that when I die to this world
I shall come to you for eternity.

May the Holy Spirit give me right judgment in all things, guide me
into the way of truth, strengthen me against temptation and bring me
after this life into the perfect knowledge and love of God.

Raymond Chapman
England

Creator God

Genesis 1

In the beginning...

Awaken Our Senses

Bless my Senses

Lord Jesus, bless my heart: that I may be more loving;
      bless my mind: that I may have understanding;
      bless my eyes: that I may have insight;
      bless my ears: that I may truly listen;
      bless my mouth: that my words may speak
          kingdom-truth;
      and bless my hands: that my actions may be open and just.

Bernard Thorogood
Australia

A Blessing for the Senses

May your body be blessed.
May you realize that your body is a faithful and beautiful friend of
    your soul.
And may you be peaceful and joyful and recognize that your senses are
    sacred thresholds.
May you realize that holiness is mindful gazing, feeling, hearing,
    and touching.
May your senses gather you and bring you home.
May your senses always enable you to celebrate the universe and the
    mystery and possibilities in your presence here.
May the *eros* of the Earth bless you.

Source Unknown

The Senses

The following three blessings can be used individually or together

To awaken to the sound of singing birds,
To recognize the sound of wind that heralds rain,
To know that a shower of rain will bring the rainbow arch,
To see the spray and curl of pounding wave
To feel the rippled beach renewed by salty wash
is to sense God's blessing on his world—
Creator and Sustainer of us all.

Smell

Bread newly lifted from the oven,
Smoke newly rising from the hearth,
Newly mown grass for a field of hay—
The *kairos* gifts of God—
Assuring us of his presence.

Sight

Open our eyes to see your daily blessings to us:
The sight of a child's expressive face,
The dazzling light of dawn as it streaks the horizon,
Vapor traces across a clear blue sky,
Dimpled footsteps in glistening, dewy grass,
Shadows playing games with lengthening light,
Shimmering light on dancing water,
Golden corn waving in the wind,
The mellow rays of sunset kissing the earth,
The twinkling stars and smiling moon
And navy canopy:

All these and more from you to us—
Thank you great giver God!

Rosemary Wass
England

A Brazilian Blessing

Leader   Touch your eyes with your hands and say:
All   Bless my eyes, Lord, that I may see more clearly.
Leader   Touch your mouth with your hands and say:

All	Bless my mouth, Lord, which breaks the silence of centuries and seek to speak now of your truth.
Leader	Touch your ears with your hands and say:
All	Bless my ears, Lord, that I may hear my own words, thoughts, and feelings and those of every person near me.
Leader	Touch your heart with your hands and say:
All	Bless my heart, Lord, that I may be open to friendship and love.
Leader	Touch your feet with your hands and say:
All	Bless my feet, Lord, so that I might travel each step firmly and with courage during my life's path.
Leader	Touch God's Word with your hands and say:
All	Bless your Word, Lord, the good news, which is a compass for my way.
Leader	Touch your friends around you and say:
All	Bless me Lord, and my sisters and brothers.

Source Unknown
Brazil

Bless the Touch!

Lord, just a word,
just a look,
can heal the hurt that people feel.
A silent presence,
    a hug,
    a smile,
can do the work of many words.
The healing power of your dear Son
is in our hands,
in the prayers we share,
in what we think
and in all we do.
So let our presence be
the healing that is needed
as you bless our words,
our touching,
or silent sharing of a grief.

Richard Becher
England

Blessing of Sight

See I am doing a new thing.
Isaiah 43:19

I see at last, my eyes are open wide.
The Spring is here, with seeds of hope,
shooting buds, and fresh new growth.
I see at last, as winter harshness goes,
the darkest coldest times of growth.
I see at last, my eyes are open wide,
you specialize in doing new things.
I see at last, the blessings of your hand,
new gifts and talents, all the very best.

Now it springs up... Do you not perceive it?
Isaiah 43:19

Frances Ballantyne
England

Bless our Tears

When we weep
bless our tears
so they may refresh
the hearts of sadness
and nurture new life
in future years.

Richard Becher
England

Bless to Me, O God

Bless to me, O God,
 Each thing mine eye sees;
Bless to me, O God,
 Each sound mine ear hears;
Bless to me, O God,
 Each odor that goes to my nostrils;
Bless to me, O God,
 Each taste that goes to my lips;
 Each note that goes to my song,

Each ray that guides my way,
Each thing that I pursue,
Each lure that tempts my will,
The zeal that seeks my living soul,
The Three that seek my heart,
The zeal that seeks my living soul,
The Three that seek my heart.

Carmina Gadelica

Sensitivity and Tenderness

May God bless you
with a mind of sensitivity,
with a heart of tenderness,
with a strength of truth,
in the name of God the Creator,
Jesus Christ the Savior,
and the Holy Spirit, the life-giver.

Per Harling
Sweden

Bless the Angel in our Presence

An angel came as we gathered,
spoke,
touched, smiled,
and sang a song
that healed my loneliness.
The angel came,
so real,
in human flesh,
then went again
among the crowd
not knowing how
in that encounter
my life was changed.
An angel came,
not with halo
or dressed in white,

but in a voice that touched my need,
gave me strength
and then was gone.
So bless the angels in our presence
and help us be like them. Amen.

Richard Becher
England

Teachers of Vision

Blessed be all those who have taught me to see:
prophets,
>   poets,
>   writers,
>   and movie-makers,
friends and lovers,
>   all teachers of vision.

May my eyes bless you this day;
>   may they be opened—prayers of gratitude,
>   as I attempt to overcome any blindness of heart
>   and any dullness of appreciation of the wonder of sight.

In the fullness of my being,
>   I bless you, incomprehensible Lord,
>   who foresees a heaven of such splendor,
>   That ear has not heard nor eye seen
>   such beauty as you have prepared.

Blessed are you, Lord my God,
>   for the wondrous gift of sight.

Vienna Cobb Anderson
USA

Beauty in Creation

Benedicite

Blessed be God
    for the grandeur and power of crashing waters, and the fearsome downwardfall of the cliffs;
    for the swoop and swing of white birds riding the waves, exultant;
    for wind hurtling over moorland miles to break battering around the house, with clawing hands eager to invade and chill;
    for the silent blanketed folds after snowfall;
    for trees etched in silver against pewter skies;
    for winter sunshine brittle as thin ice.

Sister Catherine OHP
England

In Whom All Creation Is Renewed

Blessed be Christ our Savior in whom all creation is renewed,
Let us pray in living hope,
    Lord, fill all the world with your spirit.

Ancilla Dent
England

Blessing for the Earth

That we, and all fellow creatures entrusted to our care, may praise you, we ask your blessing, heavenly Father.

Bless our houseplants and windowboxes, our birdfeeders and our animal companions. For some of us it is especially through these that we praise you.

Bless those of us who, through your Son, in the power of your living Spirit, serve you and our fellow human creatures in cities.

Bless our rivers and rain, the barrels in which we harvest the rain. Bless our compost which returns to the soil and rises again to new life as a symbol of resurrection.

Bless our parks and gardens, the living soil communities with which we praise you, and within which we too are organisms. The flowers praise you in their radiance, our vegetables and fruit praise you in their beauty. Through nurturing them we enable your will to be done on earth as it is in heaven. We contribute to biodiversity and to right relationships among all creatures.

Bless our efforts to share earth's beauty, its fruits, and life. These are yours, which you share with us, and entrust to our subordinate rule, that we too may share with your other creatures. For you love all that you have created. Through your Son, Jesus Christ our Lord, you have reconciled ourselves and all the earth's creatures which you created.

Bless us as we offer the praise of all creation to you, through your Son, in the Holy Spirit.

Edward P. Echlin
England

All You Powerful Things, Praise the Lord

All you powerful things praise the Lord:
Niagara Falls and Pacific Ocean,
Tiger and tyrannosaurus,
Killer whale and golden eagle,
Forces of gravity and pull of the tide,
Forked lightning and nuclear power,
Praise and magnify the one who created you.

All you weak things praise the Lord:
Sparkle of light and breath of the breeze,
Scuttling ant and wriggling tadpole,
Tear in the eye and hair on the head,
Soft feathers and gentle sighs,
Scent of the rose and dandelion seeds,
Praise and magnify the one who created you.

Peter Graystone
England

Creation Seen—Creation Unseen

Let all that is visible worship the Lord:
High mountain ranges and leaves on the tree,
Microscopic creatures, skyscraping towers,
Cascading waters and stars in the sky,
Colors of the rainbow, people of the nations,
Lightning and landscape, sunset and shadow,
Greatly give praise to the One who created you.

Let all that's invisible worship the Lord:
Life-giving oxygen, cool of the breeze,
Electrical current and radio waves,
Scent of the flower and taste on the tongue,
Burning emotion, mysterious sleep,
Silence and gravity, music and laughter,
Greatly give praise to the One who created you.

Peter Graystone
England

May the Light of God Fill Your Heart

As the sun in its shining brings glory
As the stars in the night scatter dark
As the moon gives us hope in its radiance
So may the light of God
fill your heart and your mind and your life.

John Johansen-Berg
England

His Love Endures Forever

In the swirling darkness before time began, God was good,
His love endures forever,
In the muds and oozes of newly created earth, God was good,
His love endures forever,
When plants began to root and sprout, God was good,
His love endures forever,
When dinosaurs crashed and scampered and swam, God was good,
His love endures forever,
When human life took to its legs, God was good,
His love endures forever,

In the ages of farms and inventions and power, God was good,
His love endures forever,
In these years of the satellite, Internet, video, God is good,
His love endures forever,
In the future uncertainty, scarce of resources, God will be good,
His love endures forever.

Peter Graystone
England

Beauty in Forms of Creation

On Smelling Fragrant Woods or Barks

Blessed art thou, O Lord our God, King of the universe,
who createst fragrant woods.

On Smelling Odorous Fruits

Blessed art thou, O Lord our God, King of the universe,
who givest a goodly scent to fruits.

On Smelling Fragrant Spices

Blessed art thou, O Lord our God, King of the universe,
who createst diverse kinds of spices.

On Smelling Fragrant Oils

Blessed art thou, O Lord our God, King of the universe,
who createst fragrant oil.

On Seeing Lightning, Falling Stars, Lofty Mountains, or Great Deserts

Blessed art thou, O Lord our God, King of the universe,
who hast made the creation.

On Hearing Thunder

Blessed art thou, O Lord our God, King of the universe,
whose strength and might fill the world.

At the Sight of the Sea

Blessed art thou, O Lord our God, King of the universe,
who hast made the great sea.

On Seeing Beautiful Trees or Animals
Blessed art thou, O Lord Our God, King of the universe,
who hast such as these in thy world.

On Seeing the Rainbow
Blessed art thou, O Lord our God, King of the universe,
who rememberest the covenant, art faithful to thy
covenant, and keepest thy promise.
The Authorized Daily Prayer Book
of the United Hebrew Congregations of the Commonwealth

A Creation Benediction

O God,
Open our ears to hear your Spirit groaning over all creation.
Open our eyes to see that when we injure the earth and its resources,
we are sinning against you.
May we have the heart of Jesus to bless the land,
the beasts
and our children that there might be a livable future for us all.
Judy Chan
Hong Kong

The Lord Bless You with Rain

The Lord bless you with rain
The Lord bless you with crops
The Lord bless you with children
The Lord grant you long life.
Prince Dibeela
Botswana

May the Rain Nourish Your Soul

May the rain softly nourish your soul
Pour the blessings of heaven upon you
May the clouds wrap your winter nights
And keep you warm while the world is sleeping

May the thunder make you strong
Stirring the life within you
May the lightning awake us all
To act in knowing our Divine keeping

May your heart ever know peace and joy
And may sweet loving be yours to keep

Radha Sahar
Aotearoa New Zealand

Dominion Over All Living Creatures

May God who made male and female bless you
May God who gave dominion over all living creatures guide you
May God who promised you the products of the earth grant you
  good harvests
May God who made everything good bless you with abundance.
May the Lord of the running deer be alongside you
May the Lord of the living water journey with you
May the Lord of the flying crane be your guide
May the Lord of the flowing air go with you.

John Johansen-Berg
England

A Garden Blessing

Open your eyes to the beauty of color and shape;
tune your ears to the rustle of leaves and the babble of water;
lift your nose to the scent of flower and fruit;
reach out your hand to the texture and touch of the living earth;
with your whole being taste the goodness of the God of creation.
So may you share your joy with the God who planted a garden
in Eden and called you to look after it;
may you find your peace in the Christ who prayed in the garden

that God's will might be done;
may you experience the love of the Lord in that garden whose
leaves are for the healing of the nations.
For the God of the garden waits to bless you and hold you in
his eternal keeping.

David L. Helyar
England

A Doxology of Flowers

Praise God from whom all blessings flow;
praise God, when gentle breezes blow.
As flowers dance on summer days,
so may our spirits dance in praise.

Praise God whose light is there to bless
when earth puts on her summer dress.
As flowers tilt their heads above,
so may we blossom in God's love.

Praise God from whom all justice flows
for every race that blooms and grows.
In Christ may colors mix and stand
in glad array and hand in hand.

Praise God from whom shalom does flow;
praise God, whose world is ours to know.
May we take time, before they're gone,
to smell the flowers, one by one.

Tune: Old Hundredth

Walter Murray
Canada

Blessing of the Flowerbeds

Blessed are you, Lord God, in your ineffable and eternal Beauty, which you have willed to show forth in all your creatures. Bless now we pray these flowering plants, that they may blossom to your glory, and grant that we who look upon them may be drawn to gaze upon the splendor of your Divine Majesty. Glory to you, O God, Father, Son, and Holy Spirit, glory to you.

The Community of the Servants of the Will of God
Crawley, England

Peace, Strength and Light

May the God of Flint and Sedge
Marsh and Dune
Lark and Bittern
Cloud and Sand
Be peace, strength and light
To you, in you, and through you.

Community of All Hallows
Ditchingham, England

Blessing at a Time of Planting Trees

God our Father in heaven, you are the source of all life and goodness. For millions of years you have prepared the earth to be the garden planet of the universe. Over the millennia, your loving care has shaped and formed these islands which we call the Philippines in a unique way so that they are a home for an incredible variety of trees, flowers, insects, birds, and all kinds of animal life. We know that all of these life forms form a single community of the living. They sustain and nourish each other in ways that we still do not understand. You have placed us human beings in this garden. We are created in your image and called to be stewards of your creation.

For the past few decades, we have been poor stewards of your creation. We have destroyed the tropical forest, the rich life system with which you have blessed this beautiful land.

Today we wish to atone for our sins. We bring here these seedlings and ask you to bless them. As you blessed our country with a wonderful variety of trees which we use for food, clothing, and shelter, we ask you to bless them again and bless us also so that we might care for them in a new way.

Open our minds to the importance of trees in the community of the living. Enlighten us so that we will clearly understand that if we continue to destroy the forest we then endanger all life forms. Open our minds also to the beauty of the trees. Trees remind us of your creation and particularly of your presence always with us. The roots reach down deeply into the soil for water and nourishment, the tree trunks are our constant companion as we walk the earth, and the branches and canopy, reaching to the heavens, remind us of your presence always with us. Our ancestors, and tribal Filipinos today, are very much aware of the presence of your spirit in the trees around them. Unfortunately we have lost this wisdom. As we bless these seedlings today, help us to recapture that sensitivity and to resolve both individually and as a community to protect our forests and care for our trees. We ask you this through Jesus your Son and our brother who died on a tree so that we might have life.

Vin McMullen
England/Philippines

An Elemental Blessing

May the blessing of the earth, our mother,
nourish and sustain you.

May the blessing of the sky, our sister,
lift up your tired heart.

May the blessing of the sun, our brother,
smile his warmth upon you.

May the voices that call in the wind
and thunder in the raging sea,
bless you with their strength.

May the flames that dance in the fire
and burn in life's longings for love
bless you with their power.

May the blessings of earth, sky, fire, wind, and water,
Grant you peace and joy as creation's son or daughter.

Jean Mortimer
England

Landscapes

Landscape Blessing

Based on an exhibition of paintings by the landscape artist Jill Hutchings.

May the living Spirit carry you as a feather on the breath of God;
May the creative Spirit enable you to flower in the earth of God;
May the airy Spirit uphold you as a cloud in the sky of God;
May the watery Spirit surround you as a reed within the stream of God;
May the powerful Spirit energize you as a leopard in the strength of God;
May the ocean Spirit hold you as a rock within the waves of God;
May the earthy Spirit support you as a tree within the landscape of God;
    So that in Wisdom you may reflect God's glory.

June Boyce-Tillman
England

A Blessing of Trees

As part of creation,
like the wood of the cross,
may God bless you.

May you know, like the oak, how to stand:
    rooted in truth;
    reaching for light;
    patiently enduring and growing;
    sheltering, without favor,
    all who come into your shade;
and becoming part of the rock
on which you rest.

May you learn, like the willow, how to bend:
    flexing in hope;
    twisting in love;
    moving with the breeze of the Spirit;
    receiving the pressures of others
    For accommodating their pain;
and trusting that, in God's time, all will return.

May you find, like the pine, an evergreen way:
    clothed in life;
    ever productive;
    bearing the color of Christ in all seasons;
    never succumbing to dark winter
    no matter how bleak today may seem;
and, when you are cut (for you shall be),
letting your fragrance spread, for God's sake.

Like the wood of the cross,
may God bless you.

Duncan L. Tuck
Wales

A Blessing on the Desert

May the God of the vast red Australian desert bless us with rivers of living water. May the mystery and loneliness of the desert transform into lush spiritual vegetation. May the God who is as inscrutable as the land send prophets from the desert to teach us.

Adapted by Alan Nichols
Australia

Blessing of the Forest

Pour down, O Lord, your heavenly blessing on this forest:
    May all the trees of this wood rejoice, for they are made holy by Christ, who planted them in the beginning and who was outstretched upon the Tree, and who now lives and reigns with you and the Holy Spirit, one God forever and ever.

The Community of the Servants of the Will of God
Crawley, England

Blessing for Prairie Sage

Creator, Christ and Spirit
bless you, prairie sage,
first of springtime's wild herbs
on our little prairie hills.
As I pass,
your aroma
surprises me and caresses me and blesses me:
winter is gone.
Survivors of the winter's wind and freeze,
your grey-green leaves beneath my feet,
through fragrance
call out "Come forth and dance."
I bend before you
and gently rub a leaf
and all creation smells of your fresh rebirth.
Welcome, little prairie sage,
blessed be you;
blessed be life.

Betty Lynn Schwab
Canada

The Blessing of the Bush

Lincoln University offers a course in Human Ecology. The tutor takes a group of about twenty students into the west coast native bush for a week. The forest is dense; within a few paces one quickly loses any sense of direction. The tracks are rudimentary; often cut along a mountain-side, sometimes with a distance to fall should one slip. The rain pours down for a time almost every day. There are streams to ford; one minute a trickle and next a torrent.

The tutor said, "God teaches these young men and women quite a lot in that week. God teaches them, there is a time to be active and a time to sleep! They learn to live by the rhythm of daylight and darkness; by the time darkness falls, they are ready for sleep. God teaches each one, they must take care. In the bush, there are dangers, things to beware of. God teaches them to look out for one another. In the forest environment we never know when we might need someone's help. God teaches them, when it comes to mealtimes, it is a lot easier when everyone pools their resources and pulls their weight in the preparation. God teaches them, without electronic music, they will hear the beautiful music of birds singing, leaves rustling and in the distance, the waves breaking. God teaches them, engaging in the natural world one can find a deep pleasure, a sense of well-being and peace which is engagement with the Creator. They find themselves with a spirit of awe and wonder and thankfulness."

He said, "At the end of the week, they are reluctant to return to the city. They return however, with some life skills not unrelated to the Scripture."

John Hunt
Aotearoa New Zealand

Seascapes

The Blessing of the Sea (1)

From silent calm to crashing splendor
—such is the blessing of the sea.
Rippling, lapping, swirling, turning,
resting.
Foaming, spraying, surging, dancing,
white horses
crescendo leaping.

Ebbing and flowing
to the moon's waxing and waning;

life is teeming
microscopic and mighty,
waters of life nurturing.

Ebbing and flowing
the waters gushing
moonlit rhythms measuring—
birthing
and re-birthing.

Ebbing and flowing
ancient
timeless
predictable
secret.

Life's heartbeat measured:
ebbing and flowing
giving and receiving
cleansing and renewing
dying and living

—such is the blessing of the sea.
Sarah Brewerton
England

Blessing for Those on the Sea

Creator God who divided the mighty ocean
Bless all who earn a living on the sea:
  fisher folk
  ferry boat crews
  naval services
  roughnecks on rigs;
Bless them with your strength and power.

Compassionate Christ who gave your life for us
Bless all those who care for people on the sea:
  lifeboat crews
  air-sea rescue pilots
  coast guards
  mission workers;
Bless them with your love and courage.

Holy Spirit who brings us inner calm
Bless all those who use the sea for leisure:
  workers in commerce, industry,
  education and care
  the home makers
  the church builders;
Bless them with your joy and peace.

The strength and power of God
The love and courage of Christ
The joy and peace of the Spirit
The blessing of the Three
Be with all on the sea.

Heather Johnston
England

Boat Blessing

Helmsman	Blest be the boat
Crew	God the Father bless her.
Helmsman	Blest be the boat
Crew	God the Son bless her.
Helmsman	Blest be the boat
Crew	God the Spirit bless her
All	God the Father,
	God the Son,
	God the Spirit,
	Bless the boat.

Helmsman	What can befall you
	And God the Father with you?
Crew	No harm can befall us.
Helmsman	What can befall you
	And God the Son with you?
Crew	No harm can befall us.
Helmsman	What can befall you
	And God the Spirit with you?
Crew	No harm can befall us.
All	God the Father,
	God the Son,
	God the Spirit,
	With us eternally.

Helmsman	What can cause you anxiety
	And the God of the elements over you?
Crew	No anxiety can be ours.
Helmsman	What can cause you anxiety
	And the King of the elements over you?
Crew	No anxiety can be ours.

Helmsman	What can cause you anxiety
	And the Spirit of the elements over you?
Crew	No anxiety can be ours.
All	The God of the elements,
	The King of the elements,
	The Spirit of the elements,
	Close over us,
	Ever eternally.

Carmina Gadelica

Blessing of a Samoan Fishing Canoe

Lord Jesus Christ, you have chosen from among the Galilean fishermen your first disciples to be your companions in your earthly ministry; you have used their fishing boats as a means of transportation; you also used them often as your preaching platforms.

Today, we place this *paopao* (smaller outrigger canoe); *va'aalo* (larger version); *alia* (double-deck) for your dedication and blessing. We thank you for the skill you've given the *tufuga* (builder) to make it, and now it is ready to go to sea.

Lord, we pray that you will bless this canoe and ask your gracious favor to keep watch over all who will use it either for travel from one place to the other, but especially when it goes out to the open seas to fish for our daily living. Keep it safe from the rough seas and keep it safe from any tidal disasters.

Hear this our prayer in Jesus' mighty name. Amen.

L. Setefano
Aotearoa New Zealand

The Blessing of the Sea (2)

Our son James, aged seventeen, has joined a surf life-saving club. The boat is a canoe type with a high prow and stern. Four young men sit in pairs with a paddle each. Launching is hazardous. They carry the boat to the beach. The boat is guided into the shallows, facing the waves. Pushing the boat into deeper water, the two in front leap in and start paddling; the second two keep pushing a little further, then leap in and paddle vigorously. Directly they are climbing a wave, the crest breaking over them; then another and another. They must keep paddling. If they get side-on to a wave, the boat will be turned over.

Last week the boys were unable to keep the boat pointed into the waves, and they were tipped out. James was treading water, holding on to his paddle. Then he realized he was being dragged out to sea in a rip! He was getting tired. He had swallowed a lot of water. He began to panic. He called out and held his arm aloft as the waves crashed over him.

It was early evening. The official life guards had gone off duty. A senior guard had been taking an interest, watching the boys. He spotted James, realized he was in trouble and swam to him. One of the other boys became aware of James being in difficulty and also swam to him. The life-guard got James into position, from behind, holding his chin above the water. He called James' friend, "Prise his fingers off his paddle!"

He got James to the beach where he sat, shaking for about an hour.

I could say—James is lucky to be alive. I could think—it was a terrible experience for him. Or I could say—thank God someone was there for James. I could think—it was a good experience when James learned the sea is to be respected, he has his own limitations, he needs friends and he has friends on whom he can depend.

John Hunt
Aotearoa New Zealand

Blessing at the End of a Canoeing Day

As the setting sun warms the shoreline rocks,
and the trees turn from green to shadow,
as the loons call their young and nestle them in,
and the coals glow deep orange and yellow,
may the Spirit fill me with peace and calm
and the Christ grant me love within.

Betty Lynn Schwab
Canada

Birds and Beasts

Peacocks and Pandas

May the glory of the Creator
Which shines forth in his creation
Shine in our hearts.

May the power of God
Seen in the might of an elephant
And the endurance of the camel
Fill you with strength.

May the gentleness of God
Like a leopard caring for her cubs
Or the flight of a dove
Fill you with compassion.

May the beauty of God
Who created peacocks and pandas,
Porpoise and platypus
Fill you with awe.

May the mystery of God
Who sustains mosquitoes and maggots,
Moose and mice
Fill you with wonder.

May the wisdom of God
Who made the animal kingdom
And the human race
Give you grace to live in harmony.

And the blessing of God the creator,
Jesus the redeemer
And the spirit, the sustainer
Be upon you and all his creation
Forever and forever.

Dominic Walker
England

Presence

*One should be perfectly at peace even (perhaps especially) when
one hasn't "got something to do"...how difficult...this acceptance of simple
presence as one's contribution.*

(Catherine de Hueck Doherty)

At sunset come the swans
    to rest, survey and bless
    the bay, and fold the kiss,
    within their down, of evening's bronze.

And with them nothing bring:
    no show of love, perform
    no ballet: only calm
    to lift and lighten everything.

Their bodies cause no rift
    of waters as they swim
    away. For this they came:
    to offer presence as their gift.

Kate Compston
England

Seagull

Wild cry
gull cry
    time haunting
cascading
    sunlight soaring
salt wind whipping
    tenderly blessing
all being.

Ancilla Dent
England

A Cat Blessing

Bless you, Creator of the Universe,
for your Word made
purr and gleaming eye—
      born in flash and rumble
      beyond the curling Milky Way
      it flashes now gold now green
      and rumbles from deep within
      the curled and purring soul
      beaming your green and gold
      into me
Bless you, Creator of the Universe,
for your Universal Word.

Norm S. D. Esdon
Canada

A Blessing for Earth's Birds

Flitting, soaring, wading
nesting, feeding, bathing,
guarding, chirping, migrating:
blessed be the birds of creation.

In jungles, forests and gardens,
on oceans, plains and peaks,
high-rise ledges and dark barn beams:
blessed be the birds of creation.

Eye ring, rump and wing bar,
crown, claw and beak,
primary, and down feathers:
blessed be the birds of creation.

Hatched and cared for in our homes,
learning to talk and perch on us,
singing gladly to the music of our lives:
blessed be the birds of creation.

Caught by cats, hunted by man, weakened by DDT,
killed by windows, pushed out by tourists,

captured for black-market trade:
blessed, oh blessed be the birds of creation.

Found when injured, healed and set free,
given seeds for winter and water for summer,
nesting boxes by roads, sanctuary for others:
blessed be the birds of creation.

Flitting, soaring, wading,
nesting, feeding, bathing,
guarding, chirping, migrating:
blessed be the birds of creation.

Betty Lynn Schwab
Canada

Great Bird of the Wide Skies

May the maker of the yellow beak, the black bird, be with you
May the maker of the broad wing, the brown thrush, be with you
May the maker of the fantail, the white dove, be near you
May the great bird of the wide skies descend upon you.

John Johansen-Berg
England

The Blessing of Cows or other Animals

Prayer written for the charity Send a Cow *for use by those sending or receiving dairy cows (and goats, hens, or other breeding animals), given for the relief of poverty and malnutrition in Africa and other countries.*

Heavenly Father, creator of all living things, we thank you for your beautiful and complex world, and for your command to take control of the earth on your behalf. We thank you, too, for the example of Our Lord Jesus Christ, in his use of the donkey, his caring sayings about the wild birds, the hen, the sheep and the ox, and his use, for food, of the fish and the Passover lamb. Give us, we pray, wisdom as we care for the animals you have made and have put in our charge.

We pray for these animals present, as they pass to their new owners. We ask for safe journeys for them, for protection from danger and disease, and for understanding and conscientious work from the new owners as they care for their new responsibilities. We ask you to help the cows *(animals)* to be a productive blessing to whole neighborhoods in the milk and fertility they bring *(eggs/young that they produce)*. Grant them long and fertile lives, that they may bring nourishment and happiness for many years.

Grant, too, Heavenly Father, that these animals may always remind those that hold them, that you are their maker and ours, and that your desire is to meet needs and create generous hearts, as we have fellowship with you, through Jesus Christ our Lord.

Anthony Bush
England

Lands and Peoples

Revelation 22:1–2

...and its leaves
are for the healing
of the nations.

A Blessing for Romania

In a country with a proud history
there has been a time of oppression.
Culture and faith were suppressed
by a brutal and atheistic power.
The longing for liberation crossed barriers,
uniting people of different languages, cultures,
and religious expressions
in the common search for freedom.
With the downfall of a dictator
came the possibility of liberty and peace.
Many have suffered and for some
the feeling of deprivation continues.

May God bless Romania
with justice and with peace.
May the varied communities within the country
live together with mutual respect.
May the land return to fruitfulness
and the cities become places of healthy living.
May those in positions of leadership
encourage unity in the nation
and offer help and assistance to the most needy.
May the various churches with their long traditions,
their different liturgies, and a common faith
express unity in caring action
and shared proclamation.

May God bless Romania
and give wisdom and strength
to those who seek to establish justice and peace.
May those who live in the cities give thanks
for those who work on the land.
May those who produce the crops
appreciate those whose labor is in industry.
May there be true cooperation between the varied people
who make up this beautiful and fruitful land.
May God bless Romania
and lead its people in the ways of true peace.

John Johansen-Berg
England

A Blessing for Rwanda

There was a strange quiet in the village;
there was an eerie silence in the forest;
the birds were silent as they flew above their nests;
the animals moved softly through the undergrowth.
The piercing cry of children, the wailing of mothers,
the shouts of dying fathers, all victims of the genocide,
left a silence in the hills and valleys.

May God restore the singing of the birds; may the loving Creator
    bring back the lowing of cattle.
May those who have suffered the anguish
of seeing loved ones killed
experience the healing grace of God.
May the children traumatized by awful sights and sounds
know the peace of God in their hearts.
May the forgiveness of God flowing through the land
cause a stream of repentance by those who wielded weapons,
releasing forgiveness from those who suffered hurt.
May the land that has experienced great darkness
now encounter even greater light.
May the light of Christ overcome the shadows
and bring hope into the hearts and minds of the people.

May a new day dawn for Rwanda,
drawing the people to renewed commitment to Christ.
May the songs of joy be heard in the land;
may neighbor live with neighbor in peace;
may Hutu live with Tutsi in mutual care;
may the divisions of the past give way to friendship.
May the grace of God cover Rwanda
and make its people a source of blessing for the world.
Let those who forgive and are forgiven
show the possibility and power of reconciliation.
May God bless Rwanda, its land, and people.

John Johansen-Berg
England

Blessings from South Africa—the Rainbow Nation

Under normal conditions it would seem that blessedness and harmony walk together. Blessing can only take place in harmony. Therefore, it seems that we can only receive blessing from God and one another within a sense of harmony with him and one another. Conversely, in an atmosphere of disharmony we can only experience unhappiness—even cursedness. But considering the source from which blessing comes, if God be the source for blessing, it is possible to convert even cursed conditions into a state of harmony. Remember the man from Gerasa, who was in a total state of disharmony, confusion and chaos—Jesus Christ, the source of blessing restored harmony, peace and order within this man—indeed a blessing!

When looking back at the history of South Africa, we find that over many centuries South Africa brought the curse of disharmony upon herself, culminating in the era of apartheid. Blessing cannot be given or received in apartness.

But the definite vision and strong willpower as well as the vision of strong leadership took it to heart to create conditions of harmony. We fought a tough battle to bring people together... Four years ago apartheid was consigned to the rubbish dump in South Africa. This released all who live here to seek harmony with one another. Despite our many problems, we have had a glimpse of how we can be a blessing, of being a rainbow nation, of learning to live in joy and harmony with one another, of celebrating the dynamic of being one in the midst of our rich diversity.

May God bless us in this adventure; may we become a blessing to the world as we become visible evidence of how many nations and cultures can live in harmony in spite of the seemingly hopeless conditions of our past. Thanks be to God, our source of blessing, and also to the respect and faith that people do have in one another!

Cathy Bott
South Africa

Bless African Women, Lord

Bless women, Lord, as they
work in the fields to earn a living
and rear their livestock with little
babies on their backs.

Bless women, Lord, as they
sell their goods from early morning
until late at night sitting by the streets
in cold or sunshine.

Bless women, Lord, when
single mothers raise their children with love
and devotion only to be told that they
will die of AIDS.

Bless women, Lord, young and old
who are emotionally and physically abused;
battered and raped by those who have no respect
for the beauty of your creation.

Bless women, Lord, our doctors
lawyers, teachers and pastors, all those who
serve your people.

Bless African women
in the name of Jesus our Savior.

Cheryl Dibeela
Botswana

Bless the Earth, Every Day

A Blessing for Botswana

Every day young woman and young man
Every day, in the morning
Every day young girl and young boy
Every day, in the morning
When you wake up early in the morning
Stretch your hands upon the earth, touch the earth
Bless the earth
Stretch your hands, call God in prayer,
Bless the earth
Bless the earth (x6)

Every day young woman and young man
Every day, in the morning
Every day young girl and young boy
Every day, in the morning

When you wake up early in the morning
Stretch your feet upon the earth, walk the earth
Bless the earth
Stretch your feet, go to God in prayer,
Bless the earth
Bless the earth (x5)

Pour your healing waters upon the earth
Pour your healing soul upon the earth
Pour your healing touch upon the earth
Pour your healing love upon the earth
Bless the earth (x6)

Every day young woman and young man
Every day, in the morning
Every day young girl and young boy
Every day, in the morning
When you wake up early in the morning
Speak your word upon the Botswana,
Bless the nation
Speak your words, speak to God in prayer,
Bless Botswana
Bless Botswana (x3)

Pour your healing waters, bless Botswana
Pour your healing soul, bless Africa
Pour your healing touch, bless the earth
Pour your healing love upon the world
Bless the earth (x6)

Musa W. Dube Shomanah
Botswana

The Liverpool Blessing

May the fire of Christ consume all indifference to God
May the light of Christ illumine our vision of God
May the love of Christ enlarge our longing for God
May the spirit of Christ empower our service to God

James Jones
England

A Blessing for London

and other great cities

Peace to you great city
Peace to you vast and unknown
Peace to you close and tangible...

A blessing on all bridges—reachings of great span
Connecting, joining, reconnecting people

A blessing on all stairwells—hidden circulations
Bearing angels on their concrete steps

A blessing on all mechanics—healers of engines
Finding order and design where we see only grime and noise

A blessing on the Junction—confluence of paths
Where the world meets and joins itself in one humanity
A blessing on traffic lights and emergency warning lights, on
        pelican crossings and zebra crossings, on round signs, square
            signs, triangular signs, on policemen and lollipop men, on
                traffic wardens
On all that channels and controls the flow of cities

A blessing on the great river: slow and uncluttered
Where it all began and which always must be...
Peace be on you, great city, peace of the great river which always
        runs through you.

J. R. Ashdown
England

A Blessing for Israel/Palestine

The author uses the term Israel/Palestine in the hope that it should be seen,
ideally, as one country occupied by two peoples who are related historically.

Lord God, we seek your blessing on this ancient place
that many call the Holy Land.
May your blessing rest on Israel
and on your ancient people, the Jews.

May your blessing rest on Palestine
and on your ancient people, the Arabs.
May the descendants of Abraham
be greatly blessed in the possession of the land.
May enmity and division cease
and a new era of peace and cooperation begin.

God of many nations, Father of many peoples,
bless the Land making it fruitful;
may the rivers not run dry;
may the wells and cisterns hold fresh water;
may the crops be sufficient to feed your people.

God of peace,
Grant your *shalom-salaam* to this shared land.
May there be justice throughout the territories
and may peace prevail for all the region.
May the words of the prophets come true
as people worship you in spirit and truth
and justice and peace become evident in the Land.

God of wisdom,
guide those who have responsibility
for government in this and neighboring countries.
May they be men and women of spiritual insight
seeking the welfare of all the people.
May they nurture the peace process
which is such a fragile plant in an environment
that can be made hostile by acts of violence.

God of grace,
may your showers of blessing descend on the land
that what was once a wilderness may become a fruitful field.
May the trees of the field and the sheep on the hills
share in the jubilation of the people.
May all your children proclaim your name
and fulfill your loving purpose.
God bless Israel/Palestine
and bring peace to Jerusalem.

John Johansen-Berg
England

Bless our People

Teach us to work for the welfare of all,
To diminish the evils that beset us
And to enlarge our nation's virtues.

Bless our people with civic courage.

Bless our striving to make real the dream of your kingdom, when we
shall put an end to the suffering we now inflict upon each other.

Bless our people with a vision of your kingdom on earth.

For you have endowed us with noble powers;
help us to use them wisely
and with compassion.

Bless our people with a wise and feeling heart.

You have given us freedom to choose between good and evil,
life and death.
May we choose life and good,
that our children may inherit from us the blessings of
dignity and freedom,
prosperity and peace.

A Jewish Blessing

North East India, Bless the Lord

North East India, bless the Lord,
And all her hundred tribes in a hundred tongues, bless the Lord.
From Tirap to Terae, all you bless the Lord.
Your high Himalayas, bless the Lord.
Praise and extol him forever and ever.

Your Broad Brahmaputra, bless the Lord.
Zapfu heights and Phawngpui sights,
Nokrek Peak and Loktak Lake,
Sohra rains and Simsang rills,
The Barak, the Manas, the Bhutan Hill
Mawsmai caves and Umiam waves;

All you floods and waters, bless the Lord.
You three-hunched hills of Tripura, bless the Lord.
You snowy slopes of Arunachal, bless the Lord.
Praise and extol him forever and ever.

You roaming rhinos, bless the Lord.
Elephant herds and mithun calves.
Oil wells and green tea leaves,
Pineapple patches and papaya plants,
The mangoes, the lichees, the mulberry bush;

The bow and the dao and the many-colored shawl.
All you wealth of the soil, bless the Lord.
All you beasts of the forest, bless the Lord.
All you hand produced goods, bless the Lord.
Praise and extol him forever and ever.

Thomas Menamparampil
India

Rahim and Afroza

Rahim and Afroza, with their three children, were returning home after two months of living in a plastic sheet temporary residence on a patch of high ground or helipad. Many families were parking there after their homes went under water. They live along the banks of Brahmaputra—the big river in the north that flows from the Indian hills. The area is low, made of river silt. There is a vast tract of land but they own only the homestead—all else belongs to big people. When asked how they were doing, they replied:

We were happy to be with many others there. Made many new friends. Our children were also happy to play with other children. And we were lucky that we received some food daily, some generous people came with it—and there was also some government ration. For the long flood—there was no work available. Of course there was opportunity we could catch some fish and enjoy a good meal. Now we are relieved that the flood is over and we can go back. We have no money left of our savings. However we can borrow some money at an interest to fix the house (a fragile structure). And there will be some work for me and for Afroza. If need be we shall go to another village for work and my neighbors will take care of everything.

Am thankful to God (Allah) for everything: I have a good wife and nice children and my neighbors are considerate. And somehow we manage to make ends meet. Even during this long flood we had a dry patch to stay on and there was also food.

Bishop Mondal
Bangladesh

A Blessing for Pakistan

O Pakistan, land of the pure
In Jesu's name we bless you:
May the gates of your cities
Open wide to the King of Glory
May corruption be banished from your courts
And your judges judge in righteousness.

May your rulers fear God
And in humility serve your people.

May the good news of salvation
Be heard in your streets
And the sound of joy ring through your marketplaces.

May your women be free
And your children be full of hope.

As the snow melts from the mountains
And feeds the rivers of your plains
May the Spirit of the Lord
Flood the hearts of your people
With the love of God.

Aie Khudavand Yesu ao
Tere Rooh Pakistan par nazil ho
Yeh hamari dua hai.
Jesu ke nam me.

Come, Lord Jesus, come
Pour out your Spirit on Pakistan
This is our prayer
In Jesus' Name
Amen.

Phil Billing
Pakistan

A Blessing for Hong Kong

Lord, you have been our dwelling place,
our refuge in all generations,
for all people
in every circumstance.
Now, as this generation of Hong Kong faces the future,
we ask your gracious blessing,
for the six million residents of Hong Kong
living in the most densely populated urban area in the world.
Grant them courage of heart and peace of mind.
May they enter the future with confidence in themselves and in you.
For the Chief Executive and the Government of the Hong Kong
        Special Administrative Region,
give them wisdom and understanding for the heavy task that lies
        before them.
May they truly be servants as well as leaders of their people.
For the freedom, security and prosperity that Hong Kong people
        cherish.
May these continue to be enjoyed for fifty years and beyond and
        shared with all the citizens of the land.
For the six hundred thousand Christians and the one thousand five
        hundred churches laboring for you in Hong Kong.
Grant them faith to continue being salt of the earth and light to the
        world.
For the nation of China,
with its one billion people, long history and proud tradition.
May they honor the promises made to the people of Hong Kong
that each might be a blessing to the other.
May the people of Hong Kong and China know our love and concern.
May the people of Hong Kong and China know your love and concern.
Your steadfast love,
O Lord,
Endures forever.

Judy Chan
Hong Kong

A Blessing for Canada

Creator of us all,
In your wisdom you brought the earth into being
And in our wisdom we brought into being
Our nation, Canada.

We bless you
for your grace
has been a part in the creation of Canada.
And we bless you
for this land,
our dwelling place among your great community of nations.

We bless you
for the wealth and glory of Canada's mountains and hills, valleys
    and plains:
for huge prairie skies and mystic sun-dogs;
for woodland trilliums, steep rocky shores and silent ancient
    rainforests;
for snow and rain, hot sun and brilliant red maple leaves—
each in their returning season;
for gold and potash beneath the earth;
for fields of wheat and waters rich with salmon farms;
for the prosperity of our business people and the inspiration of our
    artists;
for the freedoms of our governments and the privileges that come to
    all...
because here, and now, there is no war;
because here, and now, there is prosperity.
Bless us, we pray
with growing compassion for those who struggle, hunger, and hurt
    within our nation.
Bless us, we pray
with a vivid knowledge of our past and present wrongs
committed against the first nations, against each other and against
    your Earth.
Bless us, we pray
with greater skills to repent, to heal, and to forgive,
to develop, to bring justice, and to make peace.
Bless us, we pray

that we may be a blessing to our land and nation;
And she in turn, a blessing to you and to all your world.

Betty Lynn Schwab
Canada

From this Place

From this place
I am connected to you.

    Though your faith may differ from mine,
    And your language be unfamiliar to me,
    We are each created
    In a spirit of love.

From this place
I am responsible for you.

    Though we may be worlds apart,
    Boundaries of land, race, economics, and religion
    Can have no meaning
    And borders fall away if you are in need.

From this place
I reach out to you.

    And together we will seek justice,
    Respect creation,
    Grow in faith,
    And build the future.

From this place
I bless you.

    I give thanks for your being,
    I bless your creation;
    Made in the image of God
    Who delights in you and cherishes you.

Louise Margaret Granahan
Canada

A Nunavut Blessing

*Nunavut is the newest Canadian territory. It was established on
April 1, 1999, to create a separate space for the Inuit people.*

We pray with our ancestors, who by their efforts brought us to where we
are today. From the beginning of time they took care of our lives and
embraced Christian faith in our camps and communities.

May our leaders of today make the same efforts to improve our lives.

Lord, help us to enjoy today's life, to have no fear, and to care for others. Help us to have a foundation as solid as rock to build our future.

Thank you for the universe: the land, the sea, the sun, the moon, the
stars, the animals, and all life. We are very grateful that you created
them as a gift of your love.

**Jesus, our Savior, with your help may all the good things you creat-
ed be used wisely. May these gifts be better recognized and appreci-
ated by our descendants.**

Thank you God for our families. We pray that, in Nunavut, families will
continue to be strong in their faith and that the elders and the young
will work closely together to create a better future.

Pastoral Leaders of Pelly Bay
Nunavut, Canada

Nature's Blessing for Busy City Folk
An island retreat in Eastern Ontario

What about the sky in the early morning as you look out east over the misty lake?

The lake shimmers blue and green and silver. The sky is orange and yellow and bright with a striking blue and just a shadow of the moon still peeking.

It is early.

But what a blessing is this! The smell of the moss on the rocks as the dew dries on them. The sound of a distant boat as a local fisherman ventures forth to catch his breakfast.

A deeper breath catches the faint scent of a far-off fire. One imagines with relish the percolator performing its distinctive morning song and dance. Shall we have bacon and eggs this morning? Cooked in the cool outdoors, with our coffee and grilled toast? What shall we do today? Perhaps we will begin with this leisurely breakfast, eating and cooking without schedule or timeline.

Then we will go for a walk and explore parts of the Canadian Shield yet unwalked. We will climb higher and higher up the hills and cliffs, and in a short while we will feel elated, as though we have reached heaven.

We will walk and the clouds will cover quickly and a misty cool rain will drape our warm faces. Then, if we look through the trees, we will be blessed by the rare and majestic appearance of the brightest rainbow we have ever seen.

The clouds will part and we will feel we have truly experienced something. We will know we walk in the presence of God. We will look at the sky and the high billowy clouds floating by us as they dance and change shape.

When we return from our walk, we will remark that we barely spoke, although we were so glad to share our spiritual time with one another. We will hold hands and sit on the bare rock watching the minnows swim around in schools of hundreds. We will stay as still as statues as the young family of loons float by us and mother makes her unique call.

We will look at the birds in the trees, the fish in the lake, feel the cool breeze on our noses. We will concentrate on the sound and movement the canoe makes as we paddle around the island.

We are enjoying this time together, understanding and appreciating the depth at which we become one with this nature. We are both renewing our spiritual selves. We are surrounded by many blessings, and noting them in our long-term memory. We share this sermon together, sitting quietly and listening to what it says to us, as we would in a pew.

When we go home, we will be back to our fast-paced life. We will be rushing to our jobs and our friends and our responsibilities, and we will sometimes forget this. But sometimes, as we lie restless, being unable to let sleep take us for the stresses in our life, we will talk to each other and remind one another about the scents and sounds and bright colors. We will hold hands again and feel the peace we feel in the wonderful place that is our holiest place.

We are blessed for having that place and the memories of it.

Thank you, God, for giving all people that one place that they can go to, often or not, where their spirit is renewed and they find solace and peace. Thank you, God, for the water and the sky and the birds and the rocks and the trees. Thank you, God, for our island retreat in Eastern Ontario.

Karen Scarlett
Canada

Before, Behind, Below and Around Us

Before us it is blessed, behind us it is blessed,
    below us it is blessed, above us it is blessed,
    around us it is blessed as we set out with Christ.
Our speech is blessed as we set out for God.
With beauty before us, with beauty behind us,
    with beauty below us, with beauty above us,
    with beauty around us, we set out for a holy place indeed.
Traditional Navajo Prayer
North America

For Australia

This is a broad land, horizons far away
roads that get lost in the distance,
and blue, distant hills.

May breadth of mind and heart be ours.

This is a hard land,
the soils thin and weathered,
dusty and cracked with drought
or deluged with sudden flood.

    May we learn to live with stress.

This land is washed by oceans,
with mighty waves on rocky coasts,
and lazy tropical tides,
and storms from the frozen south.

    Wash our lives with your living water.

And in this land people have been at home
for many millennia,
with few possessions but much courage,
with life-sustaining skills
in harmony with all creation.

    May their quiet persistence infect our lives,
    So that land and people may together praise you,
    God of creation.

Bernard Thorogood
Australia

The Aboriginal Fire Blessing

May the fire be in our thoughts:
Making them true, good, and just,
may it protect us from the evil one.

May the fire be in our eyes:
May it open our eyes to see what is good in life.
We ask that the fire may protect us
from what is not rightfully ours.

May the fire be on our lips:
So that we may speak the truth in kindness,
that we may encourage others.
May it protect us from speaking evil.

May the fire be in our ears:
We pray that we may hear with a deep, deep listening
so that we may hear the flow of water and of all creation,
and the dreaming.
May we be protected from gossip and from those things
that harm and break down our family.

May the fire be in our arms and hands:
So that we may be of service and build up love.
May the fire protect us from all violence.

May the fire be in our whole being:
In our legs and in our feet,
enabling us to walk the earth
with reverence and care;
so that we may walk in the ways of goodness and truth
and be protected from walking away from what is true.

This is reputed to be an old Australian Aboriginal blessing.

Source Unknown
Australia

A Blessing on the Land of "Fair Go"

"Fair Go" is an Australian slang term meaning "an even chance."

May the church in Australia, the Land of the Spirit, maximize its impact on Australian life and culture. May the gospel transform Australian society, help people to recognize past failures and apologize for past mistakes, so there may be true reconciliation between indigenous Australians and others. May church leaders demonstrate their ideals with actions of care and justice.

Adapted by Alan Nichols
Australia

An Australian Celtic Blessing

May the road never seem so long to the homestead.
May the sea breeze always blow softly on your veranda.
May you always find shade from the blazing sun.
May the rain fall on your paddocks just when you need it.
Until we meet again God hold you in the lee of the thunderstorm.

Adapted by Alan Nichols
Australia

Aotearoa

Genesis 28:17

May this land of Aotearoa
    its peoples
    its cultures
    their travails
    their hopes
be for us all
the very dwelling place of God.

W. L. Wallace
Aotearoa New Zealand

Arohanui Blessing

"Arohanui" means "great love" or "with all God's love."

May the mystery of God enfold us,
may the wisdom of God uphold us,
may the fragrance of God be around us,
may the brightness of God surround us,
may the wonder of God renew us,
may the loving of God flow through us,
may the peace of God deeply move us,
may the moving of God bring us peace.

Joy Cowley
Aotearoa New Zealand

Popul Vuh

A Guatemalan phrase and the title of a book
from which this blessing was taken.

Truly now,
double thanks, triple thanks
that we've been formed, we've been given
our mouth, our faces,
we speak, we listen,
we wonder, we move,
our knowledge is good, we've understood
what is far and near,
and we've seen what is great and small
under the sky, on the earth.
Thanks to you we've been formed,
we've come to be made and modeled,
our grandmother, our grandfather.

Translated by Dennis Tedlock
USA

A Mayan Prayer

An Ecumenical Blessing

Uk'ux Kaq'iq, Uk'ux Q'aq'
Uk'ux Ja', Uk'ux Ulew
Heart of Air, Heart of Fire
Heart of Water, Heart of Earth

We invoke the energies of the hills from all of the sacred places of
our ancestors.

We invoke our grandfathers and grandmothers who formed our faces,
our hearts, our worldview
and our values of respect and harmony with God
—the only supreme being, mother and father of all the peoples of the
world—
with nature and with humanity.

Uk'ux Kaj, Uk'ux Ulew
Heart of the Sky, Heart of the Earth

Bless all of the cultures in which we are immersed in the world.

Bless our variously colored faces:
red skin, black skin,
yellow skin, white skin
—like the four cardinal points.

Bless our petitions in their distinct languages.

Bless our distinct forms of celebrations
—*kotz'i'jab'* (ceremonies), rites, services, Masses—
that we present you together with all the people of the world.

That you appear with us in the hills,
in the temples,
in the churches,
in the synagogues,
in the mosques,
in all the places
where we present our happiness,
our sorrow,
and our hope;

that in all the religious beliefs is introduced the respect and the love
and the lack of competition,
that we would complement one another;

that it may be so.

Amen.

Juan Ixchop Us
Guatemala
Translated by Garry G. Sparks
USA

Give Me a Blessing

In Venezuela complete strangers will come up to you, if you are a priest, and say *"Bendicion,"* which means "Give me a blessing." At first you are taken aback by the abruptness of the demand and it is a demand more than it is a request. Not that you would want to refuse—who can refuse to give a blessing?—but the force of the demand suggests there is a right to the blessing. Then perhaps we have got a right to God's blessing.

In Northern Europe the language is one of politeness in which requests, hardly ever demands, are couched in rather obscure terminology which must be difficult for the foreign language student. "Excuse me please, but do you think it is possible for you to make tea?" Such a question in South America, and to some extent still in Spain, will get you a "yes" reply but no action. Yes it is possible for me to make tea but this is not a request for tea to be made. The words that would be used to have tea made are simply "Make me tea." No offense would be taken at this more direct approach. There is no direction of *please*. The nearest is *por favor* which is "for a favor" but it is not a very common expression.

The demand of *"Bendicion"* also demands a reply and action. *"Dios te bendiga"* (God bless you) is how you reply and the action is to make a sign of the cross on the forehead, and you can add "in the name of the Father, and of the Son, and of the Holy Spirit" for good measure to which the recipient will reply "Amen" and be grateful for the extra words thrown in.

Large cities are often great destroyers of local culture as they impose their own culture on top of anything that the local country can produce but still in the country places that do not get touched by world commerce and international businessmen the culture stays more or less intact. In Venezuela, well away from Caracas and the ports, the children still ask their parents for a blessing and whenever friends come together, especially for some family occasion like a wedding or baptism, they will ask a blessing of each other. You do not have to be a priest to give a blessing.

In North America the young have become an all-powerful force and the myth has arisen that young, fresh ideas are of greater value than the matured wisdom of the older generations. South America tries desperately to imitate anything north of Mexico but there still remains here the view that the elderly are more wise than the young. Maybe it is because there are so few old people and those who have survived have done so on their wits and wisdom. Whatever the reason, children will seek out their grandparents for a blessing even before they say hello.

The action sets out the hierarchical scale and gives a form to the pattern of family life in a land that has few cultural boundaries that are respected and where force and violence are the only effective policing strategies.

Jesus' words and actions were a plan of how to make ties with the Almighty God of Creation that pulled him down to be our Father, "abba" from the language of the nursery. In this land where churches are seen but Jesus seems to be missing, this one cord remains as a reminder of what life might be like and what it needs to be, *"Bendicion,"* (Give me a blessing), *"Dios te bendiga,"* (God bless you). A three-word reply that carries more meaning than the more famous three words of "I love you" and yet they mean the same but with the plaintive cry that calls out to God to be here and to bless us.

Roger Dawson
Venezuela/England

Community Lifestyles

Psalm 96

Sing to the Lord, all the world!

Grow Together

Meet God in Others

As we go out to take God to others,
know that we will meet him in others,
for our God blesses us with his presence
wherever we are.
Thanks be to God.

Marjorie Dobson
England

The Daily Round of Life

Go back to the daily round of life,
    and may what you have shared here
    transform all you do and experience there.
    In the name of Christ.

Nick Fawcett
England

Thank You

We take for granted
The refuse collectors and road sweepers,
The delivery of letters and of milk bottles,
The corner shop and the supermarket,
The street lights and telephone lines,
The seats and the bridges,
And you, Lord.
So I stop on this busy corner,
To do nothing more
Than simply take it in,

And say
A very heartfelt
"Thank you, Lord!"
Martin Wallace
England

Blessing on a Shopping Center

Creator, as a new day begins
Help us to leave our shabby Sunday selves behind
And, in this place we suppose you excluded
(Looking with distaste on our bricks and commerce),
Open our eyes to see you here before us.

Bless this meeting place, this center of community,
In all the gatherings, planned or chance,
Let us see the banners of your love between us.

In all the exchanges, bless this marketplace,
Teaching us to deal justly with each other,
Seeing that value is not in goods but in your people.

Bless all who work to make this possible
Knowing that no task separates from you,
Bless those who serve or stack or sweep,
Bless those who count or cook or watch.

And may those who come here today
(to spend or steal, to play or work)
Find, in your touch that transcends concrete,
That they have glimpsed the pavements of Jerusalem.
Wendy White
England

Blessing through Struggle

The bus arrives and the jostling begins
With those who have been sitting on the wall
Lurching forward to be ahead of the line.
It is a struggle, Lord, not to be left on the pavement
Stranded with the wheelchair
And the screaming, hungry child,
After the bus has left, full.

The scene here is a symbol of so much in the city:
The struggle to keep the children from crime;
The struggle to make the money last the week;
The struggle to find energy after a heavy day at work;
The struggle to keep the house decent;
The struggle to find quiet space in overcrowded rooms.
And especially,
The struggle to find
Space to be conscious of your presence;
Energy to live out your loving forgiveness.

Yet somehow your blessing is discovered in the struggle,
Just as Jacob wrestled and struggled with you.
And although he was left with a limp
Your deeper blessing never left him.

Lord, I pray for my friends and my neighbors
That they may know your blessing
In this struggle of living.

Martin Wallace
England

Blessing upon Them!

Blessing upon those who seek earnestly
To cast their words adroitly
Like potters spinning clay in their hands
To shed guiding light upon the soul of a child

Blessings upon those who remember
To pronounce a blessing

Those who reach out to touch a child
With healing hands in a hurting world

Blessings upon those tenders of God's garden
Neighbors breaking bread of life together
Churches drinking living waters with those who thirst
Schools imparting words of wisdom to a growing child

Blessings upon the princess of our world
Stopping to rescue a child floating in water
Threatened by Pharaoh's politics of insecurity
Bless the princess who gives the child back to its mother

Blessings upon those watchful shepherds
Following the light of God's star for each child
Searching for children born in the backyards of our mansions
To generously honor them with the best gifts

Blessings upon the Marys and Josephs of our world
Heeding God's voice, riding the night away
From one country to another, from border to border
Searching for a safe haven for a child to grow
Blessings upon them all!

Musa W. Dube Shomanah
Botswana

Blessing for a New Place to Be

Holy One, you have brought me/us here.
I/We give thanks for arriving, the chance of a new beginning.
May your blessing surround my/our
going in and coming out
getting up and settling down
working and resting
eating and sleeping
loving and laughing
sighing and crying.
Your company in the everyday stuff of life,
as a vital sign that you are bringing me/us to be.

Janet Lees
England

Employed by God

So many people are unemployed and feeling rejected by society—but God can still use them. And how many of us who are employed are redundant in God's service? Reflect with this blessing.

When our feet are redundant, use them, Lord
Let us Dance for You
When our voices are redundant, use them, Lord
Let us Sing for You
When our hands are redundant, use them, Lord
Let us Work for You
So let our minds be alive
With Dreams and Visions
Let our hands be creative
For Peace and Hope
Let our voices be heard
Singing of Love and Joy
Let our feet keep on moving
To Encounter and Discover
So bless our minds
And all Our Thinking
Bless our hands
And all We Touch
Bless our voices
And all Our Words
Bless our feet
And Each Step we Take
So let us encourage and empower
with the blessing of Father, Son,
and Holy Spirit
as we work for God's kingdom
to come to earth as in heaven.

Richard Becher
England

Two Women

You are a good woman—yes
you are devoted, helpful, very sure
of duties, loyalties, the rights and wrongs
of all relationships. You know the worth
of sacrifice. You speak your truth.
But somehow, in your presence,
flowers die, the birds forget to sing.
We stand to attention, noticing
dust on the mantelpiece, raftered spiders' webs.

You are a quiet woman—in fact,
we scarcely notice you. You collect
no medals for good works, do not
impress us with your busyness,
but unaffectedly you live with gentleness.
Yet, when we stop to look, we see
the grass becoming greener where you tread,
rain falling on parched earth, the heart
lifting, expanding—like the rainbow's arch.

Kate Compston
England

May There Be Safety

God who is the father who runs down the road
to greet his children,
God who is the mother who gathers her brood together
to protect them,
Jesus who blesses the children,
Spirit of gentleness:
May the patterns of rage and abuse stop.
May there be an end to the fists shaken,
    the heads shielded,
    the bodies bruised,
    the tears shed.
May there be safety.

United Church of Canada

Love, Joy, Peace

Love—tangible and expressive—
transform you;

Joy—holy and earthy—
uplift you;

Peace—of heart, home, and community—
be within you
always.

Joy Mead
England

Asking For and Giving of Blessing

In the Visayas region where I grew up an older person's blessing is not only important and meaningful, it is believed to be powerful. A younger person asks for an older person's blessing by taking the latter's right hand and putting it on his/her forehead while bowing toward the older person and saying *"Pa-amena ko, 'Nay/'Tay."* * The younger person says *"Mano po, Inay/Itay"* ("Please give me your hand and bless me"). The respected older person responds by saying *"Kaloy-an ka sa Dyos, anak."* ("May God be merciful unto you, child").

This beautiful act of respect, asking for and giving of blessing is done whenever the younger person meets the respected older persons in the street, in any public places, or upon reaching the house. Though commonly practiced among relatives, this act of blessing is not necessarily limited among relatives only. This practice of asking and giving of blessing is done also with godparents and any other respected older person.

Muriel Orevillo-Montenegro
Philippines

Pa-amena ko means "let me put your hand on my forehead." It signifies a sign of respect and a request for a blessing. *'Nay/'Tay* are contractions of *Nanay* (mother) and *Tatay* (father).

Blessing for St. Andrew's on the Terrace

A city-center church in the midst of the business/government area of Wellington, Aotearoa New Zealand. This blessing can be used in similar areas around the world.

Renew your people, Lord
and renew our life in this place.
Give us a new spirit of unity
with all who follow Christ,
and a new spirit of love
toward all people.

Bless the city in which we live
that it may be a place
where honest dealing,
good government,
the desire for beauty,
and the care for others flourish.

Bless this church
that what we know of your will
may become what we do,
and what we believe,
the strong impulse
of our worship and work.

John Stewart Murray
Aotearoa New Zealand

Blessing for a Parish or Church Occasion

Loving God, bless this parish *(church, fellowship)*, to serve you faithfully in all ways. As you have called us to worship together, strengthen us to support each other, to make your love known by word and example, and to know ourselves part of the company of all Christian people. Pardon and correct all that is wrong among us, accept and increase what is good, and unite us in the grace of our Lord Jesus Christ, the love of the Father and the fellowship of the Holy Spirit.

Raymond Chapman
England

Blessed and Blessing

I give thanks to name ways in which I am blessed:
The laughter of children,
The songs of a choir,
The smile of a stranger,
The touch of a friend.

> **We hold blessings tenderly,**
> **For they are fragile**
> **And can slip away.**

I wonder at blessings that are given unexpectedly:
A call at the right time,
A word of encouragement,
The one who understands
And loves without question.

> **We cherish blessings thankfully,**
> **For they make dark times**
> **Easier to bear.**

I open my eyes to places where blessings are found:
The quiet of nature,
A family home,
My place of worship,
The words of a book.

> **We acknowledge blessings carefully,**
> **For so many others**
> **Have gone unnoticed.**

I pause to name times of blessing:
In joy,
Or mourning,
In celebration,
And the everyday.

> **We create blessings lovingly,**
> **For we know that God works through us**
> **To be a blessing to others.**

I take courage to name ways in which I am a blessing;
The hands to create,
An ear to listen,
A heart to care,
A soul to connect.

We await blessings faithfully,
For we know that God
Has created us to be
Blessed and Blessing.

Louise Margaret Granahan
Canada

A Blessing

In the name of God who takes the risk of creation,
Of Jesus who journeyed to Calvary and beyond,
And the Spirit who kindles our hope and strength,
Let us go in peace and be witnesses of a renewed community of
women and men
in the church.

Frances Blodwell
England

Every Living Being

Now may every living being,
Young or old,
Living near or far,
Known to us or unknown,
Living, departed, or yet to be born,
May every living being
Be full of bliss.

St. Hilda Community
England

Riches in Relationships

God Bless You for Befriending Me

God bless you for befriending me
    when I felt hurt and alone.
God bless you for providing me
    with the comfort of a home.
God bless you for preventing me
    falling into the depths of despair.
God bless you for reassuring me
    with kind words and loving care.
God bless you for saving me
    from a life of destitution.
God bless you for making me
    a godly man with direction.
God bless you for holding me
    close to your lovely, firm body.
God bless you for touching me
    with your honesty and generosity.
God bless you for helping me
    calm my troubled mind.
God bless you for showing me
    the beauty of a good time.
God bless you for teaching me
    the ways of the world.
God bless you for loving me
    with a beautiful Christian heart.

Jason Doré
England

Sharing Together

Bless this time we share together,
Bless our conversation,
Our silence,
Our friendship,
And the roads we travel when we part.

Anthea Dove
England

Blessing Words Are more than Words

May words of acknowledgment,
words of apology,
words of comfort,
words of concession,
words of conciliation,
words of encouragement,
words of sympathy,
words promising assistance,
words to meet a need,
words combined with kind actions
dispel the anger
depression
despair and
despondency
that is all around us.

May we bless our neighbors
with our mouths as well as
with our hands.

Peter Comaish
England

God of our Relating

God of our relating
    thank you
for hands across the table
for hands across the sea
for hands around the world
    thank you

for eyes meeting across a room
for eyes opened to different lifestyles
for eyes shining in new friendships
    thank you
for ears that can hear the beating of a heart
for ears that pick up the cries of the voiceless
for ears that respond to the pulses of the world
    thank you

Kate Compston
England

Blessing for Lovers

Father creator, there within our tenderness, touch us
Jesus redeemer, there within our passion, enfold us
Spirit of joy, there within our senses, delight us
Holy Trinity, dance around us and bless us now and always.

Michael Turnbull
England

This Is My Prayer, My Love

May our love be
    As deep as the ocean
    As expansive as space
    As tender as the sunrise
    As passionate as the sunset
    As whole as the circle
    As wonderfilled as the mystery

May it flower as a thousand orchids,
    Wrapped in sparkling gossamer,
And may it reflect the splendor of divinity
    As the dewdrops prism the
    Technicolor sun.

This is my prayer, my love,
    May it be so.

W. L. Wallace
Aotearoa New Zealand

Blessing on a Loved One

You, sun of my waking days,
You, moon of my sleeping nights,
You, star of my glorious heaven,
God bless you day and night,
God bless you, set you right,
God hold you with his might,
My love enfolds you tight.

Nia Rhosier
Wales

Blessing a Newlywed Couple

In the Visayas region, the practice of blessing a newlywed couple does not end with the rituals in the church. As soon as the newlyweds arrive at the house where the reception is to be held, a group of elders (older women and men in the community which may include parents and relatives) meet them at the door. Before the couple enter the house the elders take turns in giving their advice and blessings before the guests.

There are variations to some practices of blessing a newlywed couple. One practice is for an elder to comb the hair of both husband and wife while expressing the blessing for harmonious, smooth relationships and living in the new home for the couple. Another elder takes a glass of water and while saying the words of blessing for the husband and wife speaks gentle words to them. The elder asks the couple to drink from the glass. Then, another elder sprinkles grains of rice and flowers over the couple's heads while saying the words of blessing for prosperity and abundance.

After the words of blessing by the elders, the newlywed couple takes each elder's right hand, putting it on his/her forehead, and thanks the elder and wishes the elder continued blessing.

The wedding feast proceeds.

Muriel Orevillo-Montenegro
Philippines

A Wedding Blessing

The second person can be substituted for the first person throughout if desired.

May God's wisdom deep within us
Shape the joy within our hearts,
Smooth the road we travel gently
Using all our loving arts.

May fair blossoms dropping petals
On the living path we tread,
Make a cushioned, glorious carpet,
Fragrancing the way ahead.

May we root our dreams and longings
In a true integrity,
Clearing out all that will hinder
Love's own creativity.

Tune: Any 8 7 8 7 metre

June Boyce-Tillman
England

A Marriage Blessing

The all-forgiving Savior walk behind you to pick up the
broken pieces and fashion them into new beginnings;
the ever-present friend stay by you to bring you delight
and joy in your relationship with him and with each other;
the Lord of space and time go before you to keep you in
the paths of peace and hope;
Jesus Christ, who is the same yesterday, today and forever,
Bless you and make your marriage fruitful to his glory.

David L. Helyar
England

Marriage Blessing

In marriage you have exchanged hands
his hands for your hands
your hands for his hands
      weak hands for bold hands
      vulnerable hands for shared hands
      tense hands for loose hands
      cold hands for squeezed hands

uncertain hands for firm hands
his hands for your hands
your hands for his hands
      hands to affirm you
to lead you and nudge you
      open hands to receive you
      to give and forgive you
      hands to touch you
      and caress you
your hand in his hand
      two hands in God's hand
      in life and in death

Bob Commin
South Africa

A Blessing for a Marriage
and a Gift of a Bowl and Jug

May your bowl contain fruit in abundance,
dripping with juices divine;

May your love combine *eros* and *charis*,
your jug run over with wine.

Jean Mortimer
England

Take this Couple

Originally written as a song for a wedding

Lord, we call upon you now
to take this couple in your arms.
As they vow to love and cherish,
keep them free from hurt and harm.
Bless their witness, as they seek,
to love each other come what may.
Guide and keep them in their union,
ever faithful day by day.

Lord, you come eternally;
in patience you would lead us on.
May we see, in Jesus Christ,
the gift you give to everyone.
By your Spirit, lift our eyes
to gaze upon the Lamb of God.
There to see, in sacrifice,
your manifested grace and love.

Lord, we call upon you now
to bind this couple, heart and soul.
As we share their happiness,
complete their joy and light us all.
You have promised, at the end,
to join your church as Groom to Bride.
Until that moment, may we seek to
ever linger by your side.

Tune: Ode to Joy

Duncan L. Tuck
Wales

Friendship

Aren't we lucky we found one another?
Did God plan it that way?
You came into my life at a point when I really needed you.
You came and you held open your door, arms, and heart for me.
I was wayward.
I needed you.
And you needed me too, as was evidenced in your own tough times.
And now...
We laugh together, cry together, hope together, and love together.
We share many similarities, and hold up the difference as wonders
between us.
We treasure each other, and thank God regularly for this "chance" meet-
ing.
We are not family, not by blood, but we are family by choice.
I am so glad I have you,
                    dear friend.

Karen Scarlett
Canada

Blessed Be Friendship

May your delight nurture faithfulness
May your freedom ensure belonging
May your separations enrich togetherness
May your giving surpass needing.

For the terrors of failing, the grace of forgiving
For the risks of releasing, surer having and holding
For grief for what is not, pleasure in the possible
For the dull plateaus, a discipline of surprises
For the wearisome haul, little celebrations, often.

Blessed be words that form out of silence
Blessed be touch that follows restraint
Blessed be wounds known and tended
Blessed be life lived in the other.

Viv Stacey
South Africa

My Friend

Lord, I ask your blessing
on my friend in need,
holding (*Name*) before you in my love.
Grant (*Name*) your comfort, your courage,
and your hope.
Hear (*Name*)'s cry and heal her/his suffering.

Anthea Dove
England

A Blessing on Those Who Have Hurt Me

Why did you do it?
Why did you hurt me
in this way?
What have I done to you
that you should want
to wound me so?

Whatever your reason,
I forgive you.
Whatever your purpose,
I forgive you.
My response
to what you have done
is words of blessing.

May the God of peace
soothe and still you.
May the love of God
surround you and fill you.

May the God of wisdom
guide you.
May you know his blessing
on all you are and do.

Now and always,
may God bless you.

Susan Hardwick
England

The Pain of Separation

O God, the alpha and the omega, help us to see beyond the pain of separation to the wider vision of all things holding together in your love. May we not become obsessed by grief but instead use it to allow the process of letting go be accomplished in a life-giving manner.

God of love, in whom there is no guilt or resentment, may we take time to nurture our self-esteem and thus be able to let go of all guilt and resentment which may arise within the process of separation.

W. L. Wallace
Aotearoa New Zealand

A Blessing for a Relationship

The blessing of the ground of being be upon you.
The blessing of the incarnate and risen one be upon you.
The blessing of the maternal spirit be upon you.

May you live in the covenant of love so long as God wills it.
May the Sun of Righteousness shine on you all your days.
May the Spirit fill your home with welcome and affirmation.
May you be a blessing to those who are welcomed into your home.
May you not be ashamed of your love.
May your love shine as a sign of Christ the loving one, so long as you live as one.

Peter Colwell
England

Go to your Friends and Greet Them

Go to your friends and greet them,
go to strangers and find them as friends,
go to enemies and look for their peace.
What does the Lord require of you?
To act justly,
to love loyalty,
to walk humbly with your God.
Go, then, in the peace of God
and the God of all peace go with you.
May the blessing of God rest upon you
and remain with you and all you meet,
this day and forever.

Paul Sheppy
England

Sending Forth

And now, may the wildly inclusive God—
Creator, Savior, Spirit—who loves all aspects of the
beautifully created rainbow of human sexual orientation,
uphold us and keep us until we meet again

Howard Warren
USA

Anointing in Courage

To the passioned pulse of human yearning,
you step into our days and years.
With the dauntless courage of a warrior,
you walk amidst our fragile lives.
Each day and night,
you breathe among us,
sharing our life-breath,
placing your gentle hand upon our flesh
in a covenant than can never be broken.
You hear the despairing beat of human hearts
too often crushed by senseless hate.
You see the glazed stare of lonely eyes
robbed of hope by unbridled ignorance.
You feed us as children with your love
and give to us your simple will
to break that same bread of your compassion
with all those of every time and place,
of every color and hue,
of every pathway and preference.
And yet into hearts carved by your providence,
we have bidden the present of darker forces
that weave their voices into our own
with syllables of darkness, the grammar of hatred,
cadences that break all semblance of human harmony.
Rouse up your might, O Passioned Lover.
Make your strength known always in our midst.
Raise up those different in life and love
from the bashing-pit, from the blood-stained sidewalk.
Lay your hands upon them with the oil of courage
to enter with new hope into the fray of our struggle
for dignity, justice, equality, and peace.

Lay your hands on those whose human hearts
have been ravaged by senseless ignorance,
on those whose minds have abandoned peace
for the twisted logic of dark and brooding hate.
Lay your hands upon all the earth
with an anointing in courage and truth:
that all might hear the passioned pulse of
wounded earth,
that all might taste the hunger that makes us one,
that all might yearn as you do
for a new dawning of justice
in a covenant of love that never ends.
Through Jesus your beloved
who walks among us always,
whose heart ever breaks open anew
whenever the lance of human violence
pierces the beauty of creation,
we ask all these things
in the unity of the Spirit Wisdom
forever and ever.
Amen.

This prayer is dedicated to gay, lesbian, and bisexual persons in the hope of an end to discrimination in all its forms. It is well suited for occasions when all women and men of faith wish to pray for an end to violence of human discrimination and hatred. In group prayer, it may be followed by a silent laying on of hands and an anointing with blessed oil.

Edward F. Gabriele
USA

Learning and Working

Blessing for a Student

God the Creator permeate my mind
God the Son enlighten my search for truth
God the Spirit kindle my desire for discovery
God the Holy Trinity bless my curiosity and my concentration this
    day and always.

Michael Turnbull
England

Teacher

But for you, I would not be here.
Except, at school, you took the stage one day
in assembly and said that for you
Christ was all that was, and is, and shall be...

Not to be clever, not to be liked, not to gain points
in the staffroom hierarchy. You
said you loved God and something in me
woke and shivered with your heaven's "Yes!"

Later, in church, the world was made anew.
I heard your truth go speaking on and on
telling us about faith and I felt a rain
of grace enfolding every prayer.

Today I teach theology in class.
I do not have your talent or your direct
simple faith, but if I speak at all
to where the hearts of others ask of me,
it is because you offered me your own.

Your living witness to what I might become
lives now in every word I should possess.
It is what I owe you, after all.

Anne Richards
England

A Blessing on Starting Secondary School

Bless to you, my son, whom I now entrust to a widening world.

Bless to you this white school shirt, the symbol of your passage to a new, less childish life.

Bless to you this tie—may you find fellowship and a new sense of belonging.

Bless to you your brother's jacket—may you receive the care and protection of those who are older than you.

Bless to you these turned-up trousers—may you grow into the potential your new life offers you.

Bless to you these sturdy shoes—may the playground be full of new friends who play soccer.

Bless to you these pencils and pens, geometry set and calculator—may you be empowered to meet all the challenges and demands that come your way.

And bless to you your mother—may she be given the grace to know when to support and when to let you be. Amen.

Cerys Jones
England

For Someone with Learning Difficulties

Father, hold this child of yours
who has difficulty in understanding
everyday things that come easily to others.

May this life be blessed
by a supportive family,
loving caregivers,
patient teachers,
understanding friends
and helpful strangers.

Open the eyes of those who are cruel,
deliberately or thoughtlessly;
so that they are able to see
your image in this life
as much as in any other.
Reach out with your deep joy
which goes beyond understanding
and your love which has no limits,
but speaks heart to heart;
so that your child
can know the wonder
of being a member of your family.

Marjorie Dobson
England

The Blessing of the Bizarre

I had a weekly appointment at a high school. I would arrive just as the pupils were leaving for the day. The school provided something of an alternative education for young people who have had difficulty settling at one of the more traditional schools. There is no school uniform.

The appearance of these young people was something of a shock! The girls in particular wear astonishing ensembles: some with long, usually black skirts to the floor, others wearing miniskirts, tights and boots; often underwear would be worn on the outside. Boys and girls have hair either long and dyed bright colors or shaven off all together. Almost everyone is decorated with rings: pierced through ears, nostrils, eyebrows, lips, navel, sometimes tongue!

As the weeks passed, however, I began to see these youngsters differently. I got to know some of them. I discovered on the whole they are pleasant and polite, sometimes happy, sometimes sad like everyone in their age group. I began to delight in the imagination and flair revealed in the way they dress. I rejoiced in their freedom from slavery to the dress conventions which, though petty, are strong in the community.

The vision of the Pharisees persists and oppresses yet. We can rejoice in the blessing of God's love for the individuality of each and every person.

John Hunt
Aotearoa New Zealand

Tutorial

Oxford College: Virginia creeper,
scrawling on walls. I am waiting
in my room. Scent of roses,
coffee, hour after hour in a china cup...

You come in, two by two,
flushed from the river, or drama class
or love. And I love you, for your eagerness,
your cynicism, for the gifts you bring.

Students of language and theology:
each of you breaks open heaven's door
and shows me what our God has put in you—
his hands, her feet, or voices in the air

as if blessed by a beating of sudden wings
and I have nothing more to say
or teach, if we drink this common cup,
water poured out, a prayer, a fellowship.

Anne Richards
England

Home Blessing

Bless all of us Marthas, Lord,
as we prepare the meals
and do the laundry
and struggle with the shopping.

Bless all of us Marys, Lord,
as we study late at night
and love the times of worship
and treasure silence.

Bless the Lazarus within us, Lord,
dead to the world,
curled up in a private tomb.
Call us out, give us life, and bless us.

Bernard Thorogood
Australia

Blessing Before Starting a New Job or Particular Task

May Almighty God, on whom all human work depends, bless this enterprise with discernment in beginning, skill in development, and success in completion: for our labor is in vain unless we trust in him, and our repose is blessed if we labor in his name.

Raymond Chapman
England

Blessings for Business Meetings

To Show the Way

Bless this work that's ours today
Bless the lives and landscapes therein held.
May ear and mind combine to say
What's "given" by you to show the way.

Rosemary Wass
England

Speech and Spirit

May space and silence
Speech and spirit
Signal your presence in all we do.

Rosemary Wass
England

Penetrate All our Deliberating

May the love of God sustain us in our working
May the light of Jesus radiate our thinking and speaking
May the power of the Spirit penetrate all our deliberating
And may all that is done witness to your presence in our lives.

Rosemary Wass
England

At the Beginning of a Committee Meeting

At this meeting we will talk and listen,
we will discuss, disagree, and decide.

This committee, as with each,
is one in which we meet as people with a sense of commitment
and to whom certain matters have been committed.

Though our time together is short and crowded,
our work together will continue.
Some will leave with specific tasks to undertake
each will leave with the care of what we are about today.

May God who is creative
turn our deliberations
into instruments for mission.

May God who is Living Word
transform the order we create
into the companionship of the church.

May God who is Spirit
invigorate the atmosphere in which we work
that our imagination may feed the vision of the communities for
    which we are meeting.

Let us expect guidance and blessing from God today
and so look to each other with hope as we speak the words of the
    grace to each other:

The grace of our Lord Jesus Christ,
      the love of God,
           and the fellowship of the Holy Spirit,
              be with us all, now and ever more.

John Ll. Humphreys
Wales

We Must Close the Meeting

To be used after a committee meeting
which should also be a time of worship

We must close the meeting,
my people!

This is merely a resting place,
a place of transit,
where humanity and God pause
before taking to the road again.

Go, my people,
you are ready to set sail,
your country is not here.

You are a wayfaring people,
strangers, never rooted in one place,
pilgrims moving toward an abiding
city further on.

Go forth, my people,
go and pray further off,
love will be your song
and life your celebration.
Go, you are the house of God,
stones cut according to the measure
of God's love.

You are awaited, my people,
and I declare to you, Word of God.
I am going with you.

United Congregational Church
of Southern Africa

Standing the World On Its Head

One day, I was teaching about the theology of mission to a group of students when I was asked why, if we are on the road to the fulfillment of God's promises, the world is filled with dark and dreadful things. How can we make sense of it all?

This is not an uncommon question and I trotted out all the usual answers but I was bothered by the feeling that I was not seeing the answer properly. I knew plenty of arguments and illustrations about how God has made the world and how we exercise free will and how the Holy Spirit is at work to create God's world out of all our messes but there was still something missing.

When I got home, I still had the upsetting idea that I had let the students down by not giving answers which made sense to me, let alone to them. I worried about it all the way back to my car and then on the drive along winding lanes to collect my children from nursery. When I arrived, they came bounding out full of excitement and achievement. The elder one, aged four, produced his latest artwork.

It was a picture of a person: black circle for a head, fat black body and four black sticks for arms and legs apparently diving headfirst into a dark mass of brown sludge. I looked at it: the impetus of the picture seemed to be a hurtling for disaster, with pain and humiliation soon to follow as the blob-man ended up in the mud and everyone laughed at him.

"You've drawn a man falling in the mud," I said.

"Oh, no, Mummy," said my son, offended. "That's a man who is so happy, he is standing on his head."

It is like asking whether the glass is half full or half empty. Sometimes it is simply a matter of perspective. Whether you see the world as dark and bitter or as graced and blessed, depends on whether you are an adult trying to show the freshness and potential of the world. But now I have been given a gift; whenever I see life like a man descending into the mud, I remember the man who is so happy he is standing on his head.

Anne Richards
England

Rejoice!

Rejoice in Christ the teacher
    whose simple words, spoken so long ago,
    have opened worlds of discovery ever since.
Rejoice in the Spirit, the prodder,
    who plants in us a hunger for growth
    that keeps us reaching after truth our whole lives long.

Rejoice in God the Creator
  whose world is full of wonders
    to amaze and delight us at every turn.
Rejoice in the gift of learning, the gift of helping others learn,
and in rejoicing, know God's joy in you.

Roberta Rominger
USA/England

Modern Technology

Blessing for New Technology

Lord we know there is nothing new under the sun,
but for what is newly discovered by us
help us to use it wisely,
help us to share it with those less lucky than ourselves.
Help us to make the most of your good gifts to us.
Help us so that we can reconstitute your creation in all that we do.
Help us to use your bounty beautifully.

Peter Comaish
England

Blessing of Computers

Blessed are you, Lord God, for you have enabled the extension of the powers of the human mind through computers.

Bless these instruments, and protect those who use them, and those who use all such equipment throughout the world, from those temptations of the human mind which appear presumptuous in your sight; convert their use to purposes which conform to the mind of Christ, and which give glory to you, Father, Son, and Holy Spirit, One God, now and forever.

The Community of the Servants of the Will of God
Crawley, England

Blessing for My New Computer

Bless me, God, as I unpack
set up
and turn on
my new computer.

May its many parts
printer
hard drive
speakers
screen
handbooks
programs, manuals and help desks
microfloppy disks and zipdisks
remind me always of
my own intricate interconnectedness
with all of Your Creation.

May its power to produce
complex
calculations
spreadsheets
geometric designs
and to solve
sophisticated formulas from physics
remind me always of
your Mind.

May its ability to communicate
with email
through the Internet
in chatrooms
on bulletin boards
remind me always of
Your eternal yearning to commune with me,
You who are The Word.

May its creative capacity to help me
paint
draw
compose a symphony or a poem

publish
morph
play and entertain
remind me always of
Your New Life, New Earth, New Heaven
yet to come.

And, God of the computer,
as I learn to use this great and wondrous machine,
may I learn patience with myself and others.
May I always use it to your glory
and according to your will, desires, and vision for humankind.
May this computer truly help me be
a better human being
a nobler thinker
a more gifted creator
a harder worker for global justice and peace
a more faithful follower of you,
Creator of us all
and inspirer of our technologies.

Betty Lynn Schwab
Canada

A Blessing for Computer Makers, Facilitators and Users

May the Word existing from the beginning
bless those who work in communication.

On those who make the chips, construct the mainframe,
produce the software, sell the packages,
the blessing of honesty, efficiency, and goodwill,
the blessing of the Word be on you.

On those who devise the programs, put together the clip art,
operate the web and design its varied pages,
the blessing of integrity, purity and effectiveness,
the blessing of the Word be on you.

On those who write with word processors,
who utilize the programs, who surf the net,
the blessing of humor, discovery and success,
the blessing of the Word be on you.

May the God who sustains the world in time,
who sustains all being in eternity,
bless you in your coming and going.

May the Word existing at the end
draw all together in the fullness of time.

John Johansen-Berg
England

My Telephone

Bless, dear Lord, my telephone.
With it, I am not alone.
Though some callers are a pest,
I'll look forward to the rest.
Friends and family sounding near—
Voices that I love to hear.
And, when people need my time,
Keep me, Lord, upon the line.

Marjorie Dobson
England

Blessing of Tools and Machines

Blessed are you, Lord God of all creation; through your goodness you
have created man in your own image, and endowed him with skills to
fashion tools and machines from raw materials to assist him in his
work.

Bless these tools and machines, we pray, and grant to those who
use them the grace of humble and obedient service in accordance with
your will.

To you be the glory forever and ever.

The Community of the Servants of the Will of God
Crawley, England

Dedication of a Sound System

The psalmist writes: "Their voice has gone out through all the world: and their message to the ends of the earth."

Let us pray
Almighty God,
whose Son Jesus Christ
sent his apostles to proclaim the good news in all the earth,
we dedicate this sound system to your service and to your glory.
May those who hear the message of the gospel
be so filled with grace
that with Mary they may magnify your holy name
and give themselves to your service.
We ask this in Jesus' name.

Roy Williamson
England

Being Creative!

Bless the Poetry, the Art, the Music of the World

Creator God,
bless the human creativity in poetry,
the art and the music of the world.
How dull and poor life would have been
if you had not inspired poets and writers
to interpret the thoughts and the experiences
of humanity,
if you had not let artists
widen the perspectives of life
with their colors and their forms,
if you had not inspired musicians
to catch the pulse of life
and the multitude of tones,
which have given body
to the joy, the protest, and the praise of life.
Creator God, help us all
to enter the living space of creativeness,
where freedom is breathing,
where souls may mature
and where life becomes meaningful.

Per Harling
Sweden

Music

Music fills my heart and ears.
Music fills my soul and spirit.
Music fills my head and mouth.
I sing.

I sing to anything.
I listen, and I sing.
I sing when I am blue.
I sing when I am angry.
I sing when I clean, as it energizes me.

I thank God for this ability to sing.
But if I couldn't, I would anyway.
It releases my spirit and renews me.
It releases the frustrations of daily life.

I thank God for an appreciation of music.
I thank God for filling the world with music.
I love all music. I love the sounds the world makes.
I love to sing the benediction, so that it reaches heaven.

Thank you God for music.
It is something common that the world is blessed with.
Aren't we most fortunate to have music?

Karen Scarlett
Canada

Bless Musicians

God, the source of creativity, blesses your art,
enabling you to respond through the weaving of

    pitch
        rhythm
            melody
                harmony
                    and silence

To voice creation's praise.
This God, the three-in-one and one-in-three who exists
in loving counterpoint,
makes you an instrument of blessing to others.

Julian Templeton
Aotearoa New Zealand/England

Blessing before a Choral Event

Father, we thank you for those gifts you bestow on us that enable us to express our praise in music, hymn, and song.

Bless us as we lead this choral worship.

May we so glorify you that all those who listen and share may feel their souls touched with inspiration and love, and glimpse that kingdom where with the Son and Holy Spirit you reign one God, world without end.

John Petty
England

Before Worship, a Performance, or a Choir Rehearsal

A voice soft and musical
I pray for you;
a tongue loving and mild
I pray for you;
ears open and listening
I pray for you;
a mind clear and creative
I pray for you;
harmony and joy in singing
I pray for you.

Kate McIlhagga
England

A Blessing for Bands

Heavenly Father we thank you for instruments of brass and silver and for the lungs and lips that blow them. Bless all who play in our bands, and the communities they represent—especially the former mill and mining communities.

May their music inspire us to live in deep harmony with one another—and in rhythm with the abiding presence of Christ. Amen.

Nigel McCulloch
England

Solo Voice

Inspired by the third movement of Shostakovich's Violin Concerto No. 1.

Solo voice,
emerging out of deep desolation,
are you the only voice to be heard,
rising sweetly out of the pain,
born out of the creator's agony and oppression?

Solo voice,
created by the groundbass of being,
bring together beauty and tension,
    dissonance and harmony,
thank you for sweetening the bitter herb of my suffering.

May you be blessed, solo voice,
way, truth and life,
redeemer and life giver.
You tell me that there is life amidst death;
    hope amidst desolation;
And I am saved, solo voice,
by your tender, life-giving melody.

Peter Colwell
England

Blessing for Artists and Composers

Divine Creator,
your works delight us with sight, scent, and sound,
bringing sensations of joy to all living creatures.
We ask your blessing on all those whose creativity
gives a reflection of your handiwork in the universe.

Give inspiration to those whose use of paint and texture
harmonizes colors and shapes with subtle interpretation;
may they bring an extra dimension into the minds of those
who view their art with pleasure.

Give guidance to those who work and mould the clay,
chisel and shape the stone, carve and smooth the wood,

to make exquisite sculptures
which delight the heart and mind.

Grant the gift of interpretation to those who compose music,
bringing varied notes together in harmony,
uniting a variety of instruments in symphony,
so that listeners with attuned ears and hearts are joyful.

Heavenly Artist,
bless the painters, sculptors and composers
whose creative gifts are a source of blessing for others.

John Johansen-Berg
England

A Blessing for Journalists

May the God who said "Let there be light" bless you in your search for
truth and your quest to bring light to dark places.
May God give you grace to resist the temptation
to create a story with little regard for truth,
to assassinate character with little regard for mercy,
to slant reports with little regard for accuracy
in order to curry favor or earn dishonest reward.

May God give you inspiration
to tell the truth as you see it without favor,
to report oppression and violence without fear,
to stand by the innocent and defend the right,
to encourage the good and denounce evil.

May you recognize the power of the word
and not use that power irresponsibly,
or for personal gain, but rather
for the welfare of the community as a whole
and particularly the hungry, the homeless, and the poor.

May you find a blessing
as you write courageously to give true pictures,
as you seek to bring hope where there is despair,
as you influence people to search for truth,
as you increase understanding of issues
and as you contribute to the happiness of all.
May God, the compassionate and loving creator,

protect you in times of danger,
guide you in situations of perplexity,
uphold you in the experience of failure
and encourage you in times of success.

John Johansen-Berg
England

A Blessing for Writers

May the grandeur be with you which is too overwhelming to express.
May you win the daily wrestling match with the opponent whose limbs
never become material. May you outlast the struggle from which the
sweat and blood are scattered on the pages of anything the serious write.

Adapted by Alan Nichols
Australia

Clowns and Other Entertainers

May the God of grace and laughter
be with you in your multi-colored clowning,
as you bring squeals of laughter to children
and tears of joy to the old.

May God grant you a blessing in your puppetry
as you bring a multitude of characters to life,
giving instruction and entertainment to the young
and crossing barriers for older ones who listen and watch.

May God be with you in the changing faces
of the clown who, now with laughter
now with tears, shares the message of a buffoon
with those who think that they are wise.

May the divine creator be in your hands and voice
as you bring many actors to a tiny stage,
as fox and badger, owl and cat
release the imagination of the young into a new world.

May God who gave light in the heavens
and cascades of water on the earth

bless you with the creativity of an artist,
with the humor of a born entertainer,
so that you may release laughter in lives that are tense,
and bring relaxation to minds full of anxiety.

May God bless you clowns, puppeteers, and comedians.
May you bring to the art of entertainment
wholesome humor and creative talents,
a love of beauty and concern for the welfare of the young.
May the laughter and the tears
be an expression of your inner being
and an offering to God.

John Johansen-Berg
England

Eat, Drink and...Share

A Blessing on a Shared Meal

We give you thanks
—for this wonderful food
—for those whose hands
have prepared it
—for those with whom
we will share it.

May the way in which
—we eat
—and we speak
at this blessed meal,
reflect our gratitude
for these heavenly gifts
and our love
for you.

Susan Hardwick
England

Bon Appetit

Lord bless this food upon these dishes
As Jesus blessed the loaves and fishes
And that our joy may be complete
Please be with us while we eat...Bon Appetit.

John Shevlin (Adapted from Donamon Castle text)
England/USA

Table Blessings from Ewell Monastery

Before the Meal

Leader   Praise the Lord for he is good.

All   Sing to his name for he is gracious.

Leader   Blessed are you and worthy of all praise, O Lord our God, creating and sustaining all things by your will;

All   Glory to you, Father, Son, and Holy Spirit, now and forever.

After the Meal

Leader   Blessed are you and worthy of all praise, O Lord our God, creating and sustaining all things by your will;

All   O God, holy in your gifts and in all your works, now and forever.

Ewell Monastery
England

Jewish Table Blessings

Before a Meal

Before we eat, we give thanks for our food.

Thank you, God, for the blessing of bread
and for the meal we will now enjoy together.

After a Meal

We join in giving thanks for the meal we have eaten.

Thank you, God, who provides our food.
Help us to share what we have
and to care for those who are hungry.

Traditional

A New Zealand Blessing at Table

God bless our meal
God bless our ways
God give us grace
Our Lord to please.

John Stewart Murray
Aotearoa New Zealand

A Brazilian Blessing for the Table

O Lord, we give you thanks, because around this table you renew our force to fight against poverty.

Transform our gluttony, our thirst for plenteousness in a new feeling of justice and hope.

O Lord, may our dishes in a divided earth one day be divided in a reunited earth.

Forgive us, now, at this unjust meal until the whole earth be fed from your bread.

Jaci Maraschin
Brazil

Bless the Talk Around this Food

Bless this table
bless this door
bless the friends
who enter here;
bless the talk
around the food
and bless this home
forevermore.

Kate McIlhagga
England

Blessing upon Food

O God who gives all that is good,
May your blessing be upon our food,
Your grace and laughter shine upon our fellowship,
Your kindness be upon our tongues,
Your peace reside within us,
And your love reign in our hearts.

Monica Furlong
England

Bless this Food

Bless this food offered here
Made with love for all to share
Thank you Creator for our health and your care
Bless this food

Radha Sahar
Aotearoa New Zealand

Blessed Be this Meal

Blessed be this meal,
    May it nourish our bodies,
        awaken our sense of justice,
            deepen our bonds of love
        and enable us to be at one with all life.

W. L. Wallace
Aotearoa New Zealand

Bread Blessing

Lord of the Meal,
    we come to this prayer called grace
    asking that you help us eat this food gracefully
    and with gratitude;
    that we, with grace and care,
    share our lives by word and laughter,
May your grace, your life,
    touch us and our food.

(Lift up bread)

We lift up this bread,
    symbol of life and of your Son;
    may it and He nourish us this day.

Edward Hays
USA

Table Blessings

Voice One	Thank you, thank you, O Lord
Voice Two	For your loving kindness
Voice Three	Which is with us always
Voice Four	Now and evermore.

Voice One	Thank you, Father, for this food.
Voice Two	Thanks for those who made it too.
Voice Three	Keep us together, joyful forever,
Voice Four	In your love.

Declan Smith
Ireland

God is One

*Translated from the hymn Egy az Isten**

Isten, God of our confessing.
Isten, Light in deep distressing.
Isten, Grant to us thy blessing.
One the blessed God we cherish,
May this food our bodies nourish,
Faith and freedom ever flourish.

Adapted by Richard Boeke
Hungary

*"God is One"

For Food and Friendship

We give thanks for this opportunity
For food and friendship.
May both be blessed.

Richard Boeke
Hungary

Food and Celebration

For past memories,
    For continuing commitment,
    For the hope of the future,
    For love, life, and health
    and for this food and celebration,
      we thank you, God.

W. L. Wallace
Aotearoa New Zealand

Lift Up this Bread!

Lord, you who gave bread to Moses and his people
    while they traveled in the desert,
    come now, and bless these gifts of food
    which you have given to us.
As this food gives up its life for us,
    may we follow that pattern of self-surrender for each other.
May we be life to one another.

(Lift up bread)

With grateful and prayerful hearts,
    we lift up this bread to you.
May your glory surround it
    and all this meal.

Edward Hays
USA

A Breakfast Grace

For bacon, eggs, and buttered toast,
Praise Father, Son, and Holy Ghost.
Source Unknown

Not the Gourmet Touch

Bless the meal upon this table,
cooked as well as I am able.
It may not have the gourmet touch,
but we'll enjoy it very much
and, if it keeps us fit and healthy,
what need have we for being wealthy?

Marjorie Dobson
England

Give Us, O Lord, a Bit o' Sun

A grace used by the Wilson brothers, Brian, Carl and Dennis, better known as the Beach Boys. It is said to be of British origin.

Give us, Lord, a bit o' sun
A bit o' work and a bit o' fun.
Give us in all the struggle and sputter
Our daily bread and a bit o' butter.
Give us health our keep to make
And a bit to spare for others' sake.
Give us, too, a bit o' song
And a tale and a book to help us along.
Give us Lord, a chance to be
Our goodly best, brave, wise, and free.
Our goodly best for ourselves and others
'Til all folk learn to live as brothers.
Amen.

Source Unknown

...But What We Share

The holy supper is kept indeed,
In what we share with another's need.
Not what we give, but what we share,
For the gift without the giver is bare.

James Russell Lowell
USA

In a Somewhere Hungry World

In a somewhere hungry
    And sometimes lonely world,
        For food and friendship
            We give thanks.
Joy Croft
England

In Our World

In a world where so many are hungry,
We thank you for this food.
In a world where so many are lonely,
We thank you for the friendship in which we share it.
Source Unknown
England

A Hunger for Justice

To those who hunger, give bread.
To those who have bread,
Give a hunger for justice.
Source Unknown

Multi-faith Food Blessing

We eat and drink these fruits of earth
That love may grow between us all
Between us all.

We join God's holy cause and share
Our bread with all the poor of earth
The poor of earth.

To God whom many faiths adore
Be praises now and evermore
And evermore.
W. L. Wallace
Aotearoa New Zealand

Our Common Meal

O God, we recall that we are one in your eyes.
May we celebrate this unity in our common meal,
Ever mindful that our privileges here today
Require us to give thanks and to return such love
To the world in which we live.

Andrew Brown
England

Grace at a Wedding Breakfast

Blessed are you, Lord God of creation,
through your fatherly wisdom,
we have been born in families,
to grow in community.

We give you thanks,
as we gather to share in food and fellowship.
Bless *(Name)* and *(Name)*
that so strengthened and supported
by all who love them
they may share together until their lives end.

Marion Simpson
England

An Inclusive Grace for a Wedding Meal

Let us give thanks
For earth, our mother, who nurtures us;
For the sky, our father, who widens our vision
to the place of mystery;
For the sea, the womb of our living;
For the sunrise and sunset, signs of eternal
beginnings and endings;
For our participation in the cycles of nature
which this food reflects;
And for the friendship and love which this meal both
symbolizes and facilitates. Amen.

W. L. Wallace
Aotearoa New Zealand

Hearth and Home

Hail Guest!

Hail guest, we know not who thou art.
If friend, we greet thee hand and heart;
If stranger, such no longer be,
If foe, our love will conquer thee.

From a Crofter's Door
Wales

A Blessing for the Home

May the son of Mary bless you in your home.
May it be a place of friendship,
of the deepening relationship of love.
May it be a place of safety and mutual care,
of new discoveries and excitement,
of celebration and of quiet.
May it be a place where parents and children
find delight in each other's company.
May it be a place of welcome
where relatives, friends, and strangers
find an open door.
May there be a special and compassionate welcome
for the needy, the homeless, and the poor.

May God bless you in your home;
may it be filled with the harmony of music;
may there be joy in the sharing of meals;
may there be often the laughter of children;
may there be mutual support at times of distress
and encouragement in the times of celebration.
May the healer of Galilee
bestow his blessing on your home.

John Johansen-Berg
England

A Blessing for a New Home (1)

When we are cold and tired
struggling against wind, rain, and dark,
you invite us into warmth and light
and welcome us with your gifts.

**Holy wisdom of God
create a place of abundance
and bless this home with comfort.**

When the city seems alien and unfamiliar
filled with voices threatening hurt,
you draw us into a secure house
and shut the door against all harm.

**Holy wisdom of God
create a place of shelter
and bless this home with safety.**

When we are weary and drained,
harassed by constant demands,
you offer us a quiet space
where we are nurtured and refreshed.

**Holy wisdom of God
create a place of retreat
and bless this home with calm.**

When we are lost and rootless
in a world that seems strange and cold,
you surround us with treasured memories
and the assurance of knowing and being known.

**Holy wisdom of God
create a place of friendship
and bless this home with love.**

Jan Berry
England

A Blessing for a New Home (2)

God bless this house
a place to be
God bless the journey
that brings me here
God bless the door
between two worlds
God bless the solitude
to rest and pray
God bless the rooms
to welcome friends
God bless the food
the sharing of life
God bless the ground
with sun and rain and seed
God bless this place
to be my home.

John Stewart Murray
Aotearoa New Zealand

Blessing a Samoan House

God of all families, we gather as an earthly family to celebrate the completion of our *fale* (dwelling place) where our parents, our *matais* (chiefs and orators), our young men and women, and our children will live. We have worked so hard to build it under the skillful direction of our *agaiotupu* (builder) and his team.

Now we have come to you today with joy and thanksgiving placing it before you, O God, for your blessing, and at the same time ask that you will keep it safe from all dangers so that our people who will live in it will be safe from all forms of disasters. May any unforeseen perils pass over it and may all who live therein feel secure at all times. Chase away all evil and all types of epidemic that may come near us, and may this house be yours too.

So we come into your presence with dances and songs in our celebrations today to dedicate this fruit of our labor to the glory of you our Almighty God and King. And we do it in the precious name of your Son and our Savior Jesus Christ. Amen.

L. Setefano
Aotearoa New Zealand

Bless this House...

Look,
I am standing
at the door,
knocking.

Revelation 3:20

Bless this door
which leads into our home.
Bless each one
who enters through it.
May we always
greet them in your name.

May our welcome
be as warm
as if it were you
who knocks,
and waits,
on the threshold
of our lives
and of our hearts.

Susan Hardwick
England

A House of Peace

Bless this house
And the people within
May it be a house of peace for all who enter

Bless this place
And the soil and trees
May the plants and creatures and water and air be protected

Bless this house
Bless this land
Family and friends
Heart and hand
May you be blessed year by year

And bless in turn
All who enter here

Bless this house
And the people within
May it be a house of peace for all who enter
May it be a house of love for all who enter
May it be a house of joy for all who enter

Radha Sahar
Aotearoa New Zealand

Our Home

Bless this house and all that's in it—
It would be clean, if I had a minute!
But really, Lord, most folk don't mind—
It's friendship they come here to find.

Marjorie Dobson
England

Surround Us, God

Surround me, my God
and this place where I live.

Surround my children,
awake, asleep.

Surround those who visit here,
their coming and their going
that they and we may be at peace.

God of the arms of love
hold me, day and night
close to you, my heart of hearts.

John Stewart Murray
Aotearoa New Zealand

Blessing for a House

God bless this house and those whose home it is:
    may it be a radiant center of mutual love
    may it be open to receive and welcome
    may it be safe from all harm
        by the divine protection.

Raymond Chapman
England

Blessing of a New House

Outside

Lord, bless this house and all who live in it.
Hallow it with your presence and your peace.
Fill it with joy and laughter.
Let it be a place where love abounds
where hurts are healed,
where sadness finds solace,
where differences are reconciled,
and where pardon is freely given.

Inside

Bless this house from roof to floor,
and from door to door.
Bless each room
with your particular blessing.
Bless those who live here
and those who visit here,
in their going out and in their coming in,
in their work and in their rest,
in eating and in sleeping,
in silence and in speech.
May it be to them home and castle,
sanctuary and haven,
a place of joyous settings out
and of safe returns.

Study

Lord of creation,
here we give thanks for all those
who by their skills have created this house—

architects, surveyors, and draftspersons,
bricklayers, joiners, and plumbers,
electricians, heating engineers, and plasterers,
tilers, fitters, and laborers,
—may they take pleasure in work well done,
and enjoy the sense of shared endeavor,
where the work of each is fulfilled
in the achievement of all.

Kitchen

Lord of the banquet and the feast,
of lakeside breakfasts,
of long-planned suppers,
and unplanned feedings of thousands
on remote hillsides,
bless this kitchen.
For few or for many
may it be a place of miracles;
a place of skill and ingenuity,
of joy and laughter;
a place of many hands and light work.

Sitting Room

Lord of all life,
we give thanks for all that enriches our lives,
stimulates our minds, fires our hearts,
and binds us together in harmony with one another.
Here in this sitting room we ask your blessing
on this house as a home,
and all that this word implies.

Bedrooms

Lord of joy and peace and rest and sleep,
bless this bedroom.
To those who enter here
give joy of heart and peace of mind,
bodily rest and untroubled sleep,
that they may leave refreshed
for the challenges of a new day.

Conclusion

Finally, in the words of an ancient prayer:
"Visit we beseech Thee, O Lord, this house,
and drive far from it the snares of the enemy.
Let Thy holy angels dwell herein
to preserve it in peace,
and may Thy blessing be upon it forevermore."
Through Jesus Christ our Lord. Amen.

David Weston
England

All the Days of My Life

My Wish for You

Not
that no cloud of sorrow may come upon you,
not
that your life should be a bed of roses,
not
that you may never shed any tears,
not
that you may never feel any harm,
no, these are not my wishes for you.

My wish for you is
that you may keep
every golden memory of any rich day of your life forever.
Every gift which God has given you
may grow as the years are passing by.
May it help you to fill the hearts of those you love with joy.
And in every hour of joy and every hour of grief
may the love of the Son of God incarnate be with you
and may you stay close to God and remain in his grace.

After an Irish Blessing
Werner and Cornelia Schwartz
Germany

Blessing for a Woman Who Has Conceived

May the life that stirs within you now
move you in harmony with holiness.
May your child learn the love of God
from your tender life-giving embrace.

May you one day see your grandchild come
to God's holy waters of life;
And may, in time, your great grandchild
serve you God's bread and wine.

Betty Lynn Schwab
Canada

Community Blessing of a Child in the Womb of a Single Mother

Single motherhood is usually difficult for many women. This is especially true in the Philippines when it happens outside of marriage. Single motherhood is still considered taboo in the Philippines and in many other Asian countries. This ritual is written to help the community, especially the church, minister to women who were forced by circumstances or have opted to become a single mother. An important expression of this support and ministry is for a small community of family and friends to gather to bless the baby in the woman's womb.

Community Singing
People seated forming a circle

Lighting of the Candles
Candles of different sizes and color are lit to symbolize
Christ's light that brings hope and joy.

Leader   *Words of Welcome*

Blessing of the Baby in the Womb by the Mother
She puts her hands on her belly and says something like the following:

Mother: God, you are a gentle father and a compassionate
mother to us all.
Your love for us works in many mysterious
and deep ways.
I come before you and my friends with mixed feelings.
I come with awe and wonder at the thought
of becoming a mother, a co-lifegiver
but the thought of being a single mother also
brings me fears.
Mother God, please calm my fears and anxieties
and grant me courage and peace.

Help me savor this special moment of my life
and grant that I may grow in love that
I may be able to make my child feel
the warmth and security of being so loved.
Bless this child in my womb, O mother God,
with good health and bright future.

And to you, O my child, I say,
I thank God for the gift of life that is yours.
I bless you with all my love and care.

Taped Soft Music is played for Reflection

Blessing of the Baby in the Womb by the Community
*As the expectant mother puts her hands over her belly, the persons sitting on
her left and right side may put their hands over hers while the other hand
holds the hand of the person next to him/her. The rest in the circle hold hands
and say this prayer together.*

All   Loving God, the Source of Life,
You have given *(mother's name)* the gift of life
through the child in her womb.
Bless this child, O God,
Keep this child healthy and the mother too.
Embrace them in the warmth of your
compassion, love, and care.
As we await the birth of this innocent babe,
help us remember that we need to learn like children
to be humble and forgiving
of ourselves and others.
As we bless this child, we also thank you
for being blessed by you in many ways.
This is our prayer, in the name of Him
who came to us once as a poor babe
in swaddling clothes. Amen.

Song of Blessing
*People continue holding hands in a circle while singing this song adapted to
the tune of* Edelweiss.

Bless this child in her womb,
Grant your peace e'er enduring;

Of good health, warmth, and love
Through the days, safe in birthing.
Blossoms of life, may she bloom and grow,
Bloom and grow in your sight.
Bless this child in her womb,
Our delight and a star bright.

Sharing of Refreshments brought by the Community

Muriel Orevillo-Montenegro
Philippines

An Act of Blessing for a Woman Giving Birth

In the Philippines, where health care is very expensive, many women in the rural communities and even in the depressed area communities of cities, prefer to give birth to their babies at home. As the husband ran to fetch the *hilot* or *mananabang* (the village midwife), the neighbors would usually come to the woman's house to help prepare warm water that will be used to bathe the newborn and for postpartum care. If no immediate family member is around, the neighbor also takes care of making porridge, chicken soup or soup made with *til-ogon* (any white fish) for the mother to take after delivery so that she will regain her strength quickly; also she prepares food and coffee for the midwife, too. They do this because of the concern that the husband may not have the concentration to do all these things alone. Neighbors also do the errands and other aftercare chores that the midwife may require.

Usually, the midwife allows only one helper inside the bedroom which she turns into a delivery room. The other helpers stay outside the room. As everyone in the household quietly does other necessary things waiting for whatever the *mananabang* will tell them to do or prepare, they silently pray for the safety and well-being of both mother and child. As soon as the cry of the infant is heard, everyone stops and takes a deep sigh of relief and says *"Ay, Salamit sa Dyos!"* ("Oh, thanks to God!"). Then more women go to the room to assist the midwife in cleaning the baby and the mother. They make her comfortable and put her to rest. Some neighbors stay to be available at any time, making sure that the husband feeds her as soon as she wakes up. Prayers of thanksgiving and blessing are usually offered at this time. In some cases prayers are not said formally. I believe the friendly neighbors' presence is itself an act of blessing of the woman giving birth.

Muriel Orevillo-Montenegro
Philippines

Bless our Unborn Child

Thank you, God, for the growing life,
for its mystery
and kicks in the stomach!
We talk to our unknown child,
we sing with it,
dream about it
and wait impatiently
in expectant joy.
Surround our growing child
with your creative power
and your endless love
in the secure darkness of the womb.
Make our child prepared for the light,
for us and our love.
Bless our unborn child.

Per Harling
Sweden

Birth Blessing

As I cup my hand
around your head
    little one
may God hold you
and keep you.

As I rock you
in my arms
    little one
may Christ shield you
and encompass you.

As I bend to kiss your cheek
    little one
may the Spirit bless you
and encourage you.

Kate McIlhagga
England

A Child is Given

To bless and welcome a new baby or child into the family

Gathering

Leader   Like day's first light,
          This new life is promise and mystery.

All   Child of grace and wonder—
          We welcome you,
          We share our love for you.

Leader   Like a chorus of songbirds,
          This new life is joy and celebration.

All   Child of grace and wonder—
          We welcome you,
          We share our love for you.

Leader   Like spring's fragrant bouquet,
          This new life is beauty and tenderness.

All   Child of grace and wonder—
          We welcome you,
          We share our love for you.

Leader   Like earth's rhythm of abundance,
          this new life is gift and treasure.

All   Child of grace and wonder—
          We welcome you,
          We share our love for you.

Readings

Luke 1:57–58
Now the time came for Elizabeth to give birth and she bore a son. When her neighbors and relatives heard this...they came and rejoiced with Elizabeth and Zechariah.

Psalm 139:13–14
For it was you who formed me; you knit me together in my mother's womb. I praise you, O God, for I am fearfully and wonderfully made. Wonderful are your works that I know very well.

Matthew 18:1–2, 4–5
The disciples came to Jesus and asked, "Who is the greatest in the realm of heaven?" And Jesus called a child, whom he put among them, and said, "...Whoever welcomes...this child is the greatest in the realm of heaven. Whoever welcomes one such child in my name welcomes me."

Response

Through the sharing of stories, photographs, and readings, the new child is celebrated and welcomed. Those present at the birth or adoption may wish to share the story of that experience. The name of the child may be honored with stories of how it was chosen and those gathered might wish to bring poems and stories that use the child's name.

Blessing

Said by all

May your journey in life
Shine with a star's delight.

May your days and your years
Weave together a wondrous tapestry.

May your unfolding story
Dance with the grace of every blessing.

Always and ever, may you rest in God.
Always and ever, may God rest in you.

Keri Wehlander
Canada

A Blessing for the Child Among Us

The child among us is a gift,
to treasure and enfold:
a child declares the love of God
embracing young and old.

The child among us is a sign
of how we are to be:
a people of the reign of God,
of trust and liberty.

The child among us is a way
to see the face of God:
when we receive the smallest one
we meet our cross-marked Lord.

The child among us is a guest
with us, at Christ's high feast:
with bread and wine we all are fed
and sent to serve the least.

The child among us is a pledge
of what is soon to come:
a world of justice, hope, and joy,
in Christ, in us, begun.

Tune: Richmond, Bishopthorpe, or Winchester Old

Michael McCoy
South Africa

A Mother's Blessing on her Child

My dearest babe watch thou thy step
While trav'ling through the world,
Remember always mother's love
Her arms around you curled.
Her love it comes from God himself
And does not seek reward,
Remember this and you will find
For ev'ry wound a nard.

Nia Rhosier
Wales

Our Children

Lord, we ask you bless and keep
these dear children as they sleep.
But we ask, for our own sake,
help us to cope when they're awake.

Marjorie Dobson
England

A Parent's Blessing

"Unless you become
as these little children,
you will not enter
the kingdom of heaven,"
Jesus said.
And taking them
in his arms,
he blessed them.
Matthew 18:3

Your spontaneous joy of life
fills my heart with joy.

Your passionate love of life
pierces my heart with love.

Your wide-eyed wonder in life
opens my heart to wonder.

The music of your living
makes my heart sing.

You show me
what I must become.

You are my cherished child,
my heavenly gift and blessing.

May God bless you,
my angel,
my darling one.

Susan Hardwick
England

For a Teenager's Bedroom

Bless the mess behind this door—
it's just a statement, I am sure—
that says "my life is all confused"
and though I may not be amused,
Lord, keep me counting up the days—
remind me this is just a phase!
And as I love my child so much
Strengthen my will to keep my touch.

Marjorie Dobson
England

A Cook Islands Blessing Offered at a Haircutting/Ear-Piercing Ceremony

A blessing used in rites of passage ceremonies

Monu!! Monu!! Tagaloa (Thanks be to God, Yahweh)
To you my child,
this haircutting ceremony is a crossroad
where many traditions are fused into one.
The conversion of our forebearers to Christianity.
The passage of land and wealth from generation to generation
carried by you, one chosen from the many
where resources are shared in love.

Monu!! Monu!! Tagaloa (Thanks be to God, Yahweh)
Obey me says Yahweh,
and you will live.
Let my instructions be your greatest treasure. Keep them at your
    fingertips
and write them in your mind.
Let wisdom be your sister
And common sense your closest friend.
Monu!! Monu!! Tagaloa (Blessed be God)
May you grow up to be a faithful servant to God,
making sure that God's word is spoken
even in the remote places.
Be a witness to God
in deed and faith.

Monu!! Monu!! Tagaloa (Blessed be God)
This ceremony marks the transition
from childhood into adulthood.
Your families and friends have come
to share in this moment of Thanksgiving.
We thank God for giving you health,
wisdom, humility, and love.

Monu!! Monu!! Tagaloa (Blessed be God)
Kia fakamonuina he Atua a koe
(May God bless you)
Kia lukuluku e ia haau a moui
(May God embrace you)
Tuku lagi (forever)
Monu!! Monu!! Tagaloa (Blessed be God).

L. Setefano
Aotearoa New Zealand

A Child Leaving Home

God be with you in every pass,
Jesus be with you on every hill;
God be with you in every street,
Jesus be with you in every meeting;
God be with you in every difficulty,
Jesus be with you in every storm;
The sacred three surround and save you,
this day and through all your tomorrows.

Kate McIlhagga
England

On a Child Leaving Home

Go carefully little one.
May your journey be safe,
your arrival secure.
May the guarding of the great God,
be between your shoulders,
the justice of the gentle God
be in your footstep,
the love of the compassionate God
be in your hands.
May God protect you
in every situation
and grace you
to give and receive blessing.

Kate McIlhagga
England

All the Words I Like Best

All the words I like best about the family of faith begin with "G":
Grace—God's enduring kindness, generosity
    —God's self giving to human beings and our response;
Gratitude—a life transforming attribute;
    and
Glory be to the Father and to the Son and to the Holy Spirit for all
    these gifts.

Stephen Sykes
England

May Beauty Delight You

May beauty delight you,
may tenderness envelop you,
may love nurture you
and may silence give you peace.

W. L. Wallace
Aotearoa New Zealand

Delight in that Love

Now may we with delight live in that love
which surrounds us, which is within us and which connects us
to all that was and is, through the transforming power of God's love.

W. L. Wallace
Aotearoa New Zealand

In Pain

May your pain give birth to hope.
May you find that dark clouds
can bring the rain of life and growth.
May you know yourself loved and cherished
by the glorious God who walks beside you.
And may the blessing of God Almighty,
Father, Son, and Holy Spirit,
be with you always.

Duncan L. Tuck
Wales

The Blessing of a Party

I had been visiting a parishioner over six months or more as he slowly succumbed to the spreading of cancer taking over his body. George had been a farmer; he was in touch with the natural world, with every living thing growing and maturing, declining and dying. He had no quarrel with God. He looked back over his life with satisfaction and approached its end with serenity.

His family had gathered from all over the world: a son and a daughter from Britain. They faced their dear father's death with less equanimity. George was very weak. His voice was faint. He said to me, "I am not unhappy for myself but I can see the family are distressed. What can I do to help them?"

Finally he decided—we will have a party! He asked his wife if she wouldn't mind getting in a fine selection of cheeses and pâtés and crackers. He sent off one of his sons-in-law to buy half a dozen bottles of the best champagne and a bottle of malt whisky.

That evening he had them gather around his bed. He said to them, "Let's remember happy times. Let's tell old stories! Let's eat and drink and be merry!" And so the night went on: funny and wonderful occasions were recalled; there were tears and there was great laughter. George seemed to have a new burst of life; he was able to tell some stories and join in the merriment. George was honored, his life was truly celebrated, the spirit of the family was nurtured. The next evening George lapsed into unconsciousness and the following day, he slipped away. With his family's tears, there were smiles.

John Hunt
Aotearoa New Zealand

Life Blessing

Deep peace enfold you
Encircle and hold you
In youth and age
At life's every stage
At birth and in growing,
In failing and dying,
The sacred three
Your protection be.

Ann Lewin
England

Age Blessing

At ear close and tooth drop,
At sight fail and mind loss,
The sacred three enliven thee.

Ann Lewin
England

Prayer of an Old Man

Bless, O God, bless my weatherbeaten soul.

Source Unknown
West Indies

A Blessing for Old Age

May the light of your soul mind you,
May all of your worry and anxiousness
    about becoming old be transfigured,
May you be given wisdom for the eye of your soul,
    to see this beautiful time of harvesting.
May you have the commitment to harvest your life,
    to heal what has hurt you,
    to allow it to come closer to you
    and become one with you.
May you have the great dignity,
    may you have a sense of how free you are,
    and above all may you be given the wonderful gift
    of meeting the eternal light
    and beauty that is within you.
May you be blessed,
    and may you find a wonderful love in your self
    for your self.

John O'Donohue
England/USA

A Blessing

May the light of your soul guide you.
May the light of your soul bless the work
you do with the secret love and warmth of your heart.
May you see in what you do the beauty of your own soul.
May the sacredness of your work bring healing,
light, and renewal to those who work with you
and to those who see and receive your work.
May your work never weary you.
May it release within you wellsprings of refreshment,
inspiration, and excitement.
May you be present in what you do.
May you never become lost in the bland absences.
May the day never burden.
May dawn find you awake and alert,
approaching your new day with dreams,
possibilities, and promises.
May evening find you gracious and fulfilled.
May you go into the night blessed,

sheltered, and protected.
May your soul calm, console, and renew you.

John O'Donohue
England/USA

Be a Blessing

As God blesses you and all you love,
be a blessing to all you meet,
and the God who loves you—
Father, Son, and Holy Spirit—
be with you, now and always.

Dorothy M. Stewart
England

A Boomerang Blessing

I have a prayer.
It is a gift I shower upon you.
I cannot wrap it, it will not be confined in paper.
No box can be found strong enough to hold it.
Not even reinforced concrete can contain a blessing.

It comes triple stamped approved by God.
Father, Son, and Spirit sealed.
Delivery recorded.

Fits you like a glove.
The same you were born in.
It is a perfect match.

A visitation.

It is a perfect match.
The same you were born in.
Fits you like a glove.

Delivery recorded.
Father, Son, and Spirit sealed.
It comes triple stamped approved by God

Not even reinforced concrete can contain a blessing.
No box can be found strong enough to hold it.
I cannot wrap it, it will not be confined in paper
A gift I shower upon you.
I have a prayer,
A boomerang blessing.

Val Shedden
England

Toward Wholeness

1 Corinthians 12:12–26

All of you are Christ's body
and each one is a part of it.

Toward Health

A Blessing for Calm

Spirit of life:
May we yield to your love;
Resting in your spaciousness,
Mending from our frenzy,
Turning to still waters.

May we trust your quiet rhythm
To calm us back to center,
To soften brittle places,
To bring new joy in living.

May we receive this sabbath gifting,
May we honor time as friend,
May we listen for your heartbeat,
And bring peace into our own.

Keri Wehlander
Canada

Blessing for Healing

In our anxiety, you Lord;
In our pain, you Lord;
In our hopes, you Lord;
In those who will treat us, you Lord;
For our healing, you Lord;
For our peace of mind, you Lord;
For our recovery, you Lord;
For our families, you Lord;
Only you, always you, faithfully you.
Blessed are you, Lord, who heals the sick,
Blessed are you who binds up wounds,

Blessed are you whose care knows no end,
Humbly we look to you for safekeeping
and salvation
For there is no other in whom we can
so confidently put our trust.

Peter Graystone
England

Healing Blessings

Healing light, holy light
Blessings now that you receive God's light
And be healed
Healing blessings and our prayers to *(Name)*/you.

Healing word, holy word
Blessings now that you may hear God's word
And be soothed
Healing blessings and our prayers to *(Name)*/you.

Healing touch, holy touch
Blessings now that you receive God's touch
And be comforted
Healing blessings and our prayers to *(Name)*/you.

Healing food, holy food
Blessings now that you find nourishment
And be sustained
Healing blessings and our prayers to *(Name)*/you.

Healing fragrance, holy fragrance
Blessings that you breathe God's fragrance now
And be uplifted
Healing blessings and our prayers to *(Name)*/you.

Radha Sahar
Aotearoa New Zealand

A Hospital Blessing

Just a touch.
A touch of your healing robe,
A touch of your scarred hands,
A touch of your welcoming arms,
A touch of your presence of peace.

Bless us with your touch
which many know each day
in all those who care for us.

Bernard Thorogood
Australia

A Blessing for Hospitals

After visiting a medical ward

Bless you
day surgery and coronary unit,
intensive care and pharmacy,
orthopedics and neurosciences,
for you bring healing and health.

Bless you
psychiatry ward, and maternity,
physiotherapy and dialysis unit,
laboratories and anaesthesiology,
for you bring healing and health.

Bless you
chaplaincy and administration,
housekeeping and research,
homecare and nutrition services,
for you bring healing and health.

Betty Lynn Schwab
Canada

Blessing Prayer in a Time of Sickness

Lord of health and wholeness,
    in your divine plan, you have seen fit
    to include, within your marvelous creation,
    disease and sickness.
Life becomes a balance of sickness and health,
    just as time is balanced between night and day.

Your servant (*Name*) now lies sick
    and desires to be restored
    to the balance of good health.
Hear, O Lord, our prayers
    for the healing of him/her whom we love so much.

Remove from him/her this illness
    so that, fully recovered and restored to health,
    he/she may return with renewed zeal
    to the daily life that we share.
We trust fully in the divine power
    to stir the hidden healing powers of the body.
So awakened, these God-given powers
    will remove all that causes pain and sickness.

Addressing the sick person

With abounding hope and faith,
    we now place our hands upon you
    as we call forth the healing medicine of God's grace.

Persons praying may lay hands on the sick person and pray in silence.

Divine healer and Lord of wholeness,
    together we place ourselves in your hands.
We ask for healing
    but also for acceptance of your holy plan for each of us.
Help us to embrace
    whatever you have decreed for (*Name*),
    assist him/her in the acceptance of this sickness
    as you support him/her
    with the strength of your Holy Spirit.

Addressing the sick person

May you be blessed
> with the power and the love of God
> and the affection of those who love you.

Amen. +

Now make the sign of the cross on the sick person's forehead.

Edward Hays
USA

Blessing in Sickness

May God, who is never absent in health or sickness, in joy or in tribulation, look mercifully upon you. May you find relief and healing, patience in the time of waiting, and faith made stronger by health restored.

Raymond Chapman
England

For Persons with AIDS

> Hear our prayer, O God of mercy and love
> for all who suffer with AIDS.
> Grant unto them tender and loving companions
> who will support them in the midst of fear.
> Give them hope for each day to come
> that every day may be lived with courage and faith.
> Bless them with an abundance of your love
> that they may live with concern for others
> and not be obsessed with their own illness.
> Pour upon them the peace and wholeness
> which you alone can give;
> through Jesus Christ, our Savior,
> who came to give us abundant life, we pray.

Vienna Cobb Anderson
USA

Prayer to Accompany the Taking of Medicine

Lord,
    my sickness has made praying difficult.
Its pain makes me self-conscious,
    so that I find it a burden
    to think of the needs of others.
Divine healer, I need your aid.

May this medicine
    which I am about to take
    cure me and call forth
    the hidden healing powers of my body.

The medicine is taken.

I ask that through the power of the Cross of Christ,
    this medicine, blended with faith and devotion,
    may restore me to the fullness of health.

A sign of the cross or other sacred gesture is made.

Lord, with faith and abounding hope in your love,
    I pray in communion with you, my beloved,
    and with all those who desire my healing,
    my return to the wholeness of health.
I place trust in this medicine
    based on my trust in you,
    the eternal healing medicine of life.
I believe in your holy power to heal me
    of all that has combined to create my present illness.
I seek to be healed,
    but I seek even more your holy will
    as I embrace your final choice.

Bowing in loving obedience
    as did your Son, Jesus, on the Mount of Olives,
    I seek holiness in your will
    more than just health of body.
Amen. +

Edward Hays
USA

Blessing before an Operation

No journey you take
Is ever alone
There is always
The white light
On the crest
Of your mind
The dove of friendship
Always alighting
The whisper of encouragement
The beckoning stranger
To lure you on
Or to send you home
For blessings or blessings.

Bob Commin
South Africa

A Blessing for One Whom Healing Eludes

For Tyrell

Caught
you are
between health sciences and alternative medicine,
between hope and despair, death and life.
Blessed
may you be,
embraced deeply by God's love.

Chemotherapy, radiation, and surgery,
physicians, labs, and specialists
did all they can do;
yet disease ravages your organs, bones, and blood.
Blessed
may you be,
embraced deeply by God's strength.

Alternative medicine now draws you:
unverified vitamins, expensive procedures, controversial drugs,
borderline methods, frontier physicians, and anecdotal evidence.

Blessed
may you be,
embraced deeply by God's wisdom.

Family, friends, and the public rally to your side:
talking, advising, contributing, praying,
visiting, writing, discussing, campaigning.
Blessed
may you be,
embraced deeply by God's people.

And you, desperate, cherished young one,
whom will you hear? Whom can you trust?
Some say only death stands before you;
others say hope, health, and life.
Blessed
may you be,
embraced deeply by God's truth.

Betty Lynn Schwab
Canada

A Prayer for an Insight into Suffering

Lord, my God, incomprehensible one,
    your sacrament of suffering,
    the mystery of pain,
    is an integral part of my life.
I have at times been offered the cup of bitterness
    so that I may share in the sorrow
    that was freely embraced by your Son, Jesus,
    and so that I may help to heal
    the sickness that plagues our planet.

I thank you for opportunities to explore,
    with those around me and with all the world,
    the profound puzzle of pain.
May I seek only the fullness of life
    and not reject the element of pain
    inherent in all growth
    and essential in each search for wholeness.

As a disciple of Christ,
   I follow in the footsteps
   of a suffering Savior,
   asking that this pain
   have special meaning for me
   and for all the earth.

Blessed are you, Lord my God,
   who share pain and suffering
   as part of the mystery of life.

Amen. +

Edward Hays
USA

A Blessing for Someone with Alzheimer's Disease

Lord, we ask your blessing on this confused mind.
You know that the experiences and knowledge of a lifetime are
   locked away inside a complicated mechanism to which this
   disease has inappropriate keys.

Keep this troubled one safe in confusion,
happy in forgetfulness,
aware in times of lucidity
and secure in the environment of constant care.

When there is fear and anger, surround *(Name)* with your peace.
When despair strikes, give her/him your glimmer of hope.
When there seems to be no response, probe deep into the apparent
   emptiness of the mind with the reassurance of your love.

And when everything seems hopeless and this disease has full
   control, we commit her/him to your eternal compassion and care.

Marjorie Dobson
England

The Healing

In this ritual for a service of healing, people should sit together in a circle, and work together in pairs or small groups. It involves touch, and this might need to be explained beforehand so that people are prepared.

Leader One Christ is like a single body which has many parts

All It is still one body, even though it is made up of different parts

Leader Two Therefore the foot cannot say

Women I am not part of the body *(open hand toward the feet of partner/group members)*

Leader One Nor can the ear say

Men I am not part of the body *(open hand toward the ears of partner/group members)*

Leader Two The eye cannot say to the hand

Youth I don't need you *(open hand toward the eyes of partner/group members)*

Leader One Nor can the head say to the feet

Seniors I don't need you *(nod toward feet of partner/group members)*

Leader Two If one part of the body suffers

Black All other parts suffer *(link limbs in an attitude of struggle)*

Leader One If one part of the body is praised

White All other parts share its happiness *(link limbs in an attitude of celebration)*

Leader Two All of you are Christ's body:

All Each one of us is a part of it.

Janet Lees
England

Blessing for a Hard Time

Go in peace and faith.
If you are tired, may you find rest,
if you are anxious, may you find peace,
if you are lonely, may you find friends
and if you are dying, may you find new life
and know that nothing can separate you from
the love of God in Christ Jesus.

Dorothy McRae-McMahon
Australia

Escaping Danger

When we escape danger or recover from illness, we are grateful.

Thank you, God, for your comfort in my time of fear
and your kindness in my time of need.

Traditional Jewish Blessing

All Kinds of Kite Fliers

A Trinitarian Blessing

May God, the Creator, bless you
and nourish all your best ideas.

May Christ, the wounded healer, touch you
and make you whole.

May the winds of the Spirit
lift you into flight,
free as a bird
and high as a kite.

Footnote: If you have never flown a kite—try it. It is wonderful therapy for all kinds of stress. It clears the mind and stimulates creativity.

Jean Mortimer
England

Treasured Memories

Treasured Memories

Bless the memories that we treasure
Bless the friendships that we share
Bless the life that we celebrate
Bless the peace that (*Name*) has found
and, Lord, bless our journey as we seek
the friendship through the love you offer. Amen.

Richard Becher
England

A Blessing in Bereavement

May God bless you and be with you in this time of deep sorrow.

In the tears of others, know that he weeps with you.

In the touch of others, know that his arms are holding you.

In the practical work of others, know that he is helping you to cope from day to day.

In the words of others, know that he is speaking to you.

In the prayers of others, know that he hears you.

And in the desolation of this time, know that by each tear, touch, act, word and prayer, others are bringing God's love to you to filter into those empty spaces with his compassion and understanding.

Marjorie Dobson
England

A Blessing of Memories

The following was used at the end of a Memorial Service remembering the lives of people who had died during the previous twelve months and also at the end of a funeral service with slight adaptation to include the name of the deceased.

Leader   My remembering has made me cry
All   Bless my tears as a source of your compassion
Leader   My remembering has made me laugh
All   Bless my laughter as an avenue for your joy
Leader   My memories remind me of the guilty times
All   Bless my guilt as a channel for my learning
Leader   My memories remind me of the words you spoke
All   Bless those words as seeds for my growth
Leader   My remembering has given me new strength
All   Bless that strength as the movement of your spirit
Leader   My remembering has brought me healing
All   Bless that healing as an outpouring of your love
Leader   My memories remind me of the precious gift of life
All   Bless the life we had together
Bless the road I now walk alone
Bless new meetings in my life
And bless the Christ within me
So I can be your servant, Lord.

Richard Becher
England

Love Stronger than Death

May the love which is stronger than death
and which binds us together in the unity of life,
energize our spirits with divine stillness,
now and forever.

W. L. Wallace
Aotearoa New Zealand

With the Dying

The blessing of the cross of Christ be yours:
may your journey through pain be touched by him,
your burdens be shared by him,
your ending be at peace with him,
and your spirit be at one with him forever.

Bernard Thorogood
Australia

For Death and the Dying

Blessed are you Lord God
For the gift of life,
For the gift of my life.

Blessed is the life I have known
Blessed by the love of others,
Blessed by the breath of others,

Blessed is the life I have known
Blessed by your love,
Blessed by your breath,

Blessed is the life I have known
Blessed by my love…my breath.

You know my pain,
You know my fear,
You know my spent anger and deep distress.
You know how wrong this is.
Destroy death!
Please.

Quiet

Bless the curse of death
Bless the curse of my death.
Bless with my pleadings and your presence those I must leave.

Give me the breath and blessing of the Father
Who will not abandon me to death.

Give me the breath and blessing of the Son
And his gift of new Life.

Give me the breath and blessing of the Spirit
That I may depart in peace.

But God you know I don't want to die.

Peter Cruchley-Jones
Wales

Death Is the Last Great Festival

"Death is the last great festival on the road to freedom." (Bonhoeffer)

Go gently on your voyage, beloved.
Slip away with the ebb tide,
rejoice in a new sunrise.

May the moon make a path across the sea for you,
the Son provide a welcome.
May the earth receive you and the fire cleanse you
as you go from our love
into the presence of love's completeness.

Kate McIlhagga
England

A Funeral Blessing

Go then wherever you must go
Do those things that must be done,
Weep those tears that must be wept,
And learn to live with loneliness.

But go in the knowledge of the God who travels with you:
—God the Father with outstretched arms of love
—God the Son who enters the depths of our pain
—God the Spirit who heals our broken, aching hearts

And go in peace.

Edgar Ruddock
England

For a Bride Whose Father has Died

May the sun shine on the bride
and on her mother too.

May they feel her father's pride,
unseen, yet ever true.

May his love, which has not died,
bloom in their hearts anew.

Jean Mortimer
England

Sunsets and Farewells

Blessed are you, Lord our God,
whose messenger is death.

Lord and conductor of the universe,
      we acknowledge and affirm the mystery
    of sunsets and farewells,
    of departures and finales
    as integral notes in your divine chorus.
We are thankful even for the pains of daily dying,
    for the daily separations
    that are the counterpoint in our common lives.

With gratitude, we listen to the yearly song of creation,
    the melody of spring, summer and autumn
    which rises until the death-rest of winter,
    only to begin again in the evergreen resurrection of spring.
We take joy, as our hearts rise to you,
    that this divine harmony of death and life
    was sung by prophets and holy people,
    and that your Son, Jesus,
    sang that song with his whole person
    in His death and resurrection from the tomb.

We are grateful for his living example,
    for him who found it so difficult departing from his friends
    so that a greater experience of life
    might be his and theirs.

In his footsteps,
    along that path of death and resurrection,
    we process toward our own death
    and resurrection in you.
Help us, compassionate God,
    to let your ancient and eternal song of death and life
    be played out in each of us,
    as we live out our faith that death is but a doorway
    that opens unto a greater and fuller expression of life,
    that opens to a final union with you who are life!

Blessed are you, Lord of Life,
    who alone knows the hour of our death
    and ultimate union with you.

Blessed are you, Lord our God,
whose messenger is death.

Edward Hays
USA

Mixed Blessings

I carry oil in my pocket as I drive too fast to see you,
Park erratically in the deserted hospital parking lot.
Ironically tonight there is so much space I cannot choose.

Intensive care gowns always make me feel out of place,
A germ in a sterile environment.

Blue light emphasizing the lines on my face
when I want to be strong, at least appear to be brave.

You are still silent,
Machines breathe with a regularity
which proves how artificial they are.

Ideas above their station they speak to us,
Bleep and whirr with superior understanding.

I am in awe of them.
I want to kneel and thank them for keeping you alive.

The illusion is broken when I realize
doctors have made a space for me,
My sweaty palm clasping the oil, I see their faces are
calling time.

As I anoint you the machines electronically deny our fears
Unashamed I pray, may God be with you wherever you go.

Soon laughter and tears fill the blue sterile air around you.
We speak as if you can still hear us,
remind you of the love that waits to say goodbye.

God's blessing is given and taken
As we hold swollen hands.

Pain does not come always in silence
And prayers are always more
Than just words.

Val Shedden
England

Jewish Kaddish*

All remain standing as the Kaddish is sung.

Magnified and sanctified be the great name of God
in the world which he created according to his will.
May he establish his kingdom in your life and in your days,
and in the lifetime of all his people:
Quickly and speedily may it come; and let us say Amen!
Blessed be God forever!
Blessed, praised, and glorified,
exalted, extolled, and honored,
magnified and lauded by the name of the Holy One;
blessed be God!
Though he be high above all the blessings and hymns,
praises and consolations,
which are uttered in all the world; and let us say Amen!

Blessed be God forever!
May there be abundant peace from heaven
and life for us and for all people; let us say Amen!
Blessed be God forever!

Translated by Michael Vasey
England

The Kaddish is a prayer used during the eleven-month period of mourning following a death and on subsequent anniversaries.

A Blessing for Death

I pray that you will have the blessing
    of being consoled and sure about your
    own death.
May you know in your soul that there is no need
    to be afraid.
When your time comes, may you be given
    every blessing and shelter that you need.
May there be a beautiful welcome for you in the
    home that you are going to.
You are not going somewhere strange.
You are going back to the home that you never left.
May you have a wonderful urgency to live
    your life to the full.
May you live compassionately and creatively
    and transfigure everything that is negative
    within you and about you.
When you come to die may it be after a long life.
May you be peaceful and happy in the
    presence of those who really care for you.
May your going be sheltered and
    your welcome assured.
May your soul smile in the embrace of your anam cara.

John O'Donohue
England/USA

anam cara: spiritual wisdom

Always on the Move

Psalm 16

You will show me
the path of life.

Inner Strength

Earth Prayer

A prayer to the God of eight directions, the six of Native American spirituality, plus the inward and outward movements of the Spirit in all of us. Originally a song text, it was recorded on the album EarthSong *by the Medical Mission Sisters.*

O Holy One of Blessing, O Spirit of the North, hear us.
Barren are we unless you fill our emptiness.
O Wintering Warmth, come cheer us.

O Holy One of Blessing, O Spirit of the East, wake us.
Wisdom, be wise in us; let hope arise in us.
O Dawn of our days, come take us.

O Holy One of Blessing, O Spirit of the South, heed us.
Grace so abundantly flows from you, tenderly.
O Nurturing Love, come feed us.

O Holy One of Blessing, O Spirit of the West, still us.
Until you call us home, shelter us in Shalom.
O Life after life, come fill us.

O Holy One of Blessing, O Spirit from on high, see us.
Heavenly peace is ours when we can see the stars.
O Transcendent One, come free us.

O Holy One of Blessing, O Spirit of the Earth, heal us.
Touching us, teaching us, your glory reaching us,
O Flesh of our flesh, reveal us.

O Holy One of Blessing, O Spirit deep within, guide us.
Enter us, center us, patiently mentor us,
and always be there inside us.

O Holy One of Blessing, Love emanating forth, send us.
Yours is the life we share. Your love is everywhere.
Creator of all, befriend us.

Miriam Therese Winter
USA

The Spiritual Journey

May God come close to you
as you take the journey to the center,
seeking to know the ultimate,
to encounter the sublime.

May God bless you in the heart of prayer,
spirit meeting spirit,
searching, questing, discovering.
May God be alongside you
in the times of aridity,
in the experience of thirst,
in the longing for refreshing water.

May God enliven you
as you feel the heat of the day,
as you pause to drink deep,
as you draw from spiritual wells.

May God fill you
as you learn to leave the old self,
as you cease to depend on props,
as you lay aside the crutches of dependence,
as you learn to walk freely,
to breathe the air of divine encounter.

May God be with you in the joy of remembering,
in the purification of forgetting,
in the experience of refining.

May God go with you to the still center
and enable you to find true fulfillment
and deep inward peace.

John Johansen-Berg
England

Blessing on the Inner Life

May God, the great mystery, guide you
in your journey of discovery,
leading you to know more of him
as you commune with him in prayer.

May God, the divine shepherd,
protect you and lead you
as you seek the pastures
of wholesome food and still waters.

May God, the heavenly midwife,
bring you to the birthing
that gives new life in the Spirit
as you learn through the experience of suffering.

May God, the divine coach,
bring out the qualities in your spiritual life
that will enable you to serve him better,
as you express gifts of the Spirit in your discipleship.

May God, the living vine,
allow his life to flow through you
so that you may be a living branch,
grafted into the divine stem.

May God, the heavenly lover,
draw you to himself with cords of love,
enabling you to lose yourself
in the unutterable joy of communion with him.

May God the Father encircle you with his love;
may God the Son encircle you with his peace;
may God the Spirit encircle you with his joy.
May God, Father, Son and Spirit surround you to eternity.

John Johansen-Berg
England

This is Thy Blessing

Would that the clays of thee know the clays of me;
Would that the fire of thee flare within the flames of me;
Would that my breath intermingle with thy breathings;
Would that my holy fluids source all thy flowings.

For my clays are home to thy clays;
For my fire is ember for thy glowing;
For my breath is peace for thy anointing;
For my flowings are a spring for thy restoring.

Humbly, O God,

I desire the clays of me to know the clays of thee.
I yearn for fire of me to ignite from flames of thee.
I long to release my breath into thy breath.
I pray my watershed is filled by thy fountainhead.

This is thy blessing, incarnational and eternal God.
And, as Thou O God, has so blessed me,
so I say to my creature neighbor—

May I, within earth space, intuit thy creation place.
May I, within earth space, see thy radiant Christlike face.
May I, within earth space, drink thy pure outpourings.
May I, within earth space, inhale thy holy breathings.
 And, likewise, may thou do mine.
 Whether thee be existential or eternal
 may the spiritual components of me
 embrace, absorb, and rejoice in
 thy holy divinity.

Glenn Jetta Barclay
Aotearoa New Zealand/Northern Ireland

Moments of Blessing

In the mystery of a new birth,
in the baby as she discovers the world about
and the people in whom she can trust,
> we glimpse a holy moment telling of God.

In the tranquility of the silent moment,
in the music which thrills our innermost being
and the glories of nature powerfully majestic,
> we glimpse a holy moment telling of God.

In the loving word,
in the concern expressed from the heart
and the presence of friend who does not impose,
> we glimpse a holy moment telling of God.

In the opportunity to care,
in the sense of being upheld by the care of others
and the privilege of seeing deep into the solitude of another,
> we glimpse a holy moment telling of God.

In the artist's imagination,
in the composer's music,
and the scientist's leap of faith,
> we glimpse a holy moment telling of God.

In the problem being resolved,
in the transformation of decline
and the community which embraces the most vulnerable,
> we glimpse a holy moment telling of God.

God, parent,
God, companion in Jesus,
God, enlivening Spirit,
Your blessing is in all moments of our life,
> Grant us the sense to rejoice!

John Ll. Humphreys
Wales

Hold Me, Lord

Blessings can be responsive—as with the words in bold here—but this can all be said by a leader and me easily changed to us and we.

Hold me in your arms, Lord
Bless me with your Love
Whisper in the quietness, Lord
Bless me with your Word
Lead me through the darkness, Lord
Bless me with your Light
Touch me where I hurt, Lord
Bless me with your Healing
And through your blessings, Lord,
may I grow and learn
to know your presence
always walking with me. Amen.

Richard Becher
England

God of Little Things

Blessed be God for little things;
for curling lashes on a baby's face,
for snowdrops pushing through the frozen earth,
for a primrose nestling on a mossy bank,
for the intricate workings inside a watch,
for the one-celled amoeba—primitive life,
for the hazelnut, symbol of eternal love,
love of the infinitesimally small
by the one who is infinitely great.

Jean Mayland
England

To Encounter God

After Simone Weil

To resist evil, confront its lies;
To embrace good, contemplate love;
To find space, cherish silence;
To confront fear, act toward hope;

To discover courage, receive gifts;
To pray, cultivate time...

To overcome pain, attend wounds;
To experience joy, give thanks;
To sense eternity, let go...

To encounter God, enter the void
once more.

Simon Barrow
England

The Power and the Mystery

May the power and the mystery go before us, to show us the way,
    shine above us to lighten our world,
    lie beneath us to bear us up,
    walk with us and give us companionship,
and glow and flow within us to bring us joy.

St. Hilda Community
England

Be to Us Our God

Door of the sheepfold, open to your people!
Light of the world, shine before us!
Bread of life, feed us!
True vine, quench our thirst!
Good shepherd, love us with passion!
Way, truth and life, give us courage for tomorrow!

God our shelter in the storm, protect us!
God our rock, be our strength!
God our father, nurture us!
God our mother, discipline us!
God our life-breath, inspire us!
God our beginning and our end, hold us forever in your love!

O God:
Be to us the soil in which we grow;
Be to us the air we breathe;

Be to us the water we drink;
Be to us the sun that gives us light and warmth and draws us
 heavenwards;

Be to us our God, without whom we can have no being.
You are the way we shall walk.
You are the truth we shall take into ourselves.
You are the life we shall enjoy forever
And share with all.

May the mystery of God beckon us;
May the wisdom of God direct us;
May the forgiveness of God send us into the world
 to exercise justice and love,
and be a blessing to the nations.

God, imbue our souls with calm; among us stand.
God, inscribe our names on the palm of your hand.
God, touch us with your balm, give peace in our land.

Kate Compston
England

Completing the Circle

May the Great Spirit rise *(right hand reaches low before you, then spirals upward until your arm and hand are reaching high overhead and gesturing toward the heavens.)*

Like the morning sun *(hands are placed side by side, thumbs touching, to form a disk. Starting from the general region of the left hip, they are moved together in a gentle arc from the left up past the heart, and then down to the general region of the right hip—suggesting the pathway of the sun.)*

In your *(right arm and hand reach straight out in front, gracefully gesturing at the person or persons directly across the circle from you.)*

Heart *(hands are held over the heart, left hand on chest, right hand over it. Pause and hold this gesture for at least one full cycle of breath.)*

And with this *(arms are fully extended down at the sides, and held slightly away from the hips. Hands are held with the palms open and fingers spread, facing forward into the circle.)*

Our circle *(right arm and hand reach toward the person on your immediate left in the circle, pointing or gesturing not just with one finger but with the whole open hand. Then the arm and hand are slowly swept around the circle in a clockwise direction, indicating and including each person even unto the person on your immediate right.)*

Is complete *(left arm and open hand are held across the chest at heart level, about two or three inches away from the body—almost as if you were reaching across with your left hand to scratch your right biceps. The left palm faces the Earth. The right elbow is placed atop the left fingertips, with the arm and open hand pointing straight up, forming a right angle. As the words "is complete" are spoken, the right hand and arm move downward toward the left elbow, until the two arms are closed in a parallel gesture at the heart—right on top of left.)*

From a tribe of the Northeast Woodlands of Turtle Island, North America
Submitted by Steven McFadden
USA

Journeys
and
Pilgrimages

Journey with Us

May the God of history, who journeyed with our Lord Jesus on the streets of Nazareth continue to journey with us through the Holy Spirit now and forevermore.

Usha Joshua
India

A Life Blessing

Take my feet
and bless them.
Take my hands
and bless them.
Take my lips
and bless them.

May I walk
only in your Way.
May my touch
be ever gentle.
May my voice
always speak
your Word.
May my heart
beat out
your rhythm.
May my life
be given to you.

May all I do
bring glory to
your Holy Name.
Susan Hardwick
England

God Bless Us on our Way

May God bless us on our way. May he renew us, and all for whom we pray, in faith and hope and love. And may he bring us at the last to the fullness of joy in his eternal kingdom.

Robert Llewelyn
England

Going Attached

Go from this place in peace,
and if the walk is long,
praise God—he will walk it with you.
If the wind is cold,
praise God—for the warmth of his
touch.
If life is hard,
praise God—for the arms of his love
attached to you forever
by the nails that pierced hands and feet
for your sake.
Duncan L. Tuck
Wales

A Turning Season

God, my source of strength,
A season is turning in my life
Calling me to make ready:
Walk with me, I pray.

This unmapped course lies divided ahead
Urging careful determination:
Walk with me, I pray.

The gate has swung open and everything's loose
Bidding that something be left behind:
Walk with me, I pray.

Until the turbulent waters clear
I reach for your mercy
and pray for wisdom:
Walk with me, I pray.

Keri Wehlander
Canada

God of Pilgrimage

God of pilgrimage
be with me on my journey
through this life;
guard and defend me,
shelter and feed me,
challenge and inspire me,
teach me and lead me,
and when my days are ended
welcome me home at last
to rest in your love forever.

Source Unknown
Found in Ely Cathedral
England

Prompt Us

Living God, the source of all life,
prompt us into new beginnings.
Ever present God, traveling alongside us
guide us to walk in your way.
Ever loving God, surrounding us with care,
help us to detect your presence.

Jan Berry
England

A Blessing for Beginnings

Divine breath:
Each genesis daunts us;
Each sunrise rekindles us.
We cross thresholds into young stories.
One step sings hope, the other shouts doubt.
O God, midwife us into our beginnings.

We long for familiarities;
We recognize possibilities.
Rowing between the tides of transformation and resistance.
O God, midwife us into our beginnings.

Our roots stretch tender into this new soil;
Our fabrics are patterned with new colored strands.
This unknown country will reveal itself one heartbeat at a time.
O God, midwife us into all our beginnings. Amen.

Keri Wehlander
Canada

Blessing for a New Start

Face the future
for the past is over and gone.
Live with the memories.
Learn from experience.
Let go of grievances.
Resolve differences.
Live in the sight of God,
in the way of God.
Be strong.
He has seen us through
good times and bad.
He will bless our future
as he has held our past.
God go with you.

Marjorie Dobson
England

Bread for the Journey

May there be bread for the journey,
May there be friends along the way,
May we dare to dream and laugh and love,
And seek justice every day.

May God's presence give us wisdom,
May God's presence grant us peace,
May God's be the hand that gives us strength,
May we hope in the promised feast. Amen.

Keri Wehlander
Canada

New Horizons

Our God of new horizons, where do we go from here?
Our God of new experiences, how can we be the same again?
Our God of every blessing, show us how to share your love.
Our God of every dimension, thank you for being you.

Frances Ballantyne
England

Blessing for a Journey

Go in peace in the power of Christ.
And may food be found beside the road,
living water rise forth in springs around you
and the Spirit restore you in the hard places.

Dorothy McRae-McMahon
Australia

Blessed Be All Our Journeys

Blessed be the harbor hills that welcome us
Blessed be the sea that calls our holy name
Blessed be the stillness of the night,
        the morning birdsong
and at the water's edge.

Blessed be all our journeys
Blessed be all who continue to seek to flourish in
greater love and wisdom.

Anglican Women Exploring Spirituality
Aotearoa New Zealand

Journey Blessing

God be with you
on the road of life's suffering.
Christ be with you
in celebration.
The Spirit be with you
to encourage and bless you
at all times and in all time.

Kate McIlhagga
England

Journeys

May God shield you on every steep,
May Christ keep you in every path,
May Spirit bathe you in every pass.

Carmina Gadelica

In Life's Journey

In life's journey
be to me as a star;
in the wild seas
be to me as a helm.
In the times of indecision
be to me as a signpost;
in times of despair
be my loving companion.

Kate McIlhagga
England

God's Home

Make your way home this day,
knowing that God is at home in your hearts,
and that your true home is in his.
And may the blessing of God,
Father, Son, and Holy Spirit,
be in the rich joy of finding him with you
every moment of the day.

Duncan L. Tuck
Wales

Blessing for Those Who Make Journeys

May the God of travelers bless you on your journey.
May you be guided and protected
in your travel by road,
in your flight by air,
in your crossing of the seas.

May those who make possible your journey
be people of skill and integrity.
May God's blessing rest on the pilots,
on the crew members, on the drivers.
May the vehicles be well constructed
and honestly and efficiently maintained.
May God's blessing of wisdom
be on the repair crews and maintenance teams.

May you be blessed as you meet others,
finding something of God in each of them.
May you find joy in the sunrise
and contentment in the shades of evening.
May your journey be accompanied by the songs of birds;
may you find renewal in fields, rivers, and mountains.
May the God of travelers
bless you in your going and your returning.

John Johansen-Berg
England

A Blessing for Departing Travelers

Many years ago we stayed for several weeks with a nominally Muslim family in Turkey. As we were leaving, we said our goodbyes and got into the car that was to take us to the station. At this point someone threw a bucket of water over the car with the blessing—interpreted from Turkish as: "Like water you go, so like water may you return."

Source Unknown

Blessing for a Long Journey

Be in our eyes
    give us clear vision;
Be in our brains
    give us swift reactions;
Be in our hands
    give us deft coordination;
Be in our feet
    give us smooth manipulation.

Be in the people
    of the towns we are passing;
Be in their sleeping
    their playing and working;
Be in the miles behind
    with those we are leaving;
Be in the miles ahead
    with those we are greeting.
Trinity of our being
    be in our whole creating
Trinity of our creating
    be in our whole being.

Heather Johnston
England

A Blessing on your Way

May the Holy One bless and guide you
May the Holy One shine in you
    and be known through you
May the Holy One open the way before you
    and journey with you.

Norm S. D. Esdon
Canada

Blessing the Journey

On one of my visits to Kenya we prayed at the airport on arrival before start-ing our matatu (journey) and two hours later, after numerous scary near miss-es, I felt the prayer must have been answered. So here is a blessing for an African journey, but I am sure it can be adopted before getting into the car or bus in any part of the world!

Lord, this journey must begin
and so we pray that it will safely end
where people wait to welcome us home.
So, Lord, bless the hands
on the steering wheel;
bless the foot on the brake
and bless the eyes
that watch the road
for the dangers that are there
at every bend and hill.
Bless our departing,
our traveling
and our arriving
with your guidance and protection.

Richard Becher
England

God Go with Us

God go with us on our journey of faith—
    Revive us when we grow weary,
    Direct us when we go astray,
    Inspire us when we lose heart,
    Reprove us when we turn back.
Keep us traveling ever-onwards;
    a pilgrim people,
    looking to Jesus Christ
    who has run the race before us,
    and who waits to welcome us home.

Nick Fawcett
England

Walk with God

Leader   Let us walk with faith
All   where there is doubt.
Leader   Let us walk with hope
All   where there is despair.
Leader   Let us walk with love
All   where there is hate.
Leader   Let us walk with God
All   in the name of Jesus Christ, our Lord.

Per Harling
Sweden

Blessing for Walkers

May God be in our eyes
making them keen to appreciate
the color and form of his designs.

May Christ be in our feet
keeping them sure and steady
on stony paths and narrow ledges.

May the Spirit be on the wind
pure and strong to blow away
all that keeps us from inner peace.

Heather Johnston
England

A Pilgrim People

Leader	From all corners of the world:
All	God has called his pilgrim people
Leader	From all walks and ways of life:
All	God has called his pilgrim people
Leader	Black and white, male and female
All	We are signs of our world's division
Leader	Black and white, male and female
All	We are signs of God's new creation
	joined together by the love of Christ
Leader	So let us not journey alone with God.
All	So let us not journey only with our friends
	Let us be a place and a people of welcome
	Signs of God's all embracing love.

Peter Cruchley-Jones
Wales

A Penitent's Blessing

May the God who knows you
better than you know yourself,
grant you the gift of courage
to face the known and unknown,
without fear.

May the God who loves you
better than you love yourself,
grant you the gift of understanding
and acceptance.

May the God who forgives you
more fully than you can forgive yourself,

more freely than you think you deserve,
grant you the gift of release
from guilt.

So that you may let go of the past
and look to the future, unafraid,
with a brave face,
a strong heart
and a quiet spirit.

Jean Mortimer
England

Blessing for Visitors Leaving Iona

May the God of these stone walls
surround us with his strength.

May the Christ of the high crosses
encompass us with his compassion.

May the Spirit of the dove of peace
empower us as we return home.

May the light and love of Iona
shine in every corner of our existence.

Heather Johnston
England

Blessed Be Your Way

May God
to whom nothing is hidden
and to whom you belong
give you
blessing, salvation, and peace
in the days he grants you on earth.

May God keep you
and preserve you
from all perils,
from the raging of evil powers,
May God keep your body and soul.

Blessed be your way
on the roads and paths you go.
May you go in the peace of God.
May the Holy Spirit preserve you.
May God hold his hands upon you.
May God turn away all evil.

May God's angel be with you
and always be at your side.
May the moon and the sun
shine upon you
and make your way bright
so that everyone you meet
will be glad to see you.

May the love of God
and the love of all
be with you.

Following an old Tobias Blessing
From a Munich manuscript, 12th Century
Germany

A Journey for Justice

When the G8 Summit met in Birmingham, England, in May, 1998,
the agenda included the relief of debt for the developing nations. Thousands of
Christians, encouraged by the Jubilee 2000 campaign, gathered to express their
solidarity with the poor and marginalized people of the world. Jeni Parsons made
the journey by coracle along the canals and waterways. This blessing was writ-
ten for her.

Over the Canal

Bear gently upon these waters, O Lord of heaven and earth, your messenger of peace. Your word brought order in the beginning to the waters
of chaos; bring your just order in this our day to the enslaving tumult
of a world enchained by debt. Restore the harmony of the nations
according to your gracious will. Through Jesus Christ our Lord. Amen.

As we write upon these waters the name of the Prince of Peace [IHS], so
do you, O Lord, write his name upon our hearts; that in tranquility your

kingdom may go forward, till the earth is filled with the knowledge of your love as the waters cover the sea. In the + name of the Father and of the Son and of the Holy Spirit. Amen.

Over the Coracle

By your gracious command, O God, did your servant Noah build an ark so that all the species of the planet might survive the deluge. Grant that the message borne by your servant may indeed be heard so that all the inhabitants of your good earth may have abundant life in our day. Bless this coracle that Jeni may be preserved in her going out and her coming in.

Boat sprinkled

Your gracious promise, O Lord, is for seedtime and harvest not to fail; make us such good stewards of the earth that the burden of debt may not enslave us or generations yet unborn.

May the angels of God watch over you and protect you; may the prayers of the Blessed Virgin Mary and all the saints uphold you; and may the Lord bring you all safe to the haven where he would have you be;

And the blessing of God Almighty, + the Father, the Son and the Holy Spirit, be upon you and remain with you always. Amen.

Peter Selby
England

Blessing M1 Northbound

The author can see this road from her office. Michael, one of the three named angels in the Bible, is regarded as the protector of God's people.

I watch you every day,
pray for the ritual check mirror, indication, overtake.
Two lanes, continuous movement of strangers travelling.
Thinking about your arrival.

A task to accomplish, salesman's patter.
Third visit today.
Indifferent conversations.

Family funeral, dressed in black.
Wreath placed carefully.
Black tie, holding back tears, unspoken emotions.

Hospital visit, the results today.
I watch you and pray that God will bless you.

In the darkness I hear you returning.
Dull drone of engines exhausted,
A line of continuous headlights cast shadows across the wall.
I pray still, aware of a world outside full of tears and fear.

You never see me, I do not know your name.
I know your speed allows only for an occasional glance in my
    direction.

The church stands proud between junctions sixty and sixty-one.
St. Michael and all his Angels.

Do not look for me, my prayers are for strangers,
Smile at God, his answers bear your name.

Val Shedden
England

The Guarding of God

I set the keeping of Christ about you;
I send the guarding of God with you
to possess you, to protect you,
to accompany you
on all your paths,
through trouble, through danger, through loss.
And I set the dancing of the Spirit around you
to comfort and gladden and inspire you,
each day, each night,
each night, each day.

Kate McIlhagga
England

Blessing for the Person Opposite on a Train

To me you are anonymous
    God calls you by name

To me you are a mystery
    God knows your every breath

To me your destiny is unknown
    God guide you safely there
And his blessing be yours now and always.
        Michael Turnbull
        England

The Grace Enclosing Heights and Depths

The grace enclosing heights and depths
shall guide you

    and you shall walk toward your goal
    strengthened in body and mind

    and you shall feel at ease
    when you open your eyes
    to the beauty of creation

    and pain shall touch you
    but not break you—
    the pain of others
    and your own

The grace enclosing heights and depths
shall guide you

    and hope will sustain you
    and your words and deeds
    will become signs of authentic love

    and you shall avert hate and coldness
    and fight the death brought on by people's
    own fault

and you shall leave and return to the home
that offers space for the friend and the
    stranger
and for life yesterday, today, and always.

The grace enclosing heights and depths
and bringing heaven to earth
shall guide you.
Amen.

Dieter Trautwein
Germany
Translated by Martin Henninger

A Pilgrimage Prayer

O Lord God,
from whom we come,
in whom we are enfolded,
to whom we shall return,
bless us in our pilgrimage through life:
with the power of the Father protecting,
with the love of Jesus indwelling,
and the light of the Spirit guiding,
until we come to our ending,
in life and love eternal.

Peter Nott
England

Index of Titles/First Lines

Living God, Loving God

Blessing of Heart and Breath 11
Blessing of the One Who Brings
Laughter 12

Claim the Treasures 10

Everlasting to Everlasting 11

Forgiving God 11

Generous Mercy, A 9
Gift of Life 7
God for All 6
God of All Time, The 10
God of Life 4
God of Life, The 6
God of Love 4

Life Blessing, A 5
Living God 5
Living, Loving God 13
Loving God, Lead Us 12

May God Rain on You with His
Blessings 11
May God Who Is Light 5

Summit of Blessings 8

Thank You? 8
Thank You, Most Loving God 12

Your Very Best 9

Aspects of Worship

Shalom of God
A Selection of Blessings from
Sinfonia Oecumenica 30
  Glory to You, O God, Our Hope 31
  Go in Peace and Grace 33
  Let us Go in Strength 32
  May God Bless You 33
  May God's Breath Stream within Me 30
  May the Lord of Creation 32
  We Set Off 31
  Word of Benediction 33

Bless Our Worship 17
Blessed Be 28
Blessed with all Heavenly Benediction
29
Blessing for a Missionary Congregation
24
Blessing of the Protector of Life 26

Blessing with Seeds in Our Hands 30
Bulwark of Strength, A 21

Candle Blessing for Shabbat 29

Faith in God 20
Free Samples 22
Fullness of Joy, The 22

Go Forth 23
Go in Faith 20
Go in Faith and Hope 23
Go in Peace 21
Go out to Change the World 24
Go to Serve 27
God's Blessing 30
Guests of Jesus Christ 23

Hold Firm! 19

Implant the Love of God 18
In Every Place 18
In Whose Name We Have Met 24

Lord Inspire Us 19
Love Be with You 26

May God Challenge Your Ability 19

Our Offering 25

Renew the Whole Creation 18

Seeds of Your Kingdom, The 21
Shalom of God, The 16
Sing We, Sing of a Blessing 27
Story, The 16

Trust in God 20

Unity in Christ 25

Worship Does Not End 25

Your Kingdom Come 22

Praise and Thanksgiving
Ascribe Greatness to Our God 39

Bless My Soul and All that's in Me 39
Blessed Is the Spot 38
Blessing for Christian Unity, A 37

God Has Given Us Every Moment 38

Inhabited Praise 36

Praise and Glory 35
Praise Forever and Ever 35
Praising God in the Four Quarters of
the Earth 40
Prayer Over the Gifts 36

Wonder of God, The 38

Biblical Perspectives
Abound in Hope 42

Beatitude Reflection, A 49

Bible Blessings—various 51–53
Blessed Are the Poor in Spirit 47
Blessed Are the Steadfast 53
Blessed Be God 47
Blessing of Poverty, The 49
Blessing of the God of Deborah, The
44
Blessing of the God of Miriam, The 44
Blessing of the God of Sarah, The (1)
44
Blessing of Salt 50
Bodily Blessed 51

Exalt the Humiliated 46

Generous, Loving God 45
Girl Talk 55
Go Forth as the Children of God 54
God of Blessings, The 42
God's Soil 53
God Who Sang in Mary, The 46

Hail Mary! 46

May God Make You Worthy of Your
Calling 52
May Others Meet with Christ 56
Metaphor Blessing, A 53

Paraphrase of the Beatitudes, A 48
Peniel 43
People of the Book, The 42

Rich Variety of Women in the Bible,
The 56

To Whom, Jude? 45

Version of the Aaronic Blessing, A 44

Baptism Blessing Eucharist
Approaching the Communion Table 63
At the Lord's Table 64

Baptismal Blessing 62
Blessing for a Newborn Child, A 57
Blessing of a Font 62
Blessing of the Bread 64
Blessing of the Child 59

Bless this Child 59

Eucharistic Benediction 64

Naming of a Child, The 60

Parting Prayer 62
Place of Blessing and Salvation, A 61
Welcome, The 57
Welcome to the World 58

Consecration and Dedication
Blessing for Anglican Ordinands, A 66
Blessing of a Brother before Leaving
the Monastery to do Outside Work 67
Blessing of a Newly Professed Nun 66

Dedication of Those Who Work With
Children 68

For Judith—on the Occasion of Her
Ordination 68

The Sacred Three
Blessing of the Three, The 69

Great Mystery, The 71

Lullaby 71

One in Three, Three in One 69

Place, The 71

Strength, Light and Love 70

Trinitarian Blessing, A 70
Trinity Blessing, The 70
Triune God 69

Holy Wisdom
Beatitudes of a Still-seeking Christian
75
Blessed Be God, My Guide 72
Blessing, A 81
Blessing on Opposites, A 80

Fountain of Living Water 74

Glass of Blessings, A 74
Green Leaves in a White Jug 79

Holy Wisdom 72

Information, Knowledge, and Wisdom 74

Keep Your Worship True 73
May All Beings 76
May the Longtime Sun 78

Paradox 81
Purpose, The 72

Sabbath Blessing, A 77
Someone Said . . . 77

Woman of Wisdom 81

To Be Silent...
Blessing Inspired by Coleg Trefeca, A
86
Blessing Prayer for a Place to be Used
as a Hermitage 83

Prayer before Leaving a Hermitage or
Ending a Time of Solitude 84

Wallis House Blessing 85

Saints Still Alive!
Blessing from Saints of the North 89

Franciscan Blessing, A 89

Hildegard Blessing 88

Let Nothing Disturb you 90
Love of Christ Embrace You, The 88

Petition for the Life of the Martyrs and
the People, A 90
Preserve and Instruct Us 92

Places of Worship
Blessing a Banner 93
Blessing a Garden Seat in an Area of
Remembrance 95
Blessing a Place of Worship 93

Blessing an Altar Frontal 93
Blessing for Church Cleaning 95
Blessing for Churchyard Work 95

Refurbishment of a Chapel 94
Service for the Re-opening of a Church Hall 94

Fruits of the Spirit

Encourage and Challenge
Bless Me! 101
Blessing for Strength, A 99
Blessing of Flame 106

Courage Blessing 101

Give Us the Courage to Change 104
Go as Far as You Dare 98
Go Forth . . . Ask . . . Share! 107
Go with Courage 107
God Has Given Us a Dream 98

It Is So Easy to Say 100

Jesus, Courageous and Vulnerable 106

Make a Difference in the World 102
Move Us to Change 99

New Ways 104

Release Us 103
Risk Everything 98

Stir Up a Divine Restlessness 99

To Work for Change 105

We are Encouraged 105

Let Justice Flow...
Blessing, A 113
Blessing for Speaking Out, A 108
Blessing for the World's Children, A 119
Blessing for Those in Mission 108
Blessing of Liberation 117

Create a World of Equality 121

Do Justice—Love Kindness 115

For Those Who Live on the Margins 115

Gathering, The 109
Give and Take 112
God Bless 116
God of Justice 110
God Who Dances in Creation 112

Just for Me 117
Justice Blessing, A 109

May the Grace of God Sweep through this World 112

On Racial Justice Sunday 121
Open Eyes and Hearts 109
Open the Door (for one voice) 110
Open the Door (for two voices) 111

Refugee Prays for a Blessing, A 118

Smile and a Tear, A 113
Stir Up! 108
Sweet Are the Blessings 114

True Blessing, A 118

Protect Peace
Deep Peace 126
Discover the Riches of Christ 127

Go Home in Peace 129
God's Strength 124
Hilda's Blessing 125

In Times and Places of War 123

Joy of the Spirit, The 129

Live Simply, Gently 128

Peace 127
Peace, The 122
Peace Be with Us 128
Peace Harmonious 126
Peace of God 123

Receive the Gift of Peace 126
Road of Uncertainty, The 125

You Have Called Us to Peace 124

Joy, Perfect Joy
All Your Days 131
Go out Rejoicing 131
Grace of God Thrill Your Hearts, The
130

Jeu d'Esprit 132

Laughter in Your Eyes 130

May the Holy God Surprise You 132
May the World Continue to Surprise Us
132

Festivals

The Christian Year

Advent
Advent Blessing 134
An Advent Blessing 134

Christmas
At the Heart of the Manger . . . 136

Babe of Bethlehem, The 136
Blessing for Christmas 135
Blessing of the Christmas Child, A
135

Christmas Benediction 138
Christmas Blessing, A 135
Come to Us, Emmanuel 137

Motivate us 138

Orphanage 138

Your Word Made Flesh 137

Epiphany
An Epiphany Blessing 139

Epiphany 139
Epiphany Blessing 139

Ash Wednesday
Blessing of Ashes 140
Suddenly it's Wednesday 140

Lent
For Waiting in the Wilderness 142

Good Friday
Blessing the Thorn in the Flesh 143
Good Friday Blessing, A 143

Easter Day
Easter Blessing 145

Love of Jesus, Fill Me 146

Power of Your New Life, The 145

Risen Lord and Master 146

Pentecost
Pentecost 148
Pentecost Thanksgiving, A 147

Harvest
Agriculture Blessings 154

Blessing for the Wine Harvest, A 152
Blessing of a Garden Field 151
Blessing of a Herd of Cows 152
Blessing of an Orchard 151

Blessing of Beehives 152
Blessing of Bees 155
Blessing of Chickens 152
Blessing of Fish for Stocking Ponds,
Lakes or Rivers 156
Blessing of Harvest Gifts 150

For Those at Work in Food Production
and Preparation 153
Fruit of the Land, The 149

Golden Rice Harvest, The 149
Lord of the Harvest 148
On the Land 150

Prayer for the Blessing of Fishnets 156
Prayer over a Sowing 154
Prayers over a Threshing Floor or Barn
154
Prayer to Bless a Herd 155
Prayer to Bless New Honey 156
Seedtime and Harvest 149

God of Times and Seasons

Changing Splendors
Autumn 163
Autumn Is a Blazing Time 162

God of All Times and Seasons 158

I Look at a Leaf 163

New Year's Blessing, A 159

Past Present and Future 158

Signs of Spring 160
Spring 159
Spring Thanksgiving 160
Summer 161
Summer Is Extravagant 161

Winter 165
Winter Blessing, A 164

Take Us Through the Day, Lord
Any Time of Day! 170

Blessing for a Day 168
Blessing for Morning or Evening
176
Blessing for the Morning 167

Blessing for the Night 175
Blessing for the Night, A 173
Blessing on Daily Living 171
Blessing to Begin the Day, A 166

Celtic Blessing, A 169
Christ's Blessing to Start and End the
Day 169

End of the Day 175
End of the Day, The 176
Evening Blessing 172
Evening Blessing, An 172

Guarding of the God of Life, The
174
Goodnight, Lord 172

In the Bath 170

Morning Affirmations 168
Morning Blessing 167

Night Blessing 174
Night Blessing, A 173

Resting Blessing 175

Creator God

Awaken Our Senses
Bless My Senses 178

Bless Our Tears 181
Bless to Me, O God 181

Blessing for the Senses, A 178
Blessing of Sight 181
Bless the Angel in Our Presence 182
Bless the Touch! 180
Brazilian Blessing, A 179

Senses, The 179
Sensitivity and Tenderness 182

Teachers of Vision 183

Beauty in Creation
All You Powerful Things, Praise the
Lord 185

Beauty in Forms of Creation 187
Benedicite 184
Blessing at a Time of Planting Trees 191
Blessing for the Earth 184
Blessing of the Flowerbeds 191

Creation Benediction, A 188
Creation Seen—Creation Unseen
186
Dominion Over All Living Creatures
189
Doxology of Flowers, A 190

Elemental Blessing, An 192

Garden Blessing, A 189

His Love Endures Forever 186

In Whom All Creation Is Renewed 184

Lord Bless You with Rain, The 189

May the Light of God Fill Your Heart
186
May the Rain Nourish Your Soul 189

Peace, Strength and Light 191

Landscapes
Blessing for Prairie Sage 195
Blessing of the Bush, The 195
Blessing of the Forest 194
Blessing of Trees, A 193
Blessing on the Desert, A 194
Landscape Blessing 193

Seascapes
Blessing for Those on the Sea 197
Blessing at the End of a Canoeing Day
200
Blessing of a Samoan Fishing Canoe
199
Blessing of the Sea, The (1) 196
Blessing of the Sea, The (2) 199
Boat Blessing 198

Birds and Beasts
Blessing for Earth's Birds, A 203
Blessing of Cows or other Animals, The
204

Cat Blessing, A 203

Great Bird of the Wide Skies 204

Peacocks and Pandas 201
Presence 202

Seagull 202

Lands and Peoples

Aboriginal Fire Blessing, The 224
Aotearoa 226
Arohanui Blessing (Aorearoa New
Zealand) 226
Australian Celtic Blessing, An 226
Before, Behind, Below and Around Us
223

Bless African Women, Lord 210
Bless our People 215
Bless the Earth Every Day—A Blessing
for Botswana 211
Blessing for Canada, A 219
Blessing for Hong Kong, A 218
Blessing for Israel/Palestine, A 213

Blessing for London and other Great Cities, A 213

Blessing for Pakistan, A 217

Blessing for Romania, A 208

Blessing for Rwanda, A 209

Blessing on the Land of "Fair Go," A 225

Blessing from South Africa—The Rainbow Nation 210

For Australia 223

From this Place 220

Give Me a Blessing (Venezuela) 229

Liverpool Blessing, The 212

Mayan Prayer, A 227

Nature's Blessing for Busy City Folk (Canada) 222

North East India, Bless the Lord 215

Nunavut Blessing, A 221

Popul Vuh 227

Rahim and Afroza (Bangladesh) 216

Community Lifestyles

Grow Together

Asking for and Giving of Blessing 238

Blessed and Blessing 240

Blessing, A 241

Blessing for a New Place to Be 235

Blessing for a Parish or Church Occasion 239

Blessing for St. Andrew's on the Terrace 239

Blessing on a Shopping Center 233

Blessing through Struggle 234

Blessing upon Them! 234

Daily Round of Life, The 232

Employed By God 236

Every Living Being 241

Love, Joy, Peace 238

May There Be Safety 237

Meet God in Others 232

Thank You 232

Two Women 237

Riches in Relationships

Anointing in Courage 252

Blessed Be Friendship 249

Blessing a Newlywed Couple 245

Blessing for a Relationship, A 251

Blessing for a Marriage, A 247

Blessing for Lovers 244

Blessing on a Loved One 245

Blessing on Those Who have Hurt Me, A 250

Blessing Words Are more than Words 243

Friendship 249

Go to Your Friends and Greet Them 251

God Bless You for Befriending Me 242

God of Our Relating 243

Marriage Blessing 247

Marriage Blessing, A 246

My Friend 250

Pain of Separation, The 251

Sending Forth 252

Sharing Together 243

Take this Couple 248

This Is My Prayer, My Love 244

Wedding Blessing, A 246

Learning and Working
At the Beginning of a Committee
Meeting 259

Blessing before Starting a New Job or
Particular Task 258
Blessing for a Student 254
Blessing for Business Meetings 258
  To Show the Way 258
  Speech and Spirit 258
  Penetrate All Our Deliberating
  258
Blessing of the Bizarre, The 256
Blessing on Starting Secondary School,
A 255

For Someone with Learning Difficulties
255

Home Blessing 257

Rejoice! 261

Standing the World on Its Head 260

Teacher 254
Tutorial 257

We Must Close the Meeting 260

Modern Technology
Blessing for Computer Makers,
Facilitators and Users, A 265
Blessing for My New Computer 264
Blessing for New Technology 263
Blessing of Computers 263
Blessing for Tools and Machines 266
Dedication of a Sound System 267

My Telephone 266

Being Creative!
Before Worship, a Performance or a
Choir Rehearsal 270
Bless Musicians 269
Bless the Poetry, the Art, the Music of
the World 268
Blessing before a Choral Event 270
Blessing for Artists and Composers 271

Blessing for Bands, A 270
Blessing for Journalists, A 272
Blessing for Writers, A 273

Clowns and Other Entertainers 273

Music 268

Solo Voice 271

Eat, Drink and…Share
Bless the Talk Around this Food 277
Blessed Be this Meal 278
Bless this Food 278
Blessing on a Shared Meal, A 275
Blessing upon Food 277
Bon Appetit 275
Brazilian Blessing for the Table, A 277
Bread Blessing 278
Breakfast Grace, A 280
…But What We Share 281

Food and Celebration 280
For Food and Friendship 279

Give Us, O Lord, a Bit o' Sun 281
God is One 279
Grace at a Wedding Breakfast 283

Hunger for Justice, A 282

In a Somewhere Hungry World 282
In Our World 282
Inclusive Grace for a Wedding Meal, An
283

Jewish Table Blessings 276

Lift Up this Bread! 280
Multi-faith Food Blessing 282

New Zealand Blessing at Table, A 276
Not the Gourmet Touch 281

Our Common Meal 283

Table Blessings 279
Table Blessings from Ewell Monastery
276

Hearth and Home
Bless this House 287
Blessing a Samoan House 286
Blessing for a House 289
Blessing for a New Home, A (1) 285
Blessing for a New Home, A (2) 286
Blessing for the Home, A 284
Blessing of a New House 289

Hail Guest! 284
House of Peace, A 287

Our Home 288

Surround Us, God 288

All the Days of my Life
Act of Blessing for a Woman giving
Birth, An 295
Age Blessing 305
All the Words I Like Best 303

Be a Blessing 307
Birth Blessing 296
Bless our Unborn Child 296
Blessing, A 306
Blessing for a Woman Who Has
Conceived 292
Blessing for Old Age, A 306
Blessing for the Child Among Us, A
298

Blessing of a Party, The 304
Blessing offered at a Haircutting/Ear
Piercing Ceremony (Cook Islands) 301
Boomerang Blessing, A 307

Child is Given, A 297
Child Leaving Home, A 302
Community Blessing of a Child in the
Womb of a Single Mother 293
Cook Islands Blessing for Haircutting/
Ear-piercing Ceremony, A 301

Delight in that Love 304

For a Teenager's Bedroom 301

In Pain 304

Life Blessing 305

May Beauty Delight You 303
Mother's Blessing on Her Child, A 299
My Wish for You 292

On a Child Leaving Home 303
Our Children 299

Parent's Blessing, A 299
Prayer of an Old Man 305

Toward Wholeness

Toward Health...
All Kinds of Kite Fliers 320

Blessing before an Operation 316
Blessing for Calm, A 310
Blessing for Healing 310
Blessing for a Hard Time 320
Blessing for Hospitals, A 312
Blessing for One Whom Healing
Eludes, A 316
Blessing for Someone with Alzheimer's
Disease, A 318
Blessing in Sickness 314
Blessing Prayer in a Time of Sickness 313

Escaping Danger 320
For Persons with AIDS 314

Healing, The 319
Healing Blessings 311
Hospital Blessing, A 312

Prayer for an Insight into Suffering, A
317
Prayer to Accompany the Taking of
Medicine 315

Treasured Memories
Blessing for Death, A 328
Blessing in Bereavement, A 321

Blessing of Memories, A 322

Death Is the Last Great Festival 324

For a Bride Whose Father has Died 325
For Death and the Dying 323
Funeral Blessing, A 324

Jewish Kaddish 327

Love Stronger than Death 322

Mixed Blessings 326

Sunsets and Farewells 325

Treasured Memories 321

With the Dying 323

Always on the Move

Inner Strength
Be to Us Our God 336
Blessing on the Inner Life 331

Completing the Circle 337

Earth Prayer 330

God of Little Things 335
Hold Me, Lord 335

Moments of Blessing 334

Power and the Mystery, The 336

Spiritual Journey, The 331

This is Thy Blessing 333
To Encounter God 335

Journeys and Pilgrimages
Blessed Be All Our Journeys 343
Blessed Be Your Way 350
Blessing for a Journey 343
Blessing for a Long Journey 346
Blessing for a New Start 342
Blessing for Beginnings, A 342
Blessing for Departing Travelers, A 346
Blessing for the Person Opposite on a
Train 354
Blessing for Those Who Make Journeys
345
Blessing for Visitors Leaving Iona 350
Blessing for Walkers 348

Blessing M1 Northbound 352
Blessing on your Way, A 347
Blessing the Journey 347
Bread for the Journey 343

God Bless Us on Our Way 340
God Go with Us 348
God of Pilgrimage 341
God's Home 345
Going Attached 340
Grace Enclosing Heights and Depths,
The 354
Guarding of God, The 353

In Life's Journey 344

Journey Blessing 344
Journey for Justice, A 351
Journey with Us 339
Journeys 344

Life Blessing, A 339

New Horizons 343

Penitent's Blessing, A 349
Pilgrim People, A 349
Pilgrimage Prayer, A 355
Prompt Us 341

Turning Season, A 340

Walk With God 348

Index of Authors and Sources

Aboriginal Blessing 224
Adegbola, Adeolu 61
Anderson, Vienna Cobb 13, 183, 314
Anglican Women Exploring Spirituality 344
Ashdown, J. R. 213
Ashwin, Angela 146
Atwell, James E. 99

Bahá'í Community of the United Kingdom 38, 53
Ballantyne, Frances 6–9, 36, 116–117, 123, 137, 181, 343
Barclay, Glenn Jetta 9, 174, 333
Barnard, Audry 124
Barrell, Marnie 46
Barrow, Simon 141, 170, 336
Becher, Richard 134, 136, 172, 176, 180, 181, 183, 236, 321–22, 335, 347
Belletini, Mark 128
Berry, Jan 28, 285, 341
Billing, Phil 217
Blodwell, Frances 241
Boeke, Richard 279
Bott, Cathy 210
Boyce-Tillman, June 88, 101, 193, 246
Brazilian Blessing 179
Brewerton, Sarah 197
Brown, Andrew 283
Bush, Anthony 205

Carmina Gadelica 69, 174–75, 182, 199, 344
Carr-Gomm, Richard 172
Catholic Organization for Development and Peace 109
Chan, Judy 188, 218
Chapman, Raymond 95, 135, 176, 239, 258, 289, 314

Church of the Province of Kenya 149
Colwell, Peter 65, 77, 251, 271
Comaish, Peter 105, 127, 243, 263
Commin, Bob 247, 316
Community of All Hallows 191
Community of St. Peter 69
Community of the Holy Name 169
Community of the Resurrection 67
Community of the Servants of the Will of God 151–52, 191, 194, 263, 266
Compston, Kate 9, 10, 37, 50, 76, 80, 118, 139, 147, 202, 237, 244, 337
Coptic Orthodox Liturgy 150
Cora, Kalea, Lauren, Meg and Rachel 55
Coulton, Nicholas 159
Cowley, Joy 226
Croft, Joy 282
Crofter's Door, A 284
Cruchley-Jones, Peter 7, 324, 349

Dann, Jenny 58
Dawson, Roger 230
DeLisle, Ken 14
Dent, Ancilla 22, 145, 184, 202
Dibeela, Cheryl 211
Dibeela, Prince 11, 39, 188
Dobson, Marjorie 24, 26, 58, 98, 160, 162-63, 165, 232, 256, 266, 281, 288, 299, 301, 318, 321, 342
Doré, Jason 242
Dove, Anthea 243, 250

Echlin, Edward P. 185
Ely Cathedral 341
Esdon, Norm S. D. 54, 78, 137, 143–44, 203, 347

Esquierdo, Angeling B. 105, 121, 125
Ethiopian, Traditional 129
Ewell Monastery 276

Fageol, Suzanne 44
Fawcett, Nick 4, 5, 11, 12, 21, 27, 35, 38, 56, 115, 130–32, 158, 170, 232, 348
Fernando, Basil 114–15, 119
Freier, Philip 172
Furlong, Monica 277

Gabriele, Edward F. 253
Gelasian Sacramentary 29
Granahan, Louise Margaret 120, 220, 241
Gray-King, E. A. S. 5, 10
Graystone, Peter 48, 110, 112, 158, 185–87, 311

Harcourt, Giles 36, 62, 93–94, 95, 140, 150
Hardwick, Susan 174, 250, 275, 287, 300, 340
Harling, Per 20, 21, 23, 26, 42, 49, 103, 182, 268, 296, 348
Harris, Patrick B. 128
Hart, Norman 121
Harvey, Ruth 104, 164
Hays, Edward 84–85, 278, 280, 314, 315, 318, 326
Helyar, David L. 23, 190, 246
Henninger, Martin 355
Hollow, Mike 73
Humphreys, John Ll. 26, 63, 102, 259, 334
Hunt, John 196, 200, 256, 305
Husselbee, Lesley 45

Iles, Paul 146

Jewish Blessings 17–18, 29, 30, 124, 215, 276, 320, 327
Johansen-Berg, John 43, 71, 116, 126, 151, 153, 171, 186, 189, 204, 208–09, 214, 266, 272–74, 284, 331–32, 345
Johnston, Heather 167, 198, 346, 349, 350

Johnston, Rosemary 68
Jones, Cerys 255
Jones, James 212
Joshua, Usha 98, 339

Knight, Bob 108
Kooiman, Michael Jacob 39, 82

Lebans, Gertrude 12, 60, 73, 109
Lees, Janet 17, 71, 72, 235, 319
Lewin, Ann 71, 132, 305
Liddell, Fiona 86
Llewelyn, Robert 340
Long, Graham 24, 63
Lowell, James Russell 281

McCoy, Michael 299
McCulloch, Nigel 270
McFadden, Steven 338
McIlhagga, Kate 270, 277, 296, 302–3, 324, 344, 353
McMahon, Thomas 19
McMullen, Vin 192
McRae-McMahon, Dorothy 18, 20, 23, 30, 46, 54, 107–108, 128, 132, 134, 139, 167, 175, 320, 343
Maraschin, Jaci 277
Mayland, Jean 44, 47, 69, 335
Mead, Joy 4, 67, 99, 238
Menamparampil, Thomas 216
Miclat-Cacayan, Agnes N. 41
Milerepa 126
Mondal, Bishop 217
Mortimer, Jean 192, 247, 320, 325, 350
Murray, John Stewart 25, 62, 85, 239, 276, 286, 288
Murray, Walter 190

Navajo, Traditional 223
Nichols, Alan 152, 194, 225–26, 273
Northeast Woodlands of Turtle Island, Tribe of the 337
Nott, Peter 355

O'Donohue, John 306–7, 328
O, Harry 138
Obbard, Elizabeth 67
Old Tobias Blessing 350

Orevillo-Montenegro, Muriel 51, 238, 245, 293–95
Orthodox Church of the Holy Protection 154–56

Pastoral Leaders of Pelly Bay 221
Pearce, Brian Louis 80
Pencavel, Heather 75
Petty, John 70, 270
Pickard, Donald 61
Platten, Stephen 90

Rack, Henry 11, 74
Rees, Christina 88, 129
Rhosier, Nia 245, 299
Richards, Anne 255, 257, 261
Rominger, Roberta 52, 98, 107, 262
Ruddock, Edgar 135, 324

St. Hilda Community 16, 45, 72, 112, 122, 241, 336
St. Patrick of Ireland 92
Sahar, Radha 59, 76, 131, 189, 278, 288, 311
Santer, Mark 70
Scarlett, Karen 223, 249, 269
Schwab, Betty Lynn 168, 195, 200, 204, 220, 265, 293, 312, 317
Schwartz, Werner and Cornelia 292
Selby, Peter 352
Setefano, L. 199, 286, 302
Shedden, Val 170, 308, 327, 353
Sheppy, Paul 61, 110–11, 251
Shevlin, John 11, 275
Shiregreen United Reformed Church 57
Shomanah, Musa W. Dube 212, 235
Simpson, Marion 283
Sinfonia Oecumenica 30–34
Sister Catherine OHP 89, 184
Sister Michelle OHP 81
Smith, Declan 44, 279
Sparks, Garry G. 91, 228
Stacey, Viv 66, 249
Stewart, Dorothy M. 19, 20, 22, 25, 126, 149, 307
Sykes, Stephen 303

Tedlock, Dennis 227
Templeton, Julian 269
Teresa of Avila 90
Thorogood, Bernard 43, 100, 123, 178, 224, 257, 312, 323
Trautwein, Dieter 355
Tuck, Duncan L. 5, 22, 45, 51, 53, 112, 194, 248, 304, 340, 345
Turnbull, Michael 24, 244, 254, 354

United Church of Canada 56, 105–106, 237
United Congregational Church of Southern Africa 260
United Hebrew Congregations of the Commonwealth 188
Us, Juan Ixchop 91, 228

Vasey, Michael 328

Walker, Dominic 201
Wallace, Martin 233–34
Wallace, W. L. 48, 64, 136, 138–39, 148, 149, 168, 175, 226, 244, 251, 278, 280, 282–83, 303–4, 322
Warren, Howard 252
Wass, Rosemary 160, 161, 163, 165, 179, 258
Wehlander, Keri 81, 100, 106, 108, 113, 142, 166, 298, 310, 341-43
West Indian Blessing 305
Weston, David 291
White, Wendy 233
Williams, Barrie 125
Williamson, Roy 94, 267
Wilson, Lois 44
Winter, Miriam Therese 28, 74, 330
Wootton, Janet 109
World Council of Churches 46, 64, 173

Acknowledgments

*Text can be copied for use in worship on a one-time, non-commercial basis using this acknowledgment.
**Used with permission

Living God, Loving God

Blessing of Heart and Breath © John Shevlin SVD 1999
Blessing of the One who Brings Laughter from *Out of the Fire: Worship and Theology of Liberation* by Gertrude Lebans © 1992 artemis enterprises
Claim the Treasures © Kate Compston written for the United Reformed Church in the United Kingdom General Assembly 1993
Everlasting to Everlasting © Henry Rack**
Forgiving God © 1998 Nick Fawcett, taken from *Prayers for All Seasons—a Comprehensive Resource for Public Worship.* Numbers 303–20 published by Kevin Mayhew Ltd., Buxhall, Stowmarket, Suffolk IP14 3BW
Generous Mercy, A © Glenn Jetta Barclay
Gift of Life © Frances Ballantyne
God for All © Frances Ballantyne
God of All Time, The © E. A. S Gray-King 1991
God of Life © 1998 Nick Fawcett, taken from *Prayers for All Seasons*, ibid.
God of Life, The © Peter Cruchley-Jones*
God of Love © Joy Mead
Life Blessing, A © Duncan L. Tuck 1995
Living God © 1998 Nick Fawcett, taken from *Prayers for All Seasons*, ibid.
Living, Loving God © Ken DeLisle
Loving God, Lead Us © 1998 Nick Fawcett, taken from *Prayers for All Seasons*, ibid.
May God Rain on You with His Blessings © Revd Prince Dibeela
May God Who Is Light © E. A. S Gray-King 1991
Summit of Blessings © Frances Ballantyne
Thank You? © Kate Compston from *Seasons and Celebrations* published by the National Christian Education Council (NCEC)**
Thank You, Most Loving God from *Prayers of Our Hearts* by Vienna Cobb Anderson © 1993. All rights reserved. Used with permission of The Crossroad Publishing Company, New York
Your Very Best © Frances Ballantyne

Aspects of Worship

Shalom of God
A Selection of Blessings from Sinfonia Oecumenica © Feiern mit den Kirchen der Welt/Worship with the Churches in the World/Celebration avec les Eglises du monde/Comunion con las iglesias del mundo Hrsg. im Auftr. d. Evangelischen Missionswerk in Deutschland u. d. BaselerMission v. Werner, Dietrich; Aebi, Beatrice; Baltruweit, Fritz; Dithmar, Christiane; Friederich, Dirk; Lesinski, Marcus; Mettler, Armin, 2 Auflage 1999; 984 S; Gütersloher Verlagshaus, Gütersloh
Bless our Worship © Service of the Heart, Union of Liberal and Progressive Synagogues
Blessed Be © Jan Berry
Blessed with all Heavenly Benediction—Gelasian Sacramentary
Blessing for a Missionary Congregation © Rt Revd Michael Turnbull, Bishop of Durham
Blessing of the Protector of Life © Per Harling
Blessing with Seeds in our Hands © Dorothy McRae-McMahon
Bulwark of Strength, A—Author Unknown
Candle Blessing for Shabbat © from *Gates of Prayer for Young People*, Central Conference of American Rabbis—permission sought
Faith in God © Dorothy M. Stewart
Free Samples © Duncan L. Tuck from *The Word in the World*, NCEC**
Fullness of Joy, The © Ancilla Dent
Go Forth © Dorothy McRae-McMahon
Go in Faith © Dorothy McRae-McMahon
Go in Faith and Hope © David L. Helyar
Go in Peace © Per Harling
Go out to Change the World © Marjorie Dobson
Go to Serve © 1998 Nick Fawcett, taken from *Prayers for All Seasons*, ibid.
God's Blessing—Traditional Jewish Blessing—Source Unknown
Guests of Jesus Christ © Per Harling
Hold Firm! © Dorothy M. Stewart
In Every Place from © *Service of the Heart*, Union of Liberal and Progressive Synagogues
In Whose Name We Have Met © Graham Long
Lord Inspire Us © Rt Revd Thomas McMahon, Bishop of Brentwood
Love Be with You © Marjorie Dobson
May God Challenge Your Ability © Per Harling
Our Offering © John Stewart Murray
Renew the Whole Creation © Dorothy McRae-McMahon. Author of *Echoes of Our Journey—Liturgies of the People*, JBCE 1993, available from SPCK
Seeds of Your Kingdom, The © 1998 Nick Fawcett, taken from *Prayers for All Seasons*, ibid.
Shalom of God, The—from *Women Included* © SPCK**
Sing We, Sing of a Blessing from *Woman Prayer/Woman Song* © Medical Mission Sisters 1987 p. 252. Reprinted with permission
Story, The © Janet Lees, a Speech and Language Therapist and Honorary Research Fellow at the Institute of Child Health, London and an ordained minister of the United Reformed Church in the United Kingdom serving at the Sheffield Inner

City Ecumenical Mission
Trust in God © Dorothy M.Stewart
Unity in Christ © Dorothy M. Stewart
Worship Does Not End © John Ll. Humphreys
Your Kingdom Come © Dorothy M. Stewart

Praise and Thanksgiving
Ascribe Greatness to Our God © Revd Prince Dibeela
Bless My Soul and All that's in Me © Michael Jacob Kooiman 1995
Blessed Is the Spot © The Bahá'í´ Community of the United Kingdom
Blessing for Christian Unity, A © Kate Compston from *Seasons and Celebrations*, ibid.*
God Has Given Us Every Moment © 1998 Nick Fawcett, taken from *Prayers for All Seasons*, ibid.
Inhabited Praise © Frances Ballantyne
Praise and Glory © 1998 Nick Fawcett, taken from *Prayers for All Seasons*, ibid.
Praise Forever and Forever—Author Unknown
Praising God in the Four Quarters of the Earth © Agnes N. Miclat-Cacayan adapted from a Religious Sisters' Congress liturgy
Prayer Over the Gifts © Giles Harcourt
Wonder of God, The © 1998 Nick Fawcett, taken from *Prayers for All Seasons*, ibid.

Biblical Perspectives
Abound in Hope—Romans 15:13
Beatitude Reflection, A © Per Harling
Bible Blessings—various—see text
Blessed Are the Poor in Spirit © Peter Graystone
Blessed Are the Steadfast © The Bahá'í´ Community of the United Kingdom
Blessed Be God © Jean Mayland
Blessing of Poverty, The © Kate Compston from *Seasons and Celebrations*, ibid.
Blessing of the God of Deborah, The © Suzanne Fageol
Blessing of the God of Miriam, The © Jean Mayland (adapted)
Blessing of the God of Sarah, The (1) A Blessing © Lois Wilson 1982, United Church of Canada Publishing House
Blessing of Salt © Muriel Orevillo-Montenegro
Bodily Blessed © Duncan L. Tuck from *The Word in the World*, ibid.
Exalt the Humiliated © World Council of Churches
Generous, Loving God © Lesley Husselbee
Girl Talk © Girls' Spirituality Group of WATER, the Women's Alliance for Theology, Ethics and Ritual, Silver Spring, Maryland, USA. Reproduced from *Waterwheel* with permission
Go Forth as the Children of God © Dorothy McRae-McMahon
God of Blessings, The © Per Harling
God's Soil © Duncan L. Tuck 1997
God Who Sang in Mary, The © Dorothy McRae-McMahon
Hail Mary! © Marnie Barrell
May God make you worthy of your calling…Roberta Rominger adapted from 2 Thessalonians 1:11–12
May Others Meet With Christ © 1998 Nick Fawcett, taken from *Prayers for All*

Seasons, ibid.

Metaphor Blessing, A © Norm S. D. Esdon

Paraphrase of the Beatitudes, A © W. L. Wallace

Peniel © Bernard Thorogood**

People of the Book, The © Revd John Johansen-Berg, Community for Reconciliation, Barnes Close, Chadwich, Bromsgrove B61 0RA

Rich Variety of Women in the Bible, The—from *Roll Away the Stone: Lenten Reflections at the Close of the Ecumenical Decade of Churches in Solidarity with Women* edited by Caryn Douglas and Ted Dodd © United Church Publishing House 1998, p. 25

To Whom, Jude? © Duncan L. Tuck 1995

Version of the Aaronic Blessing, A © Declan Smith

Baptism, Blessing, Eucharist

Approaching the Communion Table © John Ll. Humphreys

At the Lord's Table © Peter Colwell

Baptismal Blessing © John Stewart Murray

Blessing for a Newborn Child, A © Marjorie Dobson

Blessing of a Font © Giles Harcourt

Blessing of the Bread © World Council of Churches

Blessing of the Child from *Out of the Fire: Worship and Theology of Liberation,* ibid.

Bless this Child © Radha Sahar from the collection *Songs of Universal Worship*

Eucharistic Benediction © W. L. Wallace

Naming of a Child, The © Donald Pickard in association with Adeolu Adegbola

Parting Prayer © Graham Long

Place of Blessing and Salvation, A © Revd Paul Sheppy

Welcome, The © Shiregreen United Reformed Church, Sheffield,England*

Welcome to the World © Jenny Dann

Consecration and Dedication

Blessing for Anglican Ordinands, A © Viv Stacey

Blessing for a Brother before Leaving the Monastery to do Outside Work © Community of the Resurrection, Mirfield, England

Blessing of a Newly Professed Nun © Elizabeth Obbard

Dedication of Children's Workers © Rosemary Johnston

For Judith—on the Occasion of Her Ordination © Joy Mead

The Sacred Three

Blessing of the Three, The—Floris Books**

Great Mystery, The © Revd John Johansen-Berg, Community for Reconciliation, Barnes Close, Chadwich, Bromsgrove B61 0RA

Lullaby © Ann Lewin

One in Three, Three in One © Jean Mayland

Place, The © Janet Lees

Strength, Light and Love © Rt Revd Mark Santer, Bishop of Birmingham

Trinitarian Blessing, A © John Petty, Provost of Coventry

Trinity Blessing, The—Source Unknown

Triune God © Community of St. Peter, England

Holy Wisdom
Beatitudes of a Still-seeking Christian © Kate Compston
Blessed Be God, My Guide from *Out of the Fire: Worship and Theology of Liberation,* ibid.
Blessing, A © The United Church Publishing House, from *Joy is our Banquet* by Keri Wehlander, 1996
Blessing on Opposites, A © Kate Compston
Fountain of Living Water from *Woman Prayer/Woman Song,* p. 47. © Medical Mission Sisters 1987. Reprinted with permission
Glass of Blessings, A © Henry Rack**
Green Leaves in a White Jug © Brian Louis Pearce from *Gwen John Talking*
Holy Wisdom from *Women Included* © SPCK, ibid.
Information, Knowledge and Wisdom © Heather Pencavel
Keep Your Worship True © Mike Hollow
May All Beings © Radha Sahar from the collection *Songs of Universal Worship*
May the Longtime Sun—Traditional, Source Unknown
Paradox © Sister Michelle, Order of the Holy Paraclete, England
Purpose, The © Janet Lees
Sabbath Blessing, A © Norm S. D. Esdon
Someone Said…© Peter Colwell
Woman of Wisdom by Michael J. Kooiman © United Church Publishing House; *Spirit Mourn, Spirit Dance,* edited by Rebekah Chevalier 1998, p. 93

To Be Silent…
Blessing inspired by Coleg Trefeca, A © Fiona Liddell
Blessing Prayer for a Place to be Used as a Hermitage from *Prayers for the Domestic Church* by Edward Hays © Forest of Peace Publishing, Inc., 251 Muncie Road, Leavenworth, Kansas 66048, USA
Prayer before Leaving a Hermitage or Ending a Time of Solitude from *Prayers for the Domestic Church,* © Forest of Peace Publishing, Inc., ibid.
Wallis House Blessing © John Stewart Murray

Saints Still Alive!
Blessing from Saints of the North © Sister Catherine, Order of the Holy Paraclete, England
Franciscan Blessing, A © Stephen Platten
Hildegard Blessing © June Boyce-Tillman
Let Nothing Disturb You—Teresa of Avila (1515–82)
Love of Christ Embrace You, The © Christina Rees
Petition for the Life of the Martyrs and the People, A © Juan Ixchop Us, Commission of Mayan Culture within Guatemalan Christian Action, Translation Garry G. Sparks
Preserve and Instruct Us—Source Unknown

Places of Worship
Blessing a Banner
Blessing a Garden Seat in an Area of Remembrance
Blessing a Place of Worship
Blessing an Altar Frontal

Refurbishment of a Chapel
  All of the above blessings are © Giles Harcourt
Blessing for Church Cleaning
Blessing for Churchyard Work
  The above two blessings are © Raymond Chapman
Service for the Re-opening of a Church Hall © Rt Revd Roy Williamson, former
Bishop of Southwark

Fruits of the Spirit

Encourage and Challenge
Bless Me! © John Ll. Humphreys
Blessing for Strength, A © The United Church Publishing House, from *Joy Is our
Banquet*, ibid.
Blessing of Flame © The United Church Publishing House, from *Joy Is our Banquet*,
ibid.
Courage Blessing © June Boyce-Tillman
Give Us the Courage to Change © Ruth Harvey
Go as Far as You Dare © Marjorie Dobson
Go Forth...Ask...Share © Roberta Rominger
Go with Courage © Dorothy McRae-McMahon
God has Given Us a Dream © Roberta Rominger
It is So Easy to Say © Bernard Thorogood**
Jesus, Courageous and Vulnerable from *Roll Away the Stone* © United Church
Publishing House, 1998, p. 7, ibid.
Make a Difference in the World—Source Unknown—Canada
Move Us to Change © Joy Mead
New Ways © Peter Comaish
Release Us © Per Harling
Risk Everything © Usha Joshua
Stir Up a Divine Restlessness © James Atwell, Provost of St. Edmundsbury
Cathedral
To Work for Change from *Roll Away the Stone* © United Church Publishing House,
1998, p. 19, ibid.
We are Encouraged © Angeling B. Esquierdo

Let Justice Flow...
Blessing, A © The United Church Publishing House from *Circles of Grace* by Keri K.
Wehlander, 1998
Blessing for Speaking Out, A © The United Church Publishing House, from *Joy Is
our Banquet*, ibid.
Blessing for the World's Children, A © Louise Margaret Granahan 1998
Blessing for Those in Mission © Dorothy McRae-McMahon
Blessing of Liberation © Frances Ballantyne
Create a World of Equality © Angeling B. Esquierdo
Do Justice—Love Kindness © 1998 Nick Fawcett, taken from *Prayers for All Seasons*,
ibid.
For Those Who Live on the Margins © Revd John Johansen-Berg, Community for
Reconciliation, Barnes Close, Chadwich, Bromsgrove B61 0RA

Gathering, The from *Out of the Fire: Worship and Theology of Liberation*, ibid.
Give and Take © Duncan L. Tuck
God Bless © Frances Ballantyne
God of Justice © Peter Graystone
God Who Dances in Creation from *Women Included* © SPCK
Just for Me © Frances Ballantyne
Justice Blessing, A © Janet Wootton
May the Grace of God Sweep through this World © Peter Graystone
On Racial Justice Sunday—Norman Hart
Open Eyes and Hearts © Catholic Organization for Development and Peace,
Canada. Permission sought
Open the Door (for one voice) © Paul Sheppy
Open the Door (for two voices) © Paul Sheppy
Refugee Prays for a Blessing, A © Kate Compston
Smile and a Tear, A © Basil Fernando
Stir Up © Bob Knight Toc H
Sweet are the Blessings © Basil Fernando
True Blessing, A © Basil Fernando

Protect Peace
Deep Peace taken from *Prayers for Pilgrims* by John Johansen-Berg, published
© 1993 by Darton, Longman and Todd Ltd. Used by permission of the publishers
Discover the Riches of Christ © Rt Revd Patrick B. Harris, Bishop of Southwell
Go Home in Peace—Source Unknown
God's Strength © Audry Barnard
Hilda's Blessing © Barrie Williams
In Times and Places of War © Bernard Thorogood**
Joy of the Spirit, The © Christina Rees
Live Simply, Gently © Mark Belletini**
Peace © Peter Comaish
Peace, The—from *Women Included* © SPCK**
Peace Be With Us © Dorothy McRae-McMahon
Peace Harmonious © Milerepa, Tibet
Peace of God © Frances Ballantyne
Receive the Gift of Peace © Dorothy M. Stewart
Road of Uncertainty, The © Angeling B. Esquierdo
You Have Called Us to Peace from © *Gates of Prayer*, Union of Liberal and
Progressive Synagogues

Joy, Perfect Joy
All Your Days © Radha Sahar from the collection *Songs of Universal Worship*
Go out Rejoicing © 1998 Nick Fawcett, taken from *Prayers for All Seasons*, ibid.
Grace of God Thrill Your Hearts, The © 1998 Nick Fawcett, taken from *Prayers for
All Seasons*, ibid.
Jeu d'Esprit © Ann Lewin sourced from *Candles and Kingfishers*
Laughter in Your Eyes © 1998 Nick Fawcett, taken from *Prayers for All Seasons*, ibid.
May the Holy God Surprise You © Dorothy McRae-McMahon
May the World Continue to Surprise Us © 1998 Nick Fawcett, taken from *Prayers
for All Seasons*, ibid.

Festivals

The Christian Year
    Advent
Advent Blessing © Dorothy McRae-McMahon
An Advent Blessing © Richard Becher
    Christmas
At the Heart of the Manger...© Richard Becher
Babe of Bethlehem, The © W. L. Wallace
Blessing for Christmas © Raymond Chapman
Blessing of the Christmas Child, A © Richard Becher
Christmas Benediction © W. L. Wallace
Christmas Blessing, A © Edgar Ruddock
Come to Us, Emmanuel © Frances Ballantyne
Motivate Us © W. L. Wallace
Orphanage—first appeared in the weekly journal *The Big Issue* No. 314 © Harry O.,
via Geoffrey Duncan, c/o Canterbury Press Norwich
Your Word Made Flesh © Norm S. D. Esdon
    Epiphany
An Epiphany Blessing, © Kate Compston from *Seasons and Celebrations*, ibid.
Epiphany © W. L. Wallace
Epiphany Blessing © Dorothy McRae-McMahon
    Ash Wednesday
Blessing of Ashes © Giles Harcourt
Suddenly It's Wednesday © Simon Barrow
    Lent
For Waiting in the Wilderness © The United Church Publishing House from *Circles
of Grace*, ibid.
Good Friday
Blessing the Thorn in the Flesh © Norm S. D. Esdon
Good Friday Blessing, A © Norm S. D. Esdon
    Easter Day
Easter Blessing © Ancilla Dent
Love of Jesus, Fill Me © Angela Ashwin, from *Woven into Prayer* published by the
Canterbury Press Norwich, 1999
Power of Your New Life, The © Paul Iles from *Waking with Praise* published by the
Canterbury Press Norwich, 1998
Risen Lord and Master © Paul Iles from *Waking with Praise*, ibid.
    Pentecost
Pentecost © W. L. Wallace
Pentecost Thanksgiving, A © Kate Compston from *Seasons and Celebrations*,
ibid.**

    Harvest
Agriculture Blessings (see under individual titles)
  Blessing for the Wine Harvest, A © Alan Nichols
  Blessing of a Garden Field
  Blessing of a Herd of Cows
  Blessing of an Orchard

Blessing of Beehives
Blessing of Chickens
   The above five blessings are from The Community of the Servants of the Will of God, England
Blessing of Bees
   Blessing of Fish for Stocking Ponds, Lakes or Rivers
   The above two blessings are © St. Tykon's Orthodox Theological Seminary Press, South Canaan,Pennsylvania 18459, USA
Blessing of Harvest Gifts © Giles Harcourt
   Prayer for the Blessing of Fishnets
   Prayer over a Sowing
   Prayer over a Threshing Floor or Barn
   Prayer to Bless a Herd
   Prayer to Bless New Honey
   The above five blessings are © St. Tykon's Orthodox Theological Seminary Press, South Canaan, Pennsylvania 18459, USA
For Those at Work in Food Production and Preparation © Revd John Johansen-Berg, Community for Reconciliation, Barnes Close, Chadwich, Bromsgrove B61 0RA
Fruit of the Land, The—Source Unknown
Golden Rice Harvest, The © W. L. Wallace
Lord of the Harvest—Source Unknown
On the Land © Revd John Johansen-Berg, as above
Seedtime and Harvest © Dorothy M. Stewart

God of Times and Seasons

Changing Splendors
Autumn © Rosemary Wass
Autumn Is a Blazing Time © Marjorie Dobson
God of All Times and Seasons © Peter Graystone
I Look at a Leaf © Ruth Harvey
New Year's Blessing, A © Nicholas Coulton, Provost of Newcastle
Past, Present and Future © 1998 Nick Fawcett, taken from *Prayers for All Seasons*, ibid.
Signs of Spring © Rosemary Wass
Spring © Marjorie Dobson
Spring Thanksgiving—Source Unknown
Summer © Rosemary Wass
Summer Is Extravagant © Marjorie Dobson
Winter © Rosemary Wass
Winter Blessing, A © Marjorie Dobson

Take us Through the Day, Lord
An Evening Blessing © Revd Philip Freier
Any Time of Day! © 1998 Nick Fawcett, taken from *Prayers for All Seasons*, ibid.
Blessing for a Day © Betty Lynn Schwab
Blessing for Morning or Evening © Raymond Chapman
Blessing for the Morning © Dorothy McRae-McMahon

Blessing for the Night © Dorothy McRae-McMahon
Blessing for the Night, A © World Council of Churches
Blessing on Daily Living © Revd John Johansen-Berg, Community for
Reconciliation, Barnes Close, Chadwich, Bromsgrove B61 ORA
Blessing to Begin the Day, A © The United Church Publishing House, from *Circles
of Grace*, ibid.
Celtic Blessing, A © The Community of the Holy Name, England
Christ's Blessing to Start and End the Day © Simon Barrow
End of the Day © W. L. Wallace
End of the Day, The © Richard Becher
Evening Blessing © Richard Carr-Gomm. This blessing is used in the Houses of
Abbeyfield, Carr-Gomm, Morpeth and St. Matthew societies. There are about
1600 Houses in the UK and the only qualification for residency is loneliness.
Goodnight, Lord © Richard Becher
Guarding of the God of Life, The—Floris Books**
In the Bath © Val Shedden
Morning Affirmations © W. L. Wallace
Morning Blessing © Heather Johnston
Night Blessing © Glenn Jetta Barclay
Night Blessing, A © Revd Susan Hardwick, an Anglican priest and author of a
number of books
Resting Blessing, Floris Books**

Creator God

Awaken Our Senses
Bless My Senses © Bernard Thorogood**
Bless Our Tears © Richard Becher
Bless to Me, O God—Floris Books**
Blessing for the Senses, A—Source Unknown
Blessing of Sight © Frances Ballantyne
Bless the Angel in Our Presence © Richard Becher
Bless the Touch © Richard Becher
Brazilian Blessing, A—Source Unknown
Senses, The © Rosemary Wass
Sensitivity and Tenderness © Per Harling
Teachers of Vision from *Prayers of Our Hearts* by Vienna Cobb Anderson © 1993,
the Crossroad Publishing Company, New York. All rights reserved.**

Beauty in Creation
All You Powerful Things, Praise the Lord © Peter Graystone
An Elemental Blessing © Jean Mortimer
Beauty in Forms of Creation © *The Authorized Daily Prayer Book of the United
Hebrew Congregations of the Commonwealth*
Benedicite © Sister Catherine, Order of the Holy Paraclete, England
Blessing at a Time of Planting Trees © Vin McMullen taken from *Through the Eyes
of the Poor*, Catholic Fund for Overseas Development
Blessing for the Earth © Edward P. Echlin, author of *Earth Spirituality, Jesus at the
Center*, Arthur James, 1999

Blessing of the Flowerbeds—Community of the Servants of the Will of God, England
Creation Benediction, A © Judy C. Chan, Common Global Ministries, USA/Hong Kong Christian Council
Creation Seen—Creation Unseen © Peter Graystone
Dominion over All Living Creatures © Revd John Johansen-Berg, Community for Reconciliation, Barnes Close, Chadwich,Bromsgrove B61 0RA
Doxology of Flowers, A by Walter Murray © United Church of Canada Department of Stewardship Services; Bulletins and Worship Guide 1998, p. 28
Garden Blessing, A—David L. Helyar
His Love Endures Forever © Peter Graystone
In Whom All Creation Is Renewed © Ancilla Dent
Lord Bless You with Rain, The © Revd Prince Dibeela
May the Light of God Fill Your Heart © Revd John Johansen-Berg, as above
May the Rain Nourish Your Soul © Radha Sahar from the collection *Songs of Universal Worship*
Peace, Strength and Light © Community of All Hallows, England

Landscapes
Blessing for Prairie Sage © Betty Lynn Schwab
Blessing of the Bush, The © John Hunt via Geoffrey Duncan, c/o Canterbury Press Norwich
Blessing of the Forest—Community of the Servants of the Will of God, England
Blessing of Trees, A © Duncan L. Tuck
Blessing on the Desert, A—Alan Nicholls adapted from *Caught in the Draft* © Veronica Brady, HarperCollins Publishers, Australia**
Landscape Blessing © June Boyce-Tillman

Seascapes
Blessing for Those on the Sea © Heather Johnston
Blessing at the End of a Canoeing Day © Betty Lynn Schwab
Blessing of a Samoan Fishing Canoe © L. Setefano
Blessing of the Sea, The (1) © Sarah Brewerton
Blessing of the Sea, The (2) © John Hunt via Geoffrey Duncan, c/o Canterbury Press Norwich
Boat Blessing—Floris Books**

Birds and Beasts
Blessing for Earth's Birds, A © Betty Lynn Schwab
Blessing of Cows or other Animals, The © Anthony Bush
Cat Blessing, A © Norm S. D. Esdon
Great Bird of the Wide Skies © Revd John Johansen-Berg, Community for Reconciliation, Barnes Close, Chadwich, Bromsgrove B61 0RA
Peacocks and Pandas © Rt Revd Dominic Walker, Bishop of Reading
Presence © Kate Compston
Seagull © Ancilla Dent

Lands and Peoples

Aboriginal Fire Blessing,The—Source Unknown
Aotearoa © W. L. Wallace
Arohanui Blessing (Aotearoa New Zealand) © Joy Cowley
Australian Celtic Blessing, An © Alan Nichols
Before, Behind, Below and Around Us—Source Unknown
Bless African Women, Lord © Revd Cheryl Dibeela
Bless our People © Gates of Prayer, Union of Progressive and Liberal Synagogues
Bless the Earth, Every Day © Musa W. Dube Shomanah
Blessing for Canada, A © Betty Lynn Schwab
Blessing for Hong Kong, A © Judy C. Chan,Common Global Ministries Board,
USA/Hong Kong Christian Council
Blessing for Israel/Palestine, A © Revd John Johansen-Berg, Community for
Reconciliation, Barnes Close, Chadwich, Bromsgrove B61 0RA
Blessing for London, A—and other Great Cities © J. R. Ashdown
Blessing for Pakistan, A © Phil Billing, CMS Mission Partner, Director of Murree
Christian School, Pakistan
Blessing for Romania, A
Blessing for Rwanda, A
  The above two blessings are © Revd John Johansen-Berg, as above
Blessing on the Land of "Fair Go", A—Alan Nicholas adapted from *Land of the
Spirit* by Muriel Porter © World Council of Churches
Blessings from South Africa—The Rainbow Nation © Cathy Bott, United
Congregational Church of Southern Africa
For Australia © Bernard Thorogood**
From this Place © Louise Margaret Granahan
Give Me a Blessing (Venezuela) © Roger Dawson
Liverpool Blessing, The © The Rt Revd James Jones, Bishop of Liverpool
Mayan Prayer, A © Jhuan Ixchop Us, Commission of Mayan Culture, within
Guatemalan Christian Action. Translated by Garry G. Sparks
Nature's Blessing for Busy City Folk © Karen Scarlett
North East India, Bless the Lord © Thomas Menamparampil
Nunavut Blessing, A © Pastoral Leaders of Pelly Bay, Churchill and Hudson
Diocese, Canada
Popul Vuh—Reprinted with the permission of Simon & Schuster, Inc., from *Popul
Vuh* © 1985 by Dennis Tedlock
Rahim and Afroza (Bangladesh) © Bishop B. D. Mondal via Geoffrey Duncan, c/o
Canterbury Press, Norwich

Community Lifestyles

Grow Together
Asking for and Giving of Blessing © Muriel Orevillo-Montenegro
Blessed and Blessing © Louise Margaret Granahan
Blessing, A © Frances Blodwell
Blessing for a New Place to Be © Janet Lees
Blessing for a Parish or Church Occasion © Raymond Chapman
Blessing for St. Andrew's on the Terrace © John Stewart Murray
Blessing on a Shopping Center © Wendy White

Blessing through Struggle © The Venerable Martin Wallace, Archdeacon of Colchester
Blessing upon Them! © Musa W. Dube Shomanah
Daily Round of Life, The © 1998 Nick Fawcett, taken from *Prayers for All Seasons*, ibid.
Employed By God © Richard Becher
Every Living Being from *Women Included* © SPCK
Love, Joy, Peace © Joy Mead
May there be Safety—Roll Away the Stone © United Church Publishing House 1998, p. 43, ibid.
Meet God in Others © Marjorie Dobson
Thank You © The Venerable Martin Wallace, Archdeacon of Colchester
Two Women © Kate Compston

Riches in Relationships
Anointing in Courage © 1999 Edward F. Gabriele, Ecumenical Theologian in Residence, Christ the Servant Lutheran Community, Gaithersburg, MD, USA. Author of books on liturgy and spirituality.
Blessed Be Friendship © Viv Stacey
Blessing a Newlywed Couple © Muriel Orevillo-Montenegro
Blessing for a Relationship, A © Peter Colwell
Blessing for a Marriage, A © Jean Mortimer
Blessing for Lovers © Rt Revd Michael Turnbull, Bishop of Durham
Blessing on a Loved One © Nia Rhosier*
Blessing on Those Who have Hurt Me, A © Revd Susan Hardwick, an Anglican priest and author of a number of books
Blessing Words Are more than Words © Peter Comaish
Friendship © Karen Scarlett
Go to Your Friends and Greet Them © Revd Paul Sheppy
God Bless You for Befriending Me © Jason Doré, a Big Issue vendor based in London. Contact Geoffrey Duncan, c/o Canterbury Press Norwich
God of Our Relating © Kate Compston from *Textures of Tomorrow* published by the United Reformed Church in the United Kingdom, 1996**
Marriage Blessing © Bob Commin
Marriage Blessing, A—David L. Helyar
My Friend © Anthea Dove
Pain of Separation,The © W. L. Wallace
Sending Forth © Created by Howard Warren, Director of Pastoral Care, The Damien Center, Indianapolis, Indiana, USA. Published in *More Light Update*, June–July 1992. Permission sought
Sharing Together © Anthea Dove
Take this Couple © Duncan L. Tuck included in *Stuck for a Song*
This Is My Prayer, My Love © W. L. Wallace
Wedding Blessing, A © June Boyce-Tillman

Learning and Working
At the Beginning of a Committee Meeting © John Ll. Humphreys
Blessing before Starting a New Job or Particular Task © Raymond Chapman
Blessing for a Student © Rt Revd Michael Turnbull, Bishop of Durham

Blessing for Business Meetings: To Show the Way; Speech and Spirit; Penetrate All Our Deliberating © Rosemary Wass
Blessing of the Bizarre, The © John Hunt via Geoffrey Duncan, c/o Canterbury Press Norwich
Blessing on Starting Secondary School, A © Cerys Jones
For Someone with Learning Difficulties © Marjorie Dobson
Home Blessing © Bernard Thorogood**
Rejoice! © Roberta Rominger
Standing the World on Its Head © Anne Richards
Teacher © Anne Richards
Tutorial © Anne Richards
We Must Close the Meeting © United Congregational Church of Southern Africa

Modern Technology
Blessing for Computer Makers, Facilitators and Users, A © Revd John Johansen-Berg, Community for Reconciliation, Barnes Close, Chadwich, Bromsgrove B61 0RA
Blessing for My New Computer © Betty Lynn Schwab
Blessing for New Technology © Peter Comaish
Blessing of Computers
Blessing of Tools and Machines
  The above two blessings are © The Community of the Servants of the Will of God, England
Dedication of a Sound System © Rt Revd Roy Williamson, former Bishop of Southwark
My Telephone © Marjorie Dobson

Being Creative!
Before Worship, a Performance or a Choir Rehearsal © Kate McIlhagga
Bless Musicians © Julian Templeton
Bless the Poetry, the Art, the Music of the World © Per Harling
Blessing before a Choral Event © John Petty, Provost of Coventry
Blessing for Artists and Composers © Revd John Johansen-Berg, Community for Reconciliation, Barnes Close, Chadwich, Bromsgrove B61 0RA
Blessing for Bands, A © Rt Revd Nigel McCulloch, Bishop of Wakefield
Blessing for Journalists, A © Revd John Johansen-Berg, as above
Blessing for Writers, A © Alan Nichols adapted from *Flaws in the Glass* by Patrick White
Clowns and Other Entertainers © Revd John Johansen-Berg, as above
Music © Karen Scarlett
Solo Voice © Peter Colwell

Eat, Drink And...Share
An Inclusive Grace for a Wedding Meal © W. J. Wallace
Bless the Talk Around this Food © Kate McIlhagga
Blessed Be this Meal © W. L. Wallace
Bless this Food © From the collection *Songs of Universal Worship*
Blessing on a Shared Meal, A © Revd Susan Hardwick, an Anglican priest and author of a number of books

Blessing upon Food—Monica Furlong from *Women Included* © SPCK
Bon Appetit © John Shevlin SVD 1999 adapted Donamon Castle text
Brazilian Blessing for the Table, A © Jaci Maraschin, priest of the Anglican Church in Brazil
Bread Blessing from *Prayers for the Domestic Church*, ibid.
Breakfast Grace, A—Source Unknown
...But What We Share © James Russell Lowell
Food and Celebration © W. L. Wallace
For Food and Friendship © Richard Boeke from *A Garland of Graces,* Unitarian and Free Christian Churches
Give Us, O Lord a Bit o' Sun—from *A Garland of Graces*, ibid.
God is One © Richard Boeke adapted from Egy az Isten translated *God is One*, a Hungarian Unitarian hymn
Grace at a Wedding Breakfast © Marion Simpson
Hunger for Justice, A—Anonymous
In a Somewhere Hungry World © Joy Croft from *A Garland of Graces*, ibid.
In Our World—Source Unknown
Jewish Table Blessings © Union of Liberal and Progressive Synagogues
Lift Up this Bread! from *Prayers for the Domestic Church*, ibid.
Multi-faith Food Blessing © W. L. Wallace
New Zealand Blessing at Table, A © John Stewart Murray
Not the Gourmet Touch © Marjorie Dobson
Our Common Meal © Andrew Brown from *A Garland of Graces*, ibid.
Table Blessings from Ewell Monastery © Ewell Monastery, England
Table Blessings © Declan Smith

Hearth and Home
Bless this House © Revd Susan Hardwick, an Anglican priest and author of a number of books
Blessing a Samoan House © L. Setefano
Blessing for a House © Raymond Chapman
Blessing for a New Home, A (1) © Jan Berry
Blessing for a New Home, A (2) © John Stewart Murray
Blessing for the Home, A © Revd John Johansen-Berg, Community for Reconciliation, Barnes Close, Chadwich, Bromsgrove B61 0RA
Blessing of a New House © Jill and Fred Brotherton, South Holmewood RH15 9XA
Hail Guest!—Source Unknown
House of Peace, A © Radha Sahar from the collection *Songs of Universal Worship*
Our Home © Marjorie Dobson
Surround Us, God © John Stewart Murray

All the Days of My Life
Age Blessing © Ann Lewin
All the Words I Like Best © Rt Revd Stephen Sykes, Bishop of Ely
An Act of Blessing for a Woman Giving Birth © Muriel Orevillo-Montenegro
Be a Blessing © Dorothy M. Stewart
Birth Blessing © Kate McIlhagga

Bless our Unborn Child © Per Harling
Blessing, A © John O'Donohue 1997. Extracted from *Anam Cara—Spiritual Wisdom for the Celtic World*, published by Bantam Press, a division of Transworld Publishers, a division of the Random House Group Ltd. All rights reserved
Blessing for a Woman Who Has Conceived © Betty Lynn Schwab
Blessing for Old Age, A © John O'Donohue 1997. Extracted from *Anam Cara—Spiritual Wisdom for the Celtic World*, ibid.
Blessing for the Child Among Us, A © Michael McCoy
Blessing of a Party, The © John Hunt via Geoffrey Duncan, c/o Canterbury Press Norwich
Blessing offered at a Haircutting/Ear-Piercing Ceremony © L. Setefano
Boomerang Blessing, A © Val Shedden
Child is Given, A © The United Church Publishing House from *Circles of Grace*, ibid.
Child Leaving Home, A © Kate McIlhagga
Community Blessing of a Child in the Womb of a Single Mother © Muriel Orevillo-Montenegro
Delight in that Love © W. L. Wallace
For a Teenager's Bedroom © Marjorie Dobson
In Pain © Duncan L. Tuck from *The Word in the World*, ibid.
Life Blessing © Ann Lewin
May Beauty Delight You © W. L. Wallace
Mother's Blessing on Her Child, A © Nia Rhosier*
My Wish for You © Werner and Cornelia Schwartz
On a Child Leaving Home © Kate McIlhagga
Our Children © Marjorie Dobson
Parent's Blessing, A © Revd Susan Hardwick, an Anglican priest and author of a number of books
Prayer of an Old Man from *Another Day—Prayers for the Human Family* compiled by John Carden © SPCK

Toward Wholeness

Toward Health…
All Kinds of Kite Fliers © Jean Mortimer
Blessing before an Operation © Bob Commin
Blessing for Calm, A © The United Church Publishing House, from *Joy is our Banquet*, ibid.
Blessing for Healing © Peter Graystone
Blessing for a Hard Time © Dorothy McRae-McMahon
Blessing for Hospitals, A
Blessing for One Whom Healing Eludes, A
  The above two blessings are © Betty Lynn Schwab
Blessing for Someone with Alzheimer's Disease, A © Marjorie Dobson
Blessing in Sickness © Raymond Chapman
Blessing Prayer in a Time of Sickness from *Prayers for the Domestic Church*, ibid.
Escaping Danger © Union of Liberal and Progressive Synagogues
For Persons with AIDS © Vienna Cobb Anderson. Permission sought

Healing, The © Janet Lees
Healing Blessings © Radha Sahar from the collection *Songs of Universal Worship*
Hospital Blessing, A © Bernard Thorogood**
Prayer for an Insight into Suffering, A—Reprinted from *Pray All Ways* by Edward Hays © Forest of Peace Publishing, Inc., 251 Muncie Road,Leavenworth, Kansas 66048, USA
Prayer to Accompany the Taking of Medicine from *Prayers for the Domestic Church,* ibid.

Treasured Memories

Blessing for Death, A © John O'Donohue 1997. Extracted from *Anam Cara—Spiritual Wisdom for the Celtic World,* ibid.
Blessing in Bereavement, A © Marjorie Dobson
Blessing of Memories, A © Richard Becher
Death Is the Last Great Festival © Kate McIlhagga
For a Bride Whose Father has Died © Jean Mortimer
For Death and the Dying © Peter Cruchley-Jones*
Funeral Blessing, A © Edgar Ruddock
Jewish Kaddish © The Estate of the Revd Michael Vasey
Love Stronger than Death © W. L. Wallace
Mixed Blessings © Val Shedden
Sunsets and Farewells © from *Prayers for the Domestic Church,* ibid.
Treasured Memories © Richard Becher
With the Dying © Bernard Thorogood**

Always on the Move

Inner Strength

Be to Us Our God—six different Blessings—© Kate Compston from *The Word in the World,* ibid.
Blessing on the Inner Life © Revd John Johansen-Berg, Community for Reconciliation,Barnes Close, Chadwich, Bromsgrove B61 0RA
Completing the Circle—Tribal Origin Unknown
Earth Prayer, Miriam Therese Winter © Medical Mission Sisters 1991
God of Little Things © Jean Mayland
Hold Me, Lord © Richard Becher
Moments of Blessing © John Ll. Humphreys
Power and the Mystery, The from *Women Included* © SPCK
Spiritual Journey, The © Revd John Johansen-Berg, as above
This is Thy Blessing © Glenn Jetta Barclay
To Encounter God © Simon Barrow

Journeys and Pilgrimages

Blessed Be All Our Journeys © Anglican Women Exploring Spirituality
Blessed Be Your Way—from a 12th-century Munich manuscript
Blessing for a Journey © Dorothy McRae-McMahon
Blessing for a Long Journey © Heather Johnston
Blessing for a New Start © Marjorie Dobson
Blessing for Beginnings, A © The United Church Publishing House, from *Joy is our*

Banquet, ibid.
Blessing for Departing Travelers, A—Source Unknown
Blessing for the Person Opposite on a Train © Rt Revd Michael Turnbull, Bishop of Durham
Blessing for Those Who Make Journeys © Revd John Johansen-Berg, Community for Reconciliation, Barnes Close, Chadwich, Bromsgrove B61 0RA
Blessing for Visitors Leaving Iona
Blessing for Walkers
  The above two blessings are © Heather Johnston
Blessing M1 Northbound © Val Shedden
Blessing On Your Way, A © Norm S. D. Esdon
Blessing the Journey © Richard Becher
Bread for the Journey © The United Church Publishing House from *Circles of Grace,* ibid.
God Bless Us on Our Way—Robert Llewelyn
God Go With Us © 1998 Nick Fawcett, taken from *Prayers for All Seasons—a Comprehensive Resource for Public Worship,* ibid.
God of Pilgrimage—Source Unknown
God's Home © Duncan L. Tuck
Going Attached © Duncan L. Tuck from *The Word in the World,* ibid.
Grace Enclosing Heights and Depths, The © Dieter Trautwein
Guarding of God, The © Kate McIlhagga
In Life's Journey © Kate McIlhagga
Journey Blessing © Kate McIlhagga
Journey for Justice, A © Rt Revd Peter Selby, Bishop of Worcester
Journey with Us © Usha Joshua
Journeys—Floris Books**
Life Blessing, A © Revd Susan Hardwick, an Anglican priest and author of a number of books
New Horizons © Frances Ballantyne
Penitent's Blessing, A © Jean Mortimer
Pilgrim People, A © Peter Cruchley-Jones*
Pilgrimage Prayer, A © Rt Revd Peter Nott, Bishop of Norwich
Prompt Us © Jan Berry
Turning Season, A © The United Church Publishing House from *Circles of Grace,* ibid.
Walk With God © Per Harling

Of Related Interest...

More Quips, Quotes, and Anecdotes
for Preachers and Teachers
Anthony Castle

These one hundred and fifty themes follow the liturgical calendar and includes a listing of Bible verses for any given Sunday, and an appendix of themes for the Sunday readings as well as a subject and source index.

1-58595-136-6, 624 pp, $29.95 (J-84)

BESTSELLER
A World of Stories for Preachers and Teachers
*and all who love stories that move and challenge
William J. Bausch

These 350 tales aim to nudge, provoke, and stimulate the reader and listener, to resonate with the human condition, as did the stories of Jesus.

0-89622-919-X, 534 pp, $29.95 (B-92)

Between Sundays
Daily Gospel Reflections and Prayers
Rev. Paul Boudreau

Applies gospel truths to contemporary settings and challenges readers to be disciples of Christ here and now in everyday, accessible ways.

1-58595-169-2, 360 pp, $24.95 (X-05)

TWENTY-THIRD PUBLICATIONS

185 WILLOW STREET • PO BOX 180 • MYSTIC, CT 06355
TEL: 1-800-321-0411 • FAX: 1-800-572-0788
Bayard E-MAIL: ttpubs@aol.com • www.twentythirdpublications.com